STRONG TIES

STRONG TIES

Barclay Simpson and the Pursuit of the Common Good in Business and Philanthropy

By Katharine Ogden Michaels

with

Judith K. Adamson

"Simpson Man" by Igino Pellizzari.
A sculpture made from Simpson Strong Ties.
Photo by Joseph Way.

Rare Bird Books
Los Angeles, Calif.

THIS IS A GENUINE RARE BIRD BOOK

Rare Bird Books
6044 North Figueroa Street
Los Angeles, CA 90042
rarebirdlit.com

Set in Minion Pro
Printed in the United States

10 9 8 7 6 5 4 3 2 1

Library of Congress Cataloging-in-Publication Data

Names: Michaels, Katharine Ogden, author. | Adamson, Judith K., author.
Title: Strong ties : Barclay Simpson and the Pursuit of the Common Good in Business and Philanthropy / by Katharine Ogden Michaels, with Judith K. Adamson.
Description: First paperback edition. | Los Angeles, Calif. : Rare Bird Books, [2021]
Includes bibliographical references.
Identifiers: LCCN 2021019967 | ISBN 9781644282175 (paperback)
Subjects: LCSH: Simpson, Barclay. | Simpson Manufacturing Co. |
Building materials industry—United States—History. |
Businesspeople—California—San Francisco—Biography. |
Philanthropists—California—San Francisco—Biography.
Classification: LCC HD9715.8.U64 S5665 2021 | DDC 338.7/69092 [B]—dc23
LC record available at https://lccn.loc.gov/2021019967

For Sharon

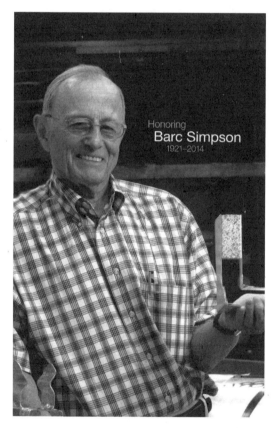

Barc holding a Strong Tie.

Acknowledgments

THANKS TO BARCLAY, SHARON, and all of their children; the staff and board of Simpson Manufacturing Company, Inc., including Earl "Budd" Cheit, Barry Williams, Jennifer Chatman, Tom Fitzmyers, Terry Kingsfather, Karen Colonias, Jacinta Pister, Kristin Lincoln, John Herrera, Mike Plunk, Joseph Way, and Laurent Versluysen, along with many others; UC Berkeley, including Chancellor Robert Birgeneau; staff and board members of Berkeley Art Museum/Pacific Film Archive, including Roselyne "Cissie" Swig, Noel Nellis, and Lawrence Rinder; Dean Rich Lyons of the UC Berkeley Haas School of Business; Sandy Barbour, formerly of UC Athletics; Neil Henry, formerly of the Bancroft Library; Jennifer Cutting of the UC Berkeley Development Office; Pat Loomes, Linda Boessenecker, Julayne Virgil, and Monica Manriquez of Girls Inc. of Alameda County; the staff and artists of the Barclay Simpson Fine Arts Gallery, including Lynda Dann and Joseph Way; Susan Avila of the California College of Arts; Lori Fogarty of the Oakland Museum of California; former BART staff and board members, including Arthur Shartsis, Mike Healy, and Joan Van Horn; the California Shakespeare Theater, including Jonathan Moscone and Sharon Simpson; Peggy White of the Diablo Regional Arts Association; Simon Baker, family friend and financial advisor to the PSB Fund; and Joe Di Prisco of the Simpson Literary Prize for his fine counsel and support throughout and for suggesting the use of the "Strong Ties" metaphor in the title.

Contents

13 Prologue
   In the Gallery

PART I
Genes and Good Luck

25 Chapter 1
   Up on the Roof: Snapshot of Pearl Harbor from the Bay

27 Chapter 2
   Origins: Scottish, Yankee, and Oakland Roots

38 Chapter 3
   From Here to Eternity: Berkeley to Alaska to Tokyo 1939–1945

42 Chapter 4
   Home Again

45 Chapter 5
   The Family Business

50 Chapter 6
   A Knock on the Door

54 Chapter 7
   Bill

PART II
Essence of a Business

59 Chapter 8
   Product: The Leap into Connectors

64 Chapter 9
   Place: From East Oakland to San Leandro

67 Chapter 10
   People: Giants and Genius

79 Chapter 11
   Principles: A Secular Catechism

93 Chapter 12
   Practice: The Making of the Simpson Brand

PART III
From Artisan Business to Technical Powerhouse

111   Chapter 13
       Two-Headed Command: Continuity and Change

125   Chapter 14
       Entrepreneurship and the Reiterative Process

129   Chapter 15
       Expansion

134   Chapter 16
       Transmitting the Creed

PART IV
Sharon and the Double Family

141   Chapter 17
       Courtship

149   Chapter 18
       The Double Family

157   Chapter 19
       After the Wedding: The Crowded Condo, Winnie in DC,
       and Rolling in the Snow

162   Chapter 20
       Special Projects, Pruning, and Housing a Marriage

PART V
Other Passions

169   Chapter 21
       Bay Area Rapid Transit District (BART)

181   Chapter 22
       Art Collecting and the Gallery

PART VI
Put Something Back: Conviction in Action

203   Chapter 23
       Motives and Methods of Philanthropy

209   Chapter 24
       The PSB Fund

212   Chapter 25
       The Art of Giving to the Arts

223 Chapter 26
   University of California at Berkeley: Pole Star

242 Chapter 27
   Girls Inc. of Alameda County, California (Girls Inc.):
   Transformational Giving

PART VII
Success and Succession: New Cooks in the Sauce

267 Chapter 28
   Tone at the Top

269 Chapter 29
   The Simpson Manufacturing Company, Inc. Board of Directors

272 Chapter 30
   Salesman in Chief Again

277 Chapter 31
   End of an Era, Beginning of an Era

282 Chapter 32
   Tweaking the Sauce and the Big Hand-Off

Part VIII
Retirement

291 Chapter 33
   The Wager

292 Chapter 34
   Letters to and from a "Servant Leader"

297 Chapter 35
   Sightings: Brilliant Plumage

299 Chapter 36
   Acknowledgments from the Community: The Berkeley Medal

302 Chapter 37
   2014: Passages

304 Chapter 38
   Legacy: Measuring Value

313 Epilogue
   Back in the Gallery

315 Interviewees
   Bios

Prologue
In the Gallery

M Y FIRST PERSONAL ENCOUNTER with Barclay Simpson[1] (Barclay or Barc; see bio)—founder and prime mover of the Simpson Manufacturing Company, Inc.[2] (Simpson Manufacturing)—was at the Barclay Simpson Fine Arts Gallery in Lafayette, California, sometime in spring of 1981. Upon knocking on the door of the gallery, I was met by a young man in a workman's apron who ushered me into a large room with white walls. I remember the sensation of walking out of the strong glare of midday sun into the gloom of the gallery, whose only window was the glass door on which I had tentatively knocked. As my eyes adjusted, I was first confused then amazed to find myself surrounded by fine prints, including those by Rembrandt and Whistler.

The young man said he would let Barclay know that I had arrived. When he disappeared, I moved closer to the prints, trying to absorb the fact of their existence in this stark, unlikely place, a converted industrial building along a strip-commercial thoroughfare in a suburban town east of the Berkeley hills and the glittering expanse of the San Francisco Bay to the west. A few moments later, Barclay found me staring fixedly at the moody prints, etched line and shadow, pulled from incised metal plates. Looking up, I was greeted by a big smile and a resounding *hello*. He asked me if I would like to see the picture-framing lab in the basement as well as other parts of the collection. Here, I also met Sharon, Barc's wife, elegant in jeans and rolled-up sleeves and a welcoming expression.

Before that day, I had only seen Barclay from a distance at a public meeting of the board of directors of the San Francisco Bay Area Rapid Transit District (BART) where, as one of nine elected members, he served between 1976 and 1988. I had recently been hired into the BART Planning Department. That day in the gallery, I was meeting him to discuss the convening of a steering committee made up of elected officials and staff from Contra Costa County cities along the transit corridor to consider the possible benefits of encouraging public-private partnerships involving the BART-owned lands.

Before my meeting with Barclay, I had been briefed by my boss on the various members of the BART Board of Directors. My memory is that Barc was described to me as a successful businessman, smart, straightforward, honest, fair, and rational. At the time, I hadn't yet realized exactly how rare that combination of qualities was in an elected official—or anybody. I don't remember if my boss also told me that Barclay was impatient—of wasted time, of pretense, of long meetings, of circuitous explanations, of the word "stress," of calculators, of wallowing and doomed pursuits, of long meetings. But whatever I knew about him in advance, when I knocked on the door of the gallery, I wasn't expecting what I found.

～

IN AUGUST 2012, THIRTY-ONE years after I first arrived at that threshold, I found myself once again at the door of the gallery. This time, when I came in from the searing hot light, there were no prints left on the walls. The Whistlers had been bequeathed to the UC Berkeley Art Museum and the Rembrandts were in storage awaiting their eventual fate. Also vanished were the brightly colored canvases and installations produced by students from the California College of Art (CCA) and by professional artists from the Mississippi to the Seine, which had intermittently graced the walls of the gallery for the thirteen years it was open to the public.

Barc met me at the front door with the same booming hello that I had known for three decades. He led me through the gloom to his library, lined floor to ceiling with *catalogues raisonné*[3] of the major artists of his and Sharon's collection as well as an assemblage of scholarly works on art and history. No noise from the street reached us in this cave, illuminated by a few desk lights bouncing off the colorful spines of books. I had often furtively imagined the pleasures one might indulge in if locked by mistake in this library with nothing to do but read and look.

For all that, it was a simple room of modest size with none of the pretensions of a millionaire's library on display. It was a room in which Barc and I had scribbled notes on the backs of envelopes before heading out to some BART meeting or other; where we had pored over books documenting different states of Rembrandt prints when we worked together on the catalogue of their collection for the 1989 gallery show; a room in which Sharon, Barc, and I met from 1997 onward to discuss the management of an old, stone farmhouse in Umbria, Italy, which I had restored after leaving BART, and which we jointly own; where I first took my husband-to-be, the writer Leonard Michaels, to meet them when we were suddenly engaged in 1996; and where I went, severely grieving, shortly after Lenny died abruptly in 2003.

Now, again, into this room full of shadows, I entered in high summer, a few months after Barc's ninety-first birthday. I had come to interview him. Self-consciously, in the spirit of full disclosure, I unpacked my tape recorder and the few pages of notes I had prepared with questions. As I fumbled with the digital controls, Barclay bluntly said he was worried that *all of this* might be a waste of my time. He reasoned that he had just completed the second version of his memoirs and distributed them to his family and a few friends and thought that should take care of it. All the answers were right there, and he was tired of thinking about himself. I replied, *The worst that can happen is that you and I will spend several hours talking together, alone in this library, uninterrupted.* As it was to turn out, our conversations were to go on from that summer until a few days before Barclay died in November 2014. That first time, not entirely convinced by my response, he said, *Do you really think there is a story here?*

This was a question I had spent a lot of time considering. More precisely, I had been trying to get at what might be the value of the story to readers who did not know Barc personally. Though well-known to many businesspeople, universities, and the arts and education communities of the East Bay, Barclay is not a universally recognized household name like Warren Buffett or Jack Walsh, not even in nearby San Francisco. He is not quoted in the *Wall Street Journal* or other business journals, even though many of the progressive business principles he exercised in the creation of Simpson Manufacturing make compelling reading to anyone interested in the unusual idea that the building of a profitable business might include the sharing of profits with a diverse employee base, as well as in finding concrete ways to make contributions to the larger community in which the business is embedded.

Against prevailing custom, Barclay managed to knit together the generally competing philosophies of bootstrap capitalism and the pursuit of the common good. Out of these often-oppositional forces, he established a professional and philanthropic practice based, for the most part, on instinct, largely without the aid of elaborate academic theories of business organization and management, or primers on how to be a good corporate citizen. Yet for those who watched him in action as a businessman or collaborated with him on public-interest projects, he was a colossal, exemplary figure whose creed one might consider bottling to sprinkle on business and institutional leaders everywhere.

Indeed, new business principles that closely resemble key aspects of Barclay's creed are just now, in the early 2020s, suddenly starting to erupt in the mission statements at the highest echelons of American business in the form of what has come to be known as "stakeholder capitalism." Though Barc probably would have scoffed at the artifice involved in giving a glossy name to what he considered to be simple fairness and good business, he would have approved of the shift in emphasis from mainly bottom-line motivations to a broader definition of the responsibilities of business in relation to local and global communities. Consider the lead-in entry on the Business Roundtable's website.[4]

"On August 19, 2019, 181 CEOs of America's largest corporations over-turned a twenty-two-year-old policy statement that defined a corporation's principal purpose as maximizing shareholder return.

"In its place, the CEOs of Business Roundtable adopted a new Statement on the Purpose of a Corporation declaring that companies should serve not only their shareholders, but also deliver value to their customers, invest in employees, deal fairly with suppliers, and support the communities in which they operate."

Echoing these principles, the World Economic Forum[5] adopted as the theme for its fiftieth annual meeting in Davos, Switzerland, in January 2020, "Stakeholders for a Cohesive and Sustainable World"—a phrase which, even five years earlier, might have surprised its powerful and wealthy clientele.

It remains to be seen how and to what degree these new corporate statements of principle will be transformed into practice.

Something like what is now being called "stakeholder capitalism" was key to the founding and abiding principles of Simpson Manufacturing. These included Barclay's adoption of a radical form of profit-sharing for workers from the early days of the business through to the present, along with a consistent increase in the company's tangible contributions to employees, their families, and their communities as the business grew in profitability. In this sense, Barclay represents an extraordinary story in American business—one that yokes apparently opposing forces by expanding the definition of "value" while still making substantial profits for shareholders and stakeholders alike.

Still, publicizing Barclay's achievements is a tough undertaking, with no scandal or celebrity to spice the sauce. How to make a compelling story based on a modern model of virtue in the archaic sense of the word? I knew going in that Barclay would not be an easy interview subject, as he had always been intrinsically distrustful of self-exploration, of indwelling tragedy, or of celebrating past triumphs. For all his palpable mental and physical vitality—his essential openness to the world—Barclay was not particularly easy, or at all suggestible. There was nothing of the "pleaser" in him. Though full of feeling, he was never a sentimentalist, never a believer in rampant subjectivity nor in the psychological desirability of protecting people from brutal truth. Committed as much as anyone I have ever known to concerted action in pursuit of the common good, he was, nevertheless, a special kind of subversive, skeptical of popularity and consensus, strange in a man so likable. Whatever story might be told of him—of his life, his family, his business, his philanthropy—this contradiction lies at its core. Or maybe this contradictory nature is just what they used to call "toughness," before a public creed of personal sensitivities confounded the old virtues.

Yes, I said, *I think there is a story worth telling.*

Turning on the microphone, I drew breath and began to ask cleverly oblique questions that I hoped would get at the contradictions, sources, and cross-currents. I was pushing for the core, trying to pry under the lid of Barc's optimism, his stoicism—coming repeatedly at the same questions from different angles. Though I did snatch from oblivion a few very telling comments—storing them away carefully—overall, I was no match for his distrust of complicated explanations. Regarding the question of his own gargantuan success—as a businessman, a family man, a public man—Barclay was concise, the way he prefers it: his story could be summed up as being a matter of *good genes and good luck and*, as an afterthought, *being in the right place at the right time.* Trying to excavate beneath these conversation-stopping statements, I asked Barc how this innately deterministic explanation squared with his twenty-year financial support of a program to teach very young girls from low-income families to read and then to mentor them through twelve years of schooling, through college, and beyond. Surely, this is an effort to stem the determinism of severely constricted circumstances.

Again, a short, undramatic response: *You do what you can.* Barclay wasn't stonewalling; he was saying exactly what he believed.

Though I wasn't able to transform Barc into a gabby, self-regarding raconteur that day or afterward, I needn't have worried about any possible awkwardness between us brought on by my role of grand inquisitor. Instead, in the magical library, and later at his home in Orinda, we enjoyed many hours of questions, digressions, and conversations enriched by the thirty years of our unlikely friendship.

～

THAT DAY, WHEN I returned to the glaring sunshine outside the gallery, I was both reassured and rueful. Yes, certainly, this is a tale of good genes and good luck; of the extreme benefits of being a white, middle-class kid of educated parents in early twentieth-century America; of enjoying innate physical and mental health; of coming of age as a businessman during the halcyon days of California and American post-war expansion. Yet it is also a story of something equally elusive—what my New England relatives call "character"—that vague but vast, implacable set of personal resources and instincts that make all the difference in life. As impossible to pin down as the explanation regarding *good genes and good luck*, character is indefinable—but you know it when you see it.

How to get hold of that tale? And harder still, how was I to tell a compelling story about an *essentially good man*? As all serious readers know, the recitation of virtue followed by good fortune violates our deepest Aristotelian longing to be vicariously thrilled and instructed by the suffering and fall from grace of highly placed men. Even Pierre Bezukhov and Konstantin Levin must suffer great loss before redemption, and Prince André must die of his wounds. Even good men must suffer to make a story. And evil is, of course, always interesting.

It would be presumptuous and untrue to say that Barclay never suffered. The unadorned facts of his life include the suicide of his older brother; the bearing of the devastating news to his parents; the loss of many dear friends to war, disease, and early death; the breakup of his first marriage; the inevitable variable fates of his children and extended family; and a prolonged personal struggle against a disease that would win in the end, and not before delivering an exaggerated payload of pain. Yet, throughout this last, stubborn battle—as during his vigorous heyday—Barc firmly rejected the idea of letting suffering or melancholy shadow his life or shake him from his path. Indeed, he never spoke of his disease, nor would he allow others to inquire or sympathize.

This willful intention to move forward rather than look back is linked to the original problem at the heart of this narrative. Barclay never believed in belaboring the past, which is an unsettling obstacle for anyone trying to be his biographer. Though he was a great reader of history, he was never much interested in the details of his own former life, preferring to probe the concrete world of daily life, the future, or the impersonal world of great art and actions. Pure subjectivity was alien to him. Though interested in the psychology of the self, his concerns were cognition, learning, and motivation. Above all, he was insistent on viewing the self in relation to other selves, especially those battling great odds.

Knowing this, I realized that most of Barc's story would need to be told from the outside, not through his own reflections but through the actual facts of his life, and even more importantly through the stories of the people and institutions whose lives he changed so profoundly. One such person, who worked at Simpson Strong-Tie (SST) for over forty-three years, describes Barclay in terms of his *passion*, but struggles to explain precisely what he means by this slippery term:

> *Barc has the presence....He's very intense. He's very direct. That intensity, though, it really is passion, but different from people who are just over the top. Barclay's words are very specific, very carefully used, yet he's not trying to sell you anything. He's not measuring or calculating. He just wants to make sure you understand....So many men could fail by not identifying their limits or their passion.* (John Herrera, SST employee, 1970–2014; see bio)

Presence...limits...passion... The weight of these words attempts to define qualities that are both concrete and inexplicable, that grapple after the texture of leadership.

Striking in the above description is the speaker's emphasis on communication and transmission rather than manipulation or coercion. *Barclay's words are very specific, very carefully used, yet he's not trying to sell you anything.* From this account and multiple conversations with other people who worked for and with Barclay over decades, what was to emerge repeatedly was the sense of how he managed by example and belief not only to "impress" people with his own passion but to "inspire" passion in them as well. The word "inspiration," from the Latin verb "to breathe or blow into," is often used in the sense of imparting a truth or idea to someone and was originally associated with divine or supernatural beings. Barclay was certainly neither of these—rather very down-to-earth—but he did have the unusual Promethean power of imparting, igniting, and inspiring through his actions and convictions rather than through control, connivance, or false comfort.

After our 2012 meeting in the gallery, I knew I was looking for a way into the story that had character and the elusive nature of leadership at its core, but that would also tell a raw tale of tangible achievement—East Bay-based, decidedly seat-of-the-pants, instinctively brilliant. It would be a story about the building from scratch of a small American manufacturing business that has survived and thrived from the immediate post-war era through the nineties and the severe technological and economic oscillations of the new century.

The pieces of the story are complex and important: creation of a brand that now bears the Simpson name throughout the world; desegregation of plants and the unions that served them during the sixties and seventies, and early promotion of diversity in hiring and retention; establishment of plants outside of North America while continuing to expand manufacturing operations in Canada and the US; development of a nonhierarchical company structure that attempts to have key decisions made at the lowest possible level; recruitment and retention of a management team and a board that was at its inception mixed in race and gender; and carrying out a collaborative CEO succession at the height of the founder's vitality. Perhaps most striking, given the current interest in business "culture," are the ways in which Barclay incorporated into the daily operations of the business and his philanthropy a set of principles that is a strange mixture of ancient Stoic philosophy, Scot's frugality, fairness, and twentieth-century inspirational literature.

Yet the core of the story is not the purity of Barclay's admirable precepts, but the rare skill with which he transformed precept into practice. In business, this meant that he never saw a conflict between making money and treating employees well, whatever their role within the company. He acted on his belief—certainly more intrinsic than schooled—that the greatest capital of any business is its people. To attract and retain both intellect and heart, the business must give people a stake and a future not based on dogged repetition of a task, but on cooperative problem-solving at every level and across reporting lines. Matrix management at SST was never a theory or a theology, but rather an organic practice that grew up with the company, seizing on several aspects of the underlying metaphor encased in the word matrix, suggesting an intertwining of purpose that breaks the classic assembly line and recasts it as communal enterprise. Though this sounds more like political manifesto than a description of the development of a successful manufacturing company, Barclay was no ideologue from either side of the political spectrum. He was a pragmatist who believed that making money and forging a community were complimentary goals.

Side by side with the narrative history of the business are the stories of Barc's public service, philanthropy, and art collecting, none in themselves unusual pursuits for a wealthy man. But here, too, Barclay operated according to his own lights, rejecting the passive display of his wealth, using principles he had perfected in building the Simpson Manufacturing Company to better the lives of people and institutions.

～

AND SO, BACK TO the starting point. This is not a biography of a man from modest origins making it big. It is an attempt at a *portrait of leadership*, which tries to analyze the structural architecture—richly symbolized by the famous Simpson Strong-Tie bent metal connector—that Barclay Simpson created in building important and lasting business, philanthropic, and familial relations. It is literally a story of *strong ties*, real and metaphorical, of the forging of economic, community, and family connections based on the careful distribution of force and burden. At the heart of the story are character and cunning, the mysteries that drive any great tale.

Note for Prologue

1 Quotations from Barclay are drawn from personal interviews with him from 2012 until a few days before his death in 2014 and from his memoirs.

2 Simpson Manufacturing Company, Inc. (Simpson Manufacturing) is the official name of the company Barclay built and is represented on the New York Stock Exchange by the symbol SSD. Throughout this manuscript, the terms "Simpson Strong-Tie (SST)," "the Simpson Company," and "Simpson" will be used interchangeably with the current official name of the company. SST is the primary subsidiary of Simpson Manufacturing.

3 A descriptive catalogue of works of art with explanations and scholarly comments.

4 The Business Roundtable (BRT) is a nonprofit association based in Washington, DC, whose members are the chief executive officers of major United States companies. https://www.businessroundtable.org.

5 "The World Economic Forum is an independent international organization committed to improving the state of the world by engaging business, political, academic and other leaders of society to shape global, regional and industry agendas." www.weforum.org

PART I
Genes and Good Luck

Perhaps after one has spent considerable time on this earth, thoughts about the past tend to occur more often. Despite these thoughts, I am even now still much more interested in ideas tied to the unknown future.

—Barclay

L to R: Barclay, Bill, Walter, and Jessie Simpson taken in 1922 or 1923.

Chapter 1

Up on the Roof: Snapshot of Pearl Harbor from the Bay

Looking toward San Francisco, it wasn't hard to imagine Japanese planes dropping bombs on the city.

—Barclay

O N DECEMBER 7, 1941, a group of guys from the Sigma Nu fraternity of UC Berkeley heard the radio announce the bombing of Pearl Harbor and scrambled onto the roof of the frat house to look for Japanese planes that might have broken off from Honolulu to bomb San Francisco. Though it never happened, the possibility of such an attack seemed real at the time.

Standing among that throng of boys scanning the bay—across the industrial flatlands of San Leandro, Oakland, Emeryville, and Berkeley to the glistening city on its many hills across the water—was a twenty-year-old Oakland native, Barclay Simpson, just two and a half years into his university education. By January of 1942, along with several other guys on the roof that day, he had met all the requirements to be admitted to the US Naval Air Corps as a member of the UC Berkeley "Flying Golden Bears." Over the next three years, Barclay was part of an anti-submarine surveillance operation in Alaska and the Aleutian Islands, and in the latter days of the war performed as a fighter pilot of a Helldiver aircraft operating off of a carrier in the South Pacific named (as it might have been in the movies of the era) the *Shangri La*. It was part of the largest fleet of war ships ever gathered in the history of the world and among the US craft that steamed into Tokyo Bay as victors in 1945.

Certainly, the years between Pearl Harbor and the surrender ceremonies in 1945 constitute one of the great sets of bookends in American history, much recalled, as is the generation coming of age on that fraternity rooftop and, soon after, on the battleships and beaches of Midway and Normandy. Famously, the twenty-year-olds who were the main protagonists of the bloody upheavals of World War II had been born into a world full of contradictory and quickly alternating visions of endless possibility and apocalypse.

The decade-long misery that preceded the outbreak of World War II naturally hit varying demographic and geographic areas of the country in different ways, depending—as usual—on race, class, climate, topography, and luck. But, somehow, out of this diverse experience emerged at least one enduring American profile, a character type that was memorably christened by one of its biographers as the "Greatest Generation."[1] The cluster of traits in this profile tells a story of American exceptionalism, a tale both philosophical and nearly religious in scope. Among the self-proclaimed virtues in this national portrait are honesty, common sense, hard work, tenacity, and a fundamentally anti-authoritarian instinct. This celebratory checklist tends to elide the greed, racism, class, and gender biases that are equally compelling parts of the story and which have started to gain recognition in the catalogue of the American national character. Yet even these essential correctives to the profile have not eradicated a prevailing sense that a native brand of self-reliance at the core of the American identity created a character type that supplied the motive force behind the global power and economic relations of the second half of the twentieth century. Whatever the underlying explanation, the American generation that was still young and still alive at the end of World War II rode the crest of—or was dashed on the shore by—the tidal wave of the United States' post-war prosperity.

Chapter 2
Origins: Scottish, Yankee, and Oakland Roots

I believe my success in life was due not to brilliance,
but to good genes and good luck.

—Barclay

O<small>F THE FRIENDS ASSEMBLED</small> at UC Berkeley and elsewhere to scout for enemy planes on Pearl Harbor Day, Barclay Simpson was one of the ones destined to survive—and prosper. Demographically, he could have served as a poster boy for the "Greatest Generation." Born on May 25, 1921, in Oakland, California, within days of the Tulsa Race Riots and eight years before the collapse of Wall Street on October 29, 1929, he was solidly located in the period between the two wars, which was ultimately to produce the leaders of American commerce and learning during the second half of the twentieth century and into the twenty-first.

Barclay later said that all his success in life was due not to brilliance or special gifts, but to a combination of *good genes and good luck*—factors over which he had no control. For this doubly fortunate inheritance he was always to give credit to his parents, Walter Chapin Simpson and Jessie Smith Simpson—the original protagonists of the Barclay doctrine. In Barc's words, his father and mother were *from totally different backgrounds*, by which he probably meant some kind of distinction between country and town with the distance of a continent in between, except that they both *came from families of modest means and both had college degrees…quite rare in the 1920s.*

Walter grew up on a farm in Greensboro, Vermont, where the rocky land produced more stone walls than crops. His grandparents, John and Janett Simpson, came in 1830 from Cardenden, Scotland, to scratch out a living in a land nearly as harsh as the one they had left. Walter's father was one of twelve children, whereas Walter was an only child, but like his father before him, he got up in the dark at 4:00 a.m. to feed the hogs before he walked to school. After high school, he sold pots and pans door to door to make enough money to go to the University of Vermont, graduated with a degree in chemistry, and migrated to Philadelphia, where he found work selling window screens. After a short time, through an affiliated Los Angeles window screen manufacturer, he was offered the opportunity to set up a screen-making venture in the San Francisco Bay Area. Accepting the offer, he headed west in 1914 and established a shop in Emeryville, a growing industrial section of the East Bay. It was known as "Butchertown" for the numerous meat-packing plants where cattle, raised on nearby ranches, were brought for processing. The stench emanating from the plants was as notorious as the numerous nearby bordellos and gambling houses. Walter took a room in a boarding house in neighboring Oakland, where he met Jessie Smith.

Jessie was born and raised in Oakland, and, rare for a woman in those days, attended college at UC Berkeley. She graduated in 1903 and became a schoolteacher, first at a grammar school and then at Oakland High School. Both in their late thirties and never before married, Walter and Jessie wed at the Oakland Courthouse in 1916. William Smith Simpson was born in 1918 and Barclay Walter Simpson was born three years later.

The two Simpson sons were born into a version of small-town America just as it was being transformed by increasing urbanization and industrialization, with all the upheavals of class, race, and economy that was to portend. The period of their childhoods represented a transitional moment in American history, normative in its middle-class status, yet chastened by recent memories of more straitened circumstances, with the Depression still looming in the near future.

∽

IN 1922, JESSIE AND Walter built a substantial house on Rosal Avenue between Lakeshore and Grand Avenues, close to where the flats begin to bend into the foothills. It was a friendly, middle-class neighborhood with ample lots and a pastoral feel, within walking distance of Lake Merritt, Lakeview Elementary School (where Jessie had taught school and where her sons were to matriculate), the local library, both Piedmont and Oakland High Schools, and, by 1926, the Grand Lake Theater, which offered vaudeville and silent movies. A hundred years earlier, the hills would have been crisscrossed with paths made by grazing cattle seeking shade under the ancient oaks that had once provided the Ohlone Tribe with a staple of their diet. A massive grove of virgin redwoods—many thirty feet in diameter and 300 feet tall—once towered atop the hills and served as a beacon to guide early ship captains through the Golden Gate into San Francisco Bay.

The Oakland of Barc's childhood was in its final decade of emergent prosperity, rising steadily as one of America's major small cities until it would be brought to its knees by the Great Depression. Due to its perfect natural harbor, it had become a thriving port and a center of the shipping industry. It boasted numerous manufacturing businesses, from canneries to shipbuilding, from metalworking to automobiles, and was the western terminus of the transcontinental railroad. Its sister across the bay might have been more famous, more glamorous, more culturally refined and cosmopolitan, but the sprawling city of Oakland was gritty and progressive, and San Franciscans, surrounded by their famous dense fogs, secretly envied its ideal Mediterranean climate.

Downtown Oakland bustled with banks, shops, insurance companies, department stores, restaurants, and early skyscrapers clustering around the convergence of San Pablo, Telegraph Avenue, and Broadway, which only a few decades earlier had been dirt roads radiating to the outlying farms and settlements of the vast Peralta Land Grant. Oakland City Hall, the first high-rise government building in the US, was considered the tallest structure this side of the Mississippi; and the Oakland Tribune building, still a beloved landmark, had begun adding a twenty-story tower, modeled after the Campanile in Venice (as was the famous bell tower on the UC Berkeley campus, completed in 1914).

Less than two miles from the house on Rosal Avenue, West Oakland bumped up against downtown from the bay side. Anchored by work on the docks and as an important railroad hub, it had long been a thriving, ethnically mixed neighborhood populated by Europeans, African Americans, Slavs, Mexicans, Portuguese, and Chinese, with schools and churches and neat, medium-sized houses surrounded by gardens.

The origins of the community go back to a small number of African Americans from the Deep South who had joined the Gold Rush and settled in West Oakland after the mining frenzy. Here, there were no Jim Crow laws to contend with and they could own a house. When Oakland was chosen in 1868 out of several possible coastal cities to anchor the final leg of the audacious Transcontinental Railroad, the Oakland rail yard became the hub of the Pullman Palace Car system. Only African Americans were hired to serve the wealthy clientele, reflecting the social structure of the country at large and playing on the retrograde imagery of the antebellum South. Drawn to the already established community and the prospect of work, southern Blacks gravitated to the far western town, causing the small, original enclave of African Americans in West Oakland to grow in size. The headquarters of the Brotherhood of Sleeping Car Porters, which was to become a militant labor union, was established in 1925 at Fifth and Wood Streets, and by the 1920s, prosperous African American–owned businesses—barber and beauty shops, eateries like the Creole Kitchen, boarding houses, and dress shops—flourished on Seventh Street. Jazz notes bending out of the clubs that lined the street set the tone for this rich hub of African American culture.

In spite of its somewhat renegade origins, the city wasn't able to escape the dangerous and prevailing racism that characterized most of the rest of the country. By the early twentieth century, the city of Oakland, threatened by possible integration of Blacks into white middle-class neighborhoods, passed an ordinance prohibiting African Americans from buying property in neighborhoods other than West Oakland. By the 1920s, the Ku Klux Klan had a firm foothold in the city.

Much of Oakland's post World War I growth, like the rest of the country's, had been energized by the escalating appetite for the automobile. East Oakland, the flat diagonal plain that stretched between Lake Merritt and San Leandro, became a nexus for an auto manufacturing frenzy, obliterating once fertile farmland. To accommodate the swell of factory workers, over 13,000 single-family houses were built in Oakland along with downtown apartment buildings designed in elegant 1920s style. By the time Chrysler built a new plant in 1929, Oakland had been dubbed "the Detroit of the West." When Walter Simpson first set up his window screen business in nearby Emeryville, his newly adopted home had a thriving economy.

～

BARC'S RECOLLECTIONS OF HIS childhood during the twenties and thirties sound like an idyll from a lost small-town America. By his own account, he grew up in *a close family* and had a home life rich in books and music. He remembers even as a small child accompanying his father to the library near Lakeview Grammar School, where he learned to love reading, a devotion that persisted throughout his life. From Jessie and Walter, he also inherited a deep enjoyment of music, especially classical, though the family repertoire also included show tunes and the alma maters of various colleges. Unable to afford to go to the opera or symphony in San Francisco, they bought records, putting together a substantial collection. The boys grew up hearing Beethoven, Bach, and Mozart issuing from the Victrola. Sunday nights Jessie would play the piano with father and sons singing along beside. Later, Barclay was to wonder whether the playing of college anthems was *a subtle impregnating of a higher education virus? If so, it worked.* A lasting legacy of these chamber music evenings was that Barclay could still sing—in his nineties—most of Cornell's "Far Above Cayuga's Waters."

Other family entertainments included ping-pong played on a plywood board fashioned by Walter and laid on top of the dining room table, a form of communal competition that was to be a central part of Barclay's family life for the next eighty-plus years. Walter and Jesse also taught their sons at an early age to play bridge, making possible the foursomes that were another central feature of Simpson Sunday evenings. Barclay's skill in these pursuits came to full fruition during his life as an anti-submarine naval pilot in the Aleutian Islands during World War II.

There was, of course, no television in the house, or the money for expensive structured entertainments or travel. Besides Saturday movies at the Grand Lake Theater or watching performances in parks, it was up to kids to seek out their own fun—street games like kick the can or racing handmade roller coasters down city streets, flying kites, baseball in the park, basketball on the school playground, or tennis at the local courts. With radio in its infancy, every kid knew how to make a crystal set and spent hours communicating with friends. In keeping with the family traditions of frugality, both boys had the proverbial paper routes.

The picture Barclay paints of his childhood represents a way of life from a more innocent and slow-paced age focused on family and neighborhood. Though he was to be swept up in the ever-escalating changes that shaped the history of the twentieth century, the almost prosaic pleasantness of his early life appears to have provided him a base of security that allowed him to weather the personal and public upheavals to come.

However, interestingly, such was not the case for his older brother, Bill. Though he should have shared in the great benefits of *good genes and good luck* that Barclay considered to be his own birthright, Bill's take-away from this inheritance was of a darker hue. Beneath the sunny surface of the Simpson family, the first and the second sons displayed radically divergent characters, springing from the same place and circumstance: *If you want an example of how important genes are, I've always been kind of a relaxed guy. But Bill had to have some genes that were really different from mine. He was tight. He had to succeed, he had to be first, he had to win. When he was in his forties, he killed himself.* Barclay, the classic second son, easygoing and only a modest achiever in his early years, turned out to be the one who emerged from the family rituals and training with a capacity for life and change that would allow him to reach the highest pinnacles in the worlds of business and philanthropy.

Perhaps in keeping with an age increasingly obsessed with personal psychology, Barclay was always interested in his placement within the family. Pulling on research outlined in *The Birth Order Book*[2] he became convinced that he and Bill were classic examples of first and second children in a two-child family. Bill was neat, organized, and looked for perfection in whatever he did, an admirable trait, but one that Barclay felt could lead to depression when carried to extremes. The research Barc read indicated that younger siblings tended to be more relaxed and less demanding of themselves. Barc points out that an unusual number of our presidents have been first-borns, but that the two most significant—Abraham Lincoln and George Washington—were second sons. This may, in small part, account for Barc's life-long obsession with Lincoln's character and leadership, though it is more likely that his interest in Lincoln's birth order was secondary to his fascination with Lincoln's dogged resilience under attack and his uncanny skills as a communicator.

～

GIVEN THE RESTRICTIVE HOUSING covenants that separated the races in Oakland, Bill and Barc attended public, predominantly white schools in their early years. Barc remembers that his time at Lakeview Grammar School was generally uneventful and even fun, except when he had a teacher who had taught Bill before him. It was too much of a temptation to compare them: Bill, the straight-A student, an Eagle Scout, and an outstanding member of the YMCA; Barclay, easily distracted in his schoolwork, never a Cub Scout nor a joiner of any organization, for that matter, who could find endless unstructured ways to amuse himself. Despite Bill's success as a student and his ability to excel at just about anything, including a more lucrative paper route than Barclay's, it seems a tribute to their parents that the boys got along well, with only rare and minor scuffles. Apparently, Jessie and Walter didn't believe that comparing Barc's imperfect performance at school with Bill's superior achievements would inspire their younger son to step up his schoolwork. Presumably they were right because Barclay managed to skip fourth grade.

Like so many thriving and not so thriving cities in the US, Oakland suffered the devastations of the Great Depression. Dilapidated encampments, like Pipe City at the foot of Nineteenth Avenue in Oakland, sprouted as hundreds of destitute, unemployed people found ingenious ways to survive day by day. As economic distress and unemployment persisted, increasing xenophobia resulted in forced deportations of Mexicans, whom white Californians blamed for taking their jobs—a sad, old tale with amazing staying power. In 1935, Congress passed the Filipino Repatriation Act, which offered free transport of Filipinos back to their native country. As Mexicans and Filipinos were forced out, refugees from dust-smothered Oklahoma, Arkansas, and Texas arrived in California expecting to find work. Instead, they were met with a paucity of jobs and open hostility. Even white skin did not protect the "Oakies."

Throughout the Depression, wealthy whites still traveled in the posh Pullman cars, generally keeping porters employed during these years of prolonged economic distress. The West Oakland music scene continued to thrive as porters brought "race music" back from their travels. While Black musicians were banned from downtown Oakland, West Oakland venues like the California Hotel and the Slim Jenkins Supper Club, which opened on the last day of Prohibition in 1933, thrived. With little interaction between Oakland's white middle-class and West Oakland's Black residents by day, a racially mixed clientele thronged to the popular nightclubs and dance halls by night to hear jazz and the distinctive, emerging West Coast Blues. Yet, it is a sign of the continuing constraints of racism that Barclay, growing up on a street near Lake Merritt, not more than 3.5 miles from the heart of West Oakland's jazz culture, had no recollection of ever being in that part of town until he went to work on the docks between high school and college. As he put it, ironically: *There weren't any race problems in those days....*

In spite of these trying times, Barc does not remember the period being one of great hardship for his family. *I didn't glean any negative information about the financial tribulations of my family until I was in my thirties. Neither of my parents ever complained within my hearing, so I had no idea of how tough the times were.* Movies were ten cents and cigarettes were fiften cents a pack, although Wings cigarettes were only a dime. An ice cream at Edy's Grand Ice Cream on Lakeshore Avenue was five cents, as was a ride on a streetcar. Tuition at UC Berkeley was seventy-five dollars per year and a nice automobile was a few hundred dollars. Whatever the cost of admission to a Cal football game, Barc didn't have it, but always a big Bears fan, he either snuck in by climbing the fence behind the Cal rooting section or, on days when that didn't work, watched the game from "Tightwad Hill." Who could have imagined that nearly eighty years later, the Simpson Center for Student-Athlete High Performance, a state-of-the-art facility for the training of high-performing scholar-competitors, would be built with funds provided by Barclay and his wife, Sharon, within yards of the famous hillside from which he had watched Bears games throughout his impecunious childhood and teenage years.

To make a few bucks, Barc got a job after school setting pins in a bowling alley in Oakland. He'd crouch behind the pins, dash out to clear the fallen ones and shoot the ball back, then stand them up for the next strike. In the summer of 1938, he also kept the books for his father at Simpson Screen Company.

In junior high school, Barc decided to cash in on his family-taught card-playing skills by learning poker. By high school he was a shark. It occurred to him that he and his poker pals might be able to make a buck or two in a game in Reno. Early Saturday mornings, they'd hide out at the Oakland freight yard and, waiting until nobody could see them, climb on top of a freight car headed east. By the time they got to Reno, with engine dust stuck on their faces, Barc said they looked like the comedians, common in those racist times, who performed in blackface. They stuck their heads in the Truckee River to clean up before heading to the Palace Club.

Though Bill attended Piedmont High School, Barclay was transferred out of the Piedmont District in the seventh grade for jurisdictional reasons and began attending Westlake Junior High and, later, Oakland High. He was invited back to Piedmont a year later, but he chose (against the desires of his mother, whom Barclay described as not insensible to questions of class) to stay in the central city district, whose student body came from *a considerably lower-income area* than Piedmont. Later, perhaps with the benefit of hindsight, he would observe, *The exposure to classmates from a variety of income levels and varied racial backgrounds had to be a plus.* Whether it was a dawning social consciousness that shaped Barclay's willed selection of Oakland High is hard to say beyond the fact that he appears to have registered the contrast with Piedmont High. He says that he made the choice because he *just didn't fit in* with the wealthy kids from Piedmont. At the very least, this choice would have introduced him to some of the tumult of the larger mixed-race world just beyond the borders of his old neighborhood.

While at Oakland High, Barc remembers being close to a Japanese American boy, who, along with his family, was to be gathered into the infamous Japanese internment camps set up in California in the early days of the Second World War. Eventually, when the government commissioned segregated Japanese American regiments to fight in Europe, Barc's friend was allowed to come out of the camp to fight the Nazis. Casualties among these troops were extremely high, as were their decorations for risk and bravery. After the war, Barc learned that his friend had been killed during the bloody slog up the boot of Italy.

As the effects of the Depression spread into every crevice of American life, a number of large and small economic stimulus efforts were undertaken in places across the land. In Oakland in the late twenties and early thirties, the city fathers tried to revive the movie business by constructing two grand theaters, known as the Fox Oakland and the Paramount. In larger-scale public works efforts during the thirties, two bridges began to rise on piers driven deep into San Francisco Bay, lifting spirits and bringing jobs. The Bay Bridge and the Golden Gate Bridge, like a couple of arms, joined the East Bay and Marin County to San Francisco by train and automobile, superseding, if not replacing, the older ferry service. These Depression-era landmarks are continuing reminders of the agony and triumph of the times.

As these momentous events unfolded, Barclay continued in the pursuits of an apparently lighthearted teenage boy who, reflecting family expectations, assumed he was headed for college. Fortunately for Barc, a "B" average was sufficient to get into UC Berkeley in those days. There seems never to have been any question that he would go to any college or university other than Berkeley.

To finance the step into higher education, Barc took a year off between high school and entering Cal, working full time on the docks in Oakland to earn his first year's tuition. This was before America entered the war officially, though by March of 1941, the country had passed the Lend-Lease Act, allowing the US to ship supplies to the Soviet Union and the UK. Barc continued to work on the docks off and on until he started training as a Navy fighter pilot in 1942. Not allowed aboard the ships since he wasn't in the Longshoremen's Union, he loaded cargo alongside. The job paid well—not so well as it would have for an official longshoreman, but enough to cover tuition, his fraternity dues, and other costs when he was to enter Cal in the fall of 1939. Coming just a few years after the general strike that had closed down the Bay Area waterfront, this period on the docks must have reflected some of the tumult and shifting demographics brought about by the earlier labor struggles. Apparently, Barclay fit in well enough as he was able to keep the job part-time during college, while he also worked the night shift at a Berkeley gas station.

Like much of the rest of the country and other struggling East Bay cities, Oakland was lifted out of the Depression by World War II, fast becoming the greatest shipbuilding center in the world as it entered a war-time production boom. In an attempt to meet the pressing demand, Moore Dry Dock in Oakland geared up to expand its shipbuilding capabilities and Henry Kaiser built four "instant shipyards" in Richmond. Following the attack on Pearl Harbor, as able-bodied men and women dropped college or work to join the armed forces, the labor surplus of the Depression suddenly turned into an extreme shortage. In Oakland, Henry Kaiser sent out a nationwide call for draft-exempt men. Tens of thousands of people, mostly poor whites (bringing their Jim Crow attitudes with them), Blacks from the Deep South, and Latinos from the Southwest poured into the East Bay. African Americans who had not been allowed to work in pre-Pearl Harbor wartime factories were hired, although there were still limitations on the jobs they were permitted to do. They primarily got the night shifts and the more dangerous assignments.

～

IT IS HARD TO know what long-term effects these turbulent events and the prevailing zeitgeist may have had on Barclay. He remembered that his parents were Republicans, though not vociferously so, and he did not recall contentious political debate or opinions on the home front. There seems to have been no obvious traces of entrenched ideological commitments in the building of his character or in the persona that solidified in later years, even when he himself entered local politics for a time. Whatever Barclay may have consciously digested, the city of Oakland provided an early stage on which core American tensions and inequalities were to play themselves out before the public eye, continuing through the twentieth century and onward into the twenty-first. The complexity of the struggles at the heart of Oakland's existence would have permeated the air Barc breathed.

Also palpable was the degree to which he was marked—young and forever—by a set of non-verbalized precepts involving fairness and honesty, will and work, physical and mental challenge. As was true of most of the generation that came of age during the Depression, he internalized a stern frugality, which in his case he attributed also to his Scottish heritage by way of hardscrabble Vermont. Though California born and bred, Barclay was always a kind of "Yankee" of the old stripe.

Chapter 3

From Here to Eternity: Berkeley to Alaska to Tokyo
1939–1945

The fighting on the Pacific islands was brutal, indeed, on both sides.

—Barclay

A S INTERNATIONAL EVENTS RUMBLED ominously in the distance, Barclay entered UC Berkeley in the fall of 1939, more than a year after the *Anschluss,* just as the Nazis invaded Poland; in quick succession, the UK and France declared war on Germany. Yet the threatening shadow cast by these events and the equally bloody incursions of Imperial Japan in the East seem not to have been in the forefront of his mind:

> *The two and one-half years that I spent at Cal before joining the Naval Air Corps were a great fun time, little disturbed by studying or learning much. I missed a lot of classes because of important activities such as chasing girls, drinking beer, playing tennis, intramural sports... bridge and poker...and various other means of avoiding intellectual elevation...including just hanging out with my buddies, some of whom have become lifelong friends.*

Barc's self-deprecating view of his own predispositions during his initial period at UC Berkeley contains little hint that he was to become one of the most important donors in the history of the university. On the other hand, his nascent love of UC Berkeley is perhaps already apparent in his description of the fun and friends that came out of his pre-war college years. Indeed, friendship was always to be of supreme importance to him and many of those friendships revolved around a group of guys he met at Cal.

In spite of what sounded like fun and games at Berkeley, he remembered a feeling of restlessness had taken hold of him. He decided to sign up for the Naval Air Corps. Many years later he explained, *I'd like to say it was patriotism that caused me to sign up. Actually, I was bored with school, and those Navy "Wings of Gold" gave the wearer status in any group anywhere. I thought that flying off of a carrier had to be a thrill. At my age and at that time danger was not a factor. It's a decision that I have never regretted.* He was impatiently awaiting his call for flight training before America officially entered the war.

In January of 1942, Barc had passed the variety of physical and mental tests required to become a Navy pilot and was eager to get started. Reading Charles Lindbergh's bestselling book *We*, published in 1927, only six weeks after the historic transatlantic flight, fired him up even more. He devoured Lindbergh's account of the Ryan monoplane's design, construction, and intimate details of the daring flight, and was especially riveted by the *spiritual partnership that had developed between himself and his airplane during the dark hours of his flight.*

Despite a desperate need for pilots, Barc and his friends had to wait several months while the Navy put together an entire flight school class from UC Berkeley, to be known as the "Flying Golden Bears." During advanced training, Barc applied to become a fighter pilot in the hope of getting to fly off of an aircraft carrier. Unfortunately, however, in the pressure chamber test required during training, he passed out at 18,000 feet, so they put him in single-engine, low-level anti-submarine patrol planes. After graduation from flight school, he joined a squadron based at the naval air station (NAS) in nearby Alameda, an island off of Oakland, joined to the mainland by a drawbridge. The first month was spent flying anti-sub patrols off the coast (a Japanese sub actually had shelled an oil field near Santa Barbara), but soon, the entire squadron was directed to fly their planes to Sitka on Alaska's panhandle, where they were to replace a scouting squadron, which had lost half its pilots due to weather, not enemy action. Shortly before leaving for Alaska, while on a training flight around the bay, Barc took it in mind to fly his plane under the Bay Bridge for the sheer thrill and beauty of it. He eased his aircraft through the narrow gap, just above the water, as people within eyeshot stopped what they were doing to watch. Then he decided that the span he had first chosen was too high and easy, so he did it again, this time under a lower part of the bridge. The Bay Area loved its fighter pilots—the rock stars of the era.

Barc spent fourteen months flying anti-sub patrols out of Alaska and then the Aleutian Islands when they took them back from the Japanese. Passing the time in unnavigable weather required inner resources and Barc wrote to UC Berkeley for a class in astronomy as well as books on several other subjects. He read the entire Bible and also became interested in Communism: *Russia was our ally, and Stalin's brutality was still buried behind the Urals. Communism's basic political philosophy—common ownership of all kinds and a stateless society—sounded wonderful; there was just one problem—it ignores human nature.*

In 1943, after many months flying patrols out of Alaska and the Aleutians, Barc was happy to get back to the lower states. Once again, he applied for carrier plane duty, either fighters or dive-bombers. This time, the record of his problem with altitude had become buried in the Navy's vast bureaucracy, and he was assigned to a squadron for training in carrier landing, gunnery, and dive-bombing. After this initial training, Barc proceeded with the unit known as Air Group 2 to the air station at Hilo, Hawaii, for additional training, including landing on various carriers off the coast of Hawaii.

Not yet assigned to a carrier, Air Group 2 spent time bombing islands that had been bypassed by the war but still had Japanese troops on them. Most of these enemy soldiers were more interested in avoiding bombs than in shooting down planes, so, according to Barc, the risks were minimal. What he was hoping for was to be in the center of the main action, a head-on fight on the scale of Midway, perhaps the greatest American naval battle of all time. But this historic confrontation had happened in 1942, before his squadron was on their way to Asia. In spite of his frustrations at being on the margins of the Pacific conflict, Barclay knew himself to be part of a savage struggle, the physical and emotional demands of which would be hard to match in normal life.

After a short time on Saipan, Air Group 2 finally was assigned to a carrier, the *Shangri La*, and joined the largest naval fleet ever assembled for war or peace. Following a handful of bombing runs, they put bundles of food and other supplies in their bomb bays instead of explosives and dropped the packages on the POW camps in Japan to desperate arms waving on the ground. Barc found life aboard a carrier exhilarating, requiring a high standard of efficiency and precision, especially during landings and takeoffs when the ship was most vulnerable to attack by hostile aircraft.

When the fighting stopped, the Shangri La steamed into Tokyo Bay, and Barc was among the first Americans to set foot in the utterly devastated capital city. He was shocked when he was told to take off his pistol before going ashore. *Jeez, a couple of days ago these people were trying to kill me!* But he heard of absolutely no incidents of Americans being bothered by the Japanese. *The Emperor had said that [the war] was over, and that was it!*

If any of them needed convincing of the horrors of war, the ruins of Tokyo would have been sufficient. It was a mass of twisted rubble where tens of thousands had died from US firebombing. Barc was appalled by the devastation, but agreed with the dominant opinion among those who fought the war in Asia:

> *I feel that if it were not for the pitiless bombing of Tokyo, as well as the atom bombing of Hiroshima and Nagasaki, the war would have continued for some time, long enough for millions more to die. During the war, not a single Japanese unit of any size surrendered; to do so was the ultimate disgrace, practically a criminal act that would result in ostracism or worse for one's family and one's self. Harry Truman made the tough decision to drop the atom bomb.*

Barc and some friends went ashore on three separate days. Barc remembered, *The first day, a handsome kimono could be bought for a cigarette, the currency of the moment. By the third day, it took at least a carton. No wonder with MacArthur's help, the Japanese built the third most important economy in the world.* On the third day in Tokyo, Barc and two of his friends decided to go beyond the boundaries of the ruined city into the relatively intact neighborhoods in the surrounding hills. Coming upon an unscathed house, they knocked on the door repeatedly until a terrified older Japanese man opened the door and prostrated himself at their feet, begging for mercy. The American kids backed off immediately, chastened by his terror and wanting to show they were not there for pillage, rape, or torture. Barc wondered whether some of the old man's fear was heightened by knowing what Japanese troops had done in Nanking and elsewhere.

Chapter 4
Home Again

These were times that caused the thought of "eat, drink, and be merry, for tomorrow you die"—an outcome that seemed more likely than it had before Hitler and Hirohito tried to rearrange the world. In that sort of atmosphere, key decisions tended to be made hurriedly, emotions often ruled over rationality. We had not had enough time together to know each other well enough to make what should be a lifetime commitment.

—Barclay

WITH THE CEREMONY ON the battleship *Missouri,* the war in the Pacific was over and it was time to head home. There was lots of space on the hangar and flight decks, and no reason for any flight operations, so they loaded up with sailors and marines and headed for California. Barc was excited to be going home; he was going to be married.

While on leave after completing flight school, Barclay had become reacquainted with Joan Devine, who had been a classmate at Oakland High. She was attending Mills College and he saw her picture in *The Oakland Tribune* as one of Mills's homecoming queens. Joan had been engaged to a fellow classmate who had been an Air Force pilot engaged in daylight bombing over Germany, a mission that accounted for perhaps the highest continuous casualty rate of any group in the entire war. His plane had been shot down and he was presumed dead. Barc and Joan saw a lot of each other during his two weeks' leave.

When the *Shangri La* anchored in San Pedro harbor on November 7, 1945, he and Joan were married in a small hotel on Wilshire Boulevard in Los Angeles. This hasty decision to marry would eventually end in divorce, but not before the marriage produced three beloved children.

Air Group 2 was disbanded a few days after their wedding and most of the pilots mustered out of the Navy, although a few decided to make it a career.

Barc had given considerable thought to that option before deciding to return to UC Berkeley to get a degree in Business Administration and from there to go on to law school. With three months before classes started, he got a job as a test pilot at the Naval Air Station, Alameda, which required him to spend one weekend a month in either a dive bomber or fighter squadron checking aircraft out at various instrument settings and altitudes. Additionally, the job involved a two-week cruise per year as a flyer in a carrier air group. Getting to fly practically all of the Navy's single-engine aircrafts in service at any given time appealed to Barc both intellectually and athletically, so much so that he stayed in the Naval reserve for fourteen years following the war.

⌢

WHEN FEBRUARY 1946 ROLLED around, Barc doffed jeans and tennis shoes, signing up for a full load at UC Berkeley's business school. Unlike his pre-war college stint, this time around he was serious and determined to be a top student. Most of his classmates were also veterans, dedicated to getting high grades in order to get the best jobs or admission to advanced degree programs. Motivated students who had just returned from life-altering experiences coupled with outstanding professors created a fertile setting for a serious pursuit of knowledge. Barc was now ready for that.

The GI Bill, which provided World War II veterans financial aid for college, meant that for the first time in US history, millions of men and women from poor and working-class backgrounds could attend college alongside their wealthier contemporaries. California, with its already well-established system of community and state colleges and universities, was more prepared than most states to meet the mass demand for higher education. Already highly regarded because of its participation in the Manhattan Project, Cal's prestige continued to rise. Between 1945 and 1948 its student body jumped to over 25,000 and over several years a massive construction program was implemented as the campus expanded. Huge dormitories and apartment buildings were hastily slapped up and property owners adjacent to the university chopped their single-family houses into apartments to rent to students.

With so many GIs returning to college before the campus expansion had begun, it was difficult to find an apartment. Luckily, Barc and his new wife, Joan, found a place right next to campus where they shared a showerless bathroom with two other apartments and bathed in locker rooms on campus. Joan got a job with the Cal admissions department and Barc's income from the GI Bill of ninety dollars per month, plus pay from the Naval Reserve, made him feel rich. In addition to a full load in regular sessions, Barc took classes throughout the summer of 1946. By that September, he was just three credits away from graduation and looked forward to entering law school, a profession that in later life he would excoriate with nearly Chaucerian passion. But, for the moment, life seemed to be getting back to normal.

Then, Barc got a fateful phone call.

His father had had a serious heart attack. He called to say that he could no longer manage his small yet resilient and modestly profitable business. With annual revenues in 1946 of around $100,000, the company did not appear saleable, and Walter asked Barc to take it over.

Chapter 5
The Family Business

The product was a commodity that made it difficult to differentiate it from competitors' screens.

—Barclay

THE SIMPSON SCREEN COMPANY, set up by Walter in Emeryville in 1914, was a small operation of four or five men, initially. Walter managed the factory and did most of the sales with a few employees handling the actual manufacturing of the screens. The early, relative success of the company may have been linked to the new construction stimulated by Oakland's growth during the 1910s and 1920s as a regional manufacturing center, port, and railroad hub.

In later years, Barclay would observe that, though a natural salesman, Walter never found a way to successfully differentiate his product from the competition; that is, he never moved from the marketing of a "commodity" to the creation of a brand. In building his own separate business a decade later, Barclay was to apply this insight in his creation of a distinctive approach to sales and manufacturing. Tellingly, he seems also to have retained another lesson from his father regarding the treatment of his customers and employees: *I think my father was totally honest. I think he had a high regard for other people's feelings.* This observation of simple virtues may explain why Simpson Strong-Tie, Barc's powerhouse company founded in 1956, took more than half a century to set up an internal human resources (HR) department or to codify decent human behavior in a company handbook.

An effective business manager, Walter was also an inventor, a capacity that Barc was to recognize and cultivate on a grand scale in the building of his own product line in the coming years. Walter's most notable invention involved the design of a roller screen for casement windows—an idea that allowed him to grow the business during the boom years. But with the stock market crash of 1929, followed by the persistent economic stagnation of the early thirties, new home construction came to a halt, bringing the Simpson Screen Company close to collapse. Walter saved the business through yet another invention—a latch hasp for gates—a niche product that allowed the business to limp through the worst of the Depression and continue at a reasonable rate of growth up until the end of World War II.

Having always intended to enter the family business, Barc's older brother, Bill, after returning from the war, joined his father in running the company. A year into Bill's tenure, Walter concluded that his elder son was on the way to wrecking the business. In what Barclay termed the toughest decision of his father's life, he told Bill how he felt and let him go. Barc always believed that this choice triggered his father's heart attack.

Whatever the medical facts of the matter, Walter's decision to fire his oldest son and long-identified successor in the business is remarkable, both in terms of personal psychology and for what it says about management practices. The question of merit versus "blood loyalty" is a fundamental issue in any family-owned and operated business, and such businesses often founder on variations of the dilemma faced by Walter in 1946. This rather radical example of hard decision-making seems not to have been lost on Barclay.

Though he had never had any desire to go into the family business, when the phone rang that day, Barc felt that he could not turn down his father's desperate request. In accepting, he made one key stipulation: *I had his pledge that I would be in complete charge.* He had no interest in serving an apprenticeship. With this concession, the Simpson business genes were now to be tested through the performance of the second son.

Having been guaranteed his place at the helm, Barclay took over the running of Simpson Screen Company, leaving UC Berkeley in the fall of 1946, just three credits short of his degree in Business Administration. He had no idea that he would not complete those credits for a bachelor's degree from UC Berkeley for another twenty years. Nor did he likely realize that he was to lead Simpson-named businesses for nearly sixty-seven years, increasing annual revenues over the years from $100,000 in 1946 to net sales of $706.3 million in 2013, the year he retired from the board of directors of Simpson Manufacturing, to $1.27 billion in 2020.[3] In the process, he was to utterly transform the "family business" into a "blood blind" enterprise open to those with the competency, will, originality, and tenacity to seize the day.

⌇

THE ADMINISTRATIVE AND MANUFACTURING facility for the Simpson Screen Company, originally located in Emeryville, was later moved to East Oakland where a handful of employees continued to build the product line. In spite of difficulties squeezing much profit from the business, Barclay described the first years as satisfying in other ways:

> *While the hours were long out of necessity and the initial compensation not very exciting, being my own boss in a real business could only be described as exhilarating. Whether it succeeded or not, I would have no one to blame but myself. The opportunity to make real money was there. I had a substantial piece of the action.*

Barclay's early interest in having a "piece of the action" was to characterize the rest of his business career, in the double sense of his wanting to run things and in the implied impatience for action itself, as opposed to slow deliberation and hesitation.

During the late forties, in search of more reliable profits, Barclay began to shift the emphasis of the business from wooden window screens to the construction of vents, louvers, and kitchen fans. This change in focus resulted in the company assembling kitchen fans for the west coast stores of Sears and Roebuck and Montgomery Ward. Soon after, he bought some more metal-working equipment, including a sixty-ton punch press, and went in search of profitable contract metal work. The proceeds of one such job for the Bechtel Corporation in Oakland allowed him to build his first family house on Miner Road in Orinda, California.

By 1949, Barclay got out of the window screen business entirely, and in 1950 successfully wooed a Sears buyer in the Chicago office to list one of his kitchen fans in their nationwide summer catalogue that was mailed to thousands of American homes across the country. Barc's competitive instincts were roused: *It was really exciting, as we were competing with firms many times our size. It would be six more years before we became Simpson Manufacturing.* During these first hectic years running the Simpson Company, Barclay and Joan gave birth to three children: John Barclay Simpson in 1947, Anne

Katheryn Simpson in 1949, and Jean Devine Simpson in 1952 (see bios). From the outside, the Simpsons appeared to be a classic post-World War II American family of the forties and fifties.

~

THROUGHOUT THE EARLY POST-WAR era, the world Barclay and his family had known while he was growing up in Oakland saw its demographics and economy change radically, altering the face and social relations of the city and the region at large. By the early 1950s, freeways sanctioned by Oakland's city fathers—often with little regard for neighborhood integrity—sprouted like weeds. The Nimitz Freeway cut off the Oakland waterfront, and when the double-decker Cypress Street Viaduct completed the connection between the freeway and the Bay Bridge, it not only made a gash through West Oakland, but isolated the neighborhood from downtown as well. Urban renewal further destroyed elegant Victorian houses and businesses to make room for high-rise apartments. What was left of the Latino community moved to the flats of Fruitvale and much of the displaced African American community relocated to East Oakland. By the time BART roared through West Oakland in the sixties, the blues could no longer compete with the rumble of trains overhead, and Slim Jenkins closed his doors for good.

Between 1950 and 1960, the freeways carried over 100,000 white property owners north, south, and over the hills to the developing suburbs where jobs and housing boomed. Wealthy Oaklanders moved to Berkeley, Kensington, Albany, and El Cerrito and east to Walnut Creek, Orinda, Lafayette, and Concord; middle- and working-class residents joined the primarily Portuguese-American population in San Leandro, and onward down to Hayward and Fremont. Oakland's version of the national trend of "white flight" left in its wake increasing poverty and hardened racial divisions. Restrictive covenants in the primarily white suburbs remained throughout the 1960s. Oakland and the entire East Bay were about to enter a new period of their history in which questions of race and economic development would become ever more compelling and fractured—even as the new California economy was set to boom.

~

From 1949 to 1955, the Simpson Company grew in size and profitability, but in Barclay's mind he was not *accomplishing the element essential to building a long-range business: creating a brand name and encouraging specifiers, distributors, and users to prefer our product over the competition.* Barc had long felt that this failure to create a brand name for his product was at the heart of his father's inability to build a truly profitable business in spite of Walter's natural skill as a salesman and designer. The concept of branding— the transformation of a generic tissue into a "Kleenex," or the "Xerox" copier machine into an internationally used verb—is an ancient precept of American business, perhaps all business. More recently, the "FAANGS" (Facebook, Apple, Amazon, Netflix, and Google) offer dramatic versions of what branding can mean to market share. Barclay's early focus on the importance of creating a named product was transformative, ultimately changing him from a small local businessman to the chief executive of a global company, whose brand name—Simpson Strong-Tie—became interchangeable with a set of core products that have become essential to modern construction. In considering this transformation, however, Barclay always believed that it was *good luck,* not ingenuity or brilliance that provided him with the necessary catapult. It depends, of course, on how one understands both luck and brilliance.

Chapter 6
A Knock on the Door

Then, something happened that proved that it was better to be lucky than smart.

—Barclay

O NE SUNDAY EVENING IN 1956, Barc answered the ring of the doorbell and found a stranger standing on the porch with a piece of bent metal in his hand. The stranger's name was Warner Odenthal. He was the brother of a neighbor, who had heard that Barc owned a punch press. After Barc invited him in, Odenthal held up the shaped object and asked whether Barc might be able to fabricate 25,000 metal connectors for him—*at the right price*. Odenthal and his partner had invented a new system of furnishing and erecting roof structures for commercial and industrial buildings such as warehouses and shopping centers. This "panelized roof system" needed a metal connector, known as a joist hanger, to tie together the ends of the horizontal beams with the cross beams that supported the four by eight plywood panels.[4] In Barc's world at the time, 25,000 units of anything was potentially a very large order. He told Odenthal he would call him first thing in the morning and took the metal piece to the head machinist at the plant. After brief consideration, his shop foreman told him that his crew could make the piece for ten cents per unit, though it would involve retooling the punch press for automatic production. Barc decided to take the risk, quoted a total price to Odenthal of $2,500 for the run, and got the order. This first experimental run did not result in great profits, but it was done on time and paid for. Characteristically, Barc noted: *We learned a lot…and Warner paid the bill on time, not a sure thing with a new business.*

Tom Fitzmyers (see bio), who was to be hired by Barc in 1978 to take over much of the daily operations of Simpson Manufacturing, laughingly recalled the now nearly mythic story of the Simpson screen business seamlessly morphing into a connector company: *I think it's kind of funny. Warner asked Barc if he could make these connectors and he said "sure," but I don't think he knew what the part was. So, he brought it back to the plant and gave it to somebody who was building vents for roofs and said, "Figure this out," and the guy did.*

Fitzmyers was undoubtedly correct when he observed that Barc did not know what a joist hanger was when Odenthal brought him the first connector. Yet something deep inside of him appears to have clicked as the job rolled forward. Like most successful entrepreneurs, he was drawn to risk, which is apparent even in his original market research and back-of-the-envelope calculations as he was quickly digesting the implications of Odenthal's commission. While his machinists were doing the tooling and punching out of the connector, Barc called on building material wholesalers and retailers throughout the Bay Area. Most of them were selling a structural connector made by the Timber Engineering Company (TECO), which was the only business selling the part nationwide. Although there were many sheet metal shops throughout the country making a few relatively simple connectors, TECO had, through lack of concerted competition, been able to build something of a brand name, and was the only product then being specified by engineers. Ascertaining that TECO had separated the manufacturing of its products from distribution and sales, Barc learned that the company had a rather limited line of products, with a small sales force composed of a few engineers. *Not a great business model,* he was later to observe. He estimated that the company's sales were between $2 and $5 million a year—quite a spread on which to make a major business decision. By his own admission, Barc confessed that this analysis was *based on little fact.* But his nose was twitching. As one of his long-term employees, John Herrera, was to put it years later, *He's a big gambler...he rolled the dice...he doesn't want to fail, but you can't take a risk if you're not prepared to fail....*

Having done the cursory research and with an instinct for opportunity, Barc estimated that the possible nationwide market for connectors might be ten times TECO's gross annual revenues. A born salesman, he appears to have recognized an important gap in the rival business plan, gleaning the chance to create a brand based on the integration of manufacturing, marketing, and customer service that would directly target engineers, architects, construction firms, and other end users. In 1956, strict building codes were neither widely diffused nor systematically enforced. In this, Barc saw a chance to link product development to engineering, and from that baseline to the establishment of precise building specifications. This realization turned out to be prescient, especially in California, where the threat and reality of earthquakes created strong impetus for the drafting, diffusion, and enforcement of ever more exacting building codes in the coming decades. Simpson fortunes were to ride side by side with this new art and science of specification, which in large part the company also helped to shape first at the local and, eventually, at the global level.

Ever ready for a bit of risk and with the sensitive nerve endings of a natural competitor, Barclay, almost overnight, radically shifted the direction of the Simpson Company: *The connector industry appeared to be in its infancy.... Having decided that there was a promising future in the structural connector field, we jumped in with both feet. The company was still called the Simpson Company. We incorporated and changed the name to Simpson Strong-Tie after the name of the core product* (Barc). The evocative metaphor at the heart of this product descriptor—which was the winning entry in an intra-company contest to select a name—captures some of the spirit of the new company's inception. Indeed, the term "strong ties" and the business that was to come into being to refine, fabricate, test, and market this core product and its many descendants goes to the heart of the company's culture and remarkable success over more than six decades.

The story behind the launching of Simpson Strong-Tie (SST) reflects a different era and ethic—a seat-of-the-pants approach wedded to a simple, driving entrepreneurial instinct—that allowed chance and raw opportunity to become the springboard for the creation of an extremely profitable business based on a fundamental product. No McKinsey, no computers, no lawyers, no headhunters. At the heart of the story is an apparent contradiction: Barclay was an archetypal generalist, yet he went on to create a highly technical business based on intricately engineered products that helped set the standard for the US residential and, later, industrial construction industry for the next half century and beyond. In time, of course, computers and even a few lawyers were to figure in the expansion of the business across America into Canada, the UK, Europe, Asia/Pacific, and South America. The genius of the company was always to be inextricably tied to Barclay's willingness to take a risk and think quick and deep.

Warner Odenthal's knock on the door brought into being the now-famous *F24*, the first "Simpson Strong-Tie," whose initial limited aim was to join one framing element or material to another. If luck was the spark that launched a major new manufacturing enterprise, Barc's instinct that the basic product might have wide application beyond Warner's innovative roofing systems fanned the blaze. From early on, he saw in this emerging twentieth century form of joinery the opportunity to do something much bigger in scope than simply mass produce a standard lumberyard commodity for the linking together of two-by-fours with two-by-eights. This perception proved golden.

To the unpracticed eye, the original connector might appear a prosaic piece—what Fitzmyers comically referred to as *sleepy metal benders. Just a bunch of sleepy metal benders.* But it was Barclay's original inspiration to see in this simple object the key to a much more complex interlocking system of possibilities. Even before he perceived the full structural potential of connectors, he imagined an enterprise devoted to a comprehensive system of technical support that emphasized painstaking customer service, training of end users, product testing, and an absolute cross-fertilization between specific customer needs and product development. For him, the piece of bent metal was always the object but not the essence of the business.

Chapter 7
Bill

I have lost nothing that belongs to me; it was not something of mine that was torn from me, but something that was not in my power has left me.

—"The Discourses," by Epictetus (c 50–c 135 AD)

FOLLOWING THE EXPULSION OF his older son, Bill, from the Simpson Screen Company in 1946, Walter set him up in a drapery business, located in an industrial building fronting on Mt. Diablo Boulevard—the main artery connecting the Contra Costa County cities of Orinda, Lafayette, and Walnut Creek. Although Barclay speculated openly on the agonies that firing Bill had caused his father, he expressed only vague theories as to what the firing meant to Bill himself. Nor did he speak of any resulting friction between him and his older brother. Whatever the weight of the event may have been, in 1960, Bill committed suicide by carbon monoxide poisoning in his garage. Barc got the call from Bill's wife and the police. Bill had closed the doors and windows in his car and redirected the fumes. He was in his forties. His second marriage was breaking up. Barc had the wrenching task of going to his parents' apartment in Oakland to tell them the dreadful news. He believed it hastened the onset of his mother's Alzheimer's, as symptoms manifested shortly afterward. She would live another eight years, mainly in an institution; his father predeceased her, dying in 1968 at the age of eighty-nine, staying mentally sharp until the end and very much at Barc's side. Outside of his family at least, Barclay never spoke of Bill's suicide except to state the plain facts and to allude to the philosophy of the Stoics, who counsel no suffering over things that can't be changed. The rest is opaque.

Notes for Part I

1 *The Greatest Generation,* Tom Brokaw, 1998, Random House.

2 *The Birth Order Book,* Dr. Kevin Leman, 1985, Revell.

3 See 2020 Annual Report. https://www.simpsonmfg.com.

4 A revolutionary method for framing a roof on industrial and commercial buildings. Originally called the Berkeley Panelized System, this method of framing became the mainstay for large wood roof structures throughout the West Coast. https://www.wood-works.org.

PART II
Essence of a Business

It's simple and it's revolutionary. The so-called "secret sauce" is pretty straight-forward: treat people well, give them a vested interest, pay them properly, support their kids, and make a community out of the business.

—Jennifer Chatman, Professor UC Berkeley Haas Business School, Simpson Manufacturing Board of Directors, 2004 to the present; see bio

Picture of SST employees with Barc in front of the San Leandro Office and Manufacturing Facility, 1976

Chapter 8
Product: The Leap into Connectors

*There was a moment of transition—early on—when Barc and Tye Gilb said,
"We're not a job shop making pieces of metal on demand. We're making a technical
piece that carries loads throughout a structure." That was the beginning...*

—Kristin Lincoln, Simpson Strong-Tie Employee from 1995–2016; see bio

The F24 Connector[1]

FOR THOUSANDS OF YEARS, wood-frame buildings were joined by
mortise and tenon, without the benefit of nails. Then came toenailing,
which involved the nail being angled through the base of one board into
another as a crude form of structural connector. That was fine in general,
but under abnormal pressure—from hurricanes, earthquakes, or other
extreme weather events—the old technology couldn't be counted on to hold.
During an earthquake, for instance, as soon as the earth started rumbling,
the house would rock, with the top going one way and the bottom another,
often carrying the building off of its foundations. With larger or multistoried
structures, engineering considerations become even more complex. Replacing
these older systems for tying together the component parts of wood-frame
buildings, structural connectors provide a modern system of joinery that

has transformed the construction industry. SST has been a central player in this transformation.

> *Before structural connectors, wood-frame buildings were held together by a hope and a prayer. They used whatever pieces of metal they had, combined with screws and nails, and anything else they could find, and hoped it would all stand up. The structural connector streamlined all of that, and ultimately also provided important technical innovations in the distribution of loads. This latter factor changed architecture while also providing much greater structural stability in the case of seismic or high-wind events.* (Barclay)

The SST website provides a simple definition of the F-24 connector—its core part: "Structural connectors are pieces of steel, engineered to connect and strengthen the frame of a building."[2] Over time, the original part designed by Simpson Manufacturing to meet the specific needs of Warner's panelized roofing system became the prototype for over 4,000 different products, including variations on the original metal part such as joist hangers, hurricane ties, straps, and hold-downs, as well as a variety of metal and non-metal anchor and structural systems that eventually also comprised epoxies and premanufactured shear walls—all aimed at tying together framing and foundation materials such as wood, masonry, and concrete. Brilliant as was Barc's initial perception that he could build a new business based on simple pieces of bent metal joinery, it was the next imaginative leap that transformed the core product from a knock-off lumberyard commodity into a brand.

From a construction engineering standpoint, the most important change in the connector business came when a simple, generic metal piece was redesigned to be one element in an integrated structural system of metal and non-metal products that both tied together individual framing materials and created what came to be known as "a continuous load path" aimed at lashing together the entire building through the systematic distribution of loads. A basic structural connector was already in use before Barclay got into the business; what SST did was transform that piece into a complete, highly engineered load-bearing system. As detailed in the company catalogue, the core concept behind the SST system is:

"To tie the [building] together from the roof to the foundation… [guaranteeing] a continuous load path is important because it helps redistribute outside pressures or forces caused by earthquakes and high winds, transferring these external forces from the frame to the foundation, which, [in turn], is securely anchored to the ground."

Terry Kingsfather (SST employee, 1979–2014; see bio)—one of the pioneering SST salesmen in the Northwest for eighteen years before moving to the home office in Pleasanton in 1997 as a part of the management team— synthesizes the concept further:

> *The thing you need to understand, it's not just connectors. It's not just screws. It's not just epoxy or tools. It's a whole systems approach to building. It's not like we sell carpet or linoleum or tile or cabinets or roofing material. All our stuff, once it's in and covered up, you don't even know it's there. You only know it's there if your house doesn't fall down. This is what we sell.*

Engineers loved the products produced out of the continuous load path system, especially when SST started to systematically test and design connectors that both met and helped modify key specifications for residential building. These products offered engineers a new level of security in an era when seismic- and wind-related codes were becoming ever more stringent— especially in the earthquake-prone West and the hurricane-beleaguered South.

Architects loved them, too, because they offered much greater design flexibility in dealing with the load-bearing elements of a structure. Kingsfather explains that by *using our stuff*, architects could design *a pretty cool house*, allowing them to come up with open-plan layouts that wouldn't have been possible before. Where they might have once had to place a large beam or wall to carry the structural load, they could now replace the cumbersome element with an integrated system of connectors that could bear and distribute loads and spans. And the strong ties were out of sight behind walls or in roofs, ceilings, floors, and foundations.

Kingsfather says that, initially, not all contractors loved the product as much as the engineers and architects, because it added a new element— particularly from the point of view of the older guys. Who, for instance, was to supply the connectors—the framers or the general contractors? But they could also see the benefits, and the connectors provided an efficient way to deal with new code requirements. The younger guys coming up really liked the ingenuity and efficiency of the "gadgetry." Plus, the connectors offered guarantees backed by the faith and insurance of SST and made up a relatively small portion of the overall cost of construction. A businessman, Barry Williams, observes:

> *If you were a contractor building a $400,000 house, the Simpson portion of your house is probably—I'm winging it—400 bucks. So why would you care? The reason you care is that with that $400 worth of Simpson stuff, you can build your house incredibly faster and stronger.* (Barry Lawson Williams, Business Executive and Simpson Manufacturing Board of Directors, 2004–2014; see bio)

Though the original SST connector was used in the framing of roofs for commercial buildings, the company's early marketing efforts focused on residential construction, taking advantage of the post-war housing boom sweeping California and the rest of the country. Betting on residential put the business on the map, but the inevitable, periodic bust cycles (such as those experienced in the early nineties and then dramatically in 2006–2009) made clear that SST needed to expand its product line. By the nineties, the company began to focus increasingly on more diversified applications, developing a range of new products for the non-residential market, and for construction systems organized around mortar and concrete in addition to wood-frame buildings.

From the time he took over his father's window screen business, Barclay had been looking for a product that he could put his name on, that could move the business beyond the narrow horizons of a job-shop. His first achievement was in recognizing that there were myriad applications for the kind of metal connector Odenthal had asked him to machine for his specialized roofing system. But what is perhaps more remarkable is Barc's transformation of the single, simple piece of bent metal into a vast system of load-bearing parts and anchors that have become fundamental to man-made structures around the world.

His particular form of entrepreneurial genius was in making this special blend of the basic and the complex both intrinsically useful and conceptually compelling for his employees and his customers—and, in time, to his board of directors and to people and markets outside of North America. The basic part was both elemental and elegant, as described by Jacinta Pister, one of the company's superstar woman engineers, who also armed herself with a business management degree in the pursuit of a demanding career (Jacinta Pister, SST employee, 1986–present; currently senior vice president; see bio). Hired in 1986 out of the glitter of the corporate world into SST's homely cave in San Leandro, Pister is both contemplative and comical in describing the rudimentary power of Barc's chosen product. Holding up a recent copy of SST's original F24 connector, she jokingly observes: *Maybe I already had this bent and I didn't know it. I wanted something concrete, something tangible. Neither the electronics industry nor banking felt tangible. And you can't get a lot more tangible than this.*

Tangible certainly—but Pister's feel for the piece suggests something more than just admiration for its essentialist form. As she continues, one hears respect for both its simplicity and its protean potential as a modern capstone for distributing force fields: *It's really cool...so down and dirty. That's what I think is so much fun. You can pick up a connector, and even though you may not be able to visualize exactly how the wood would all fit together (although some people can), you know that piece is something that makes a difference in people's lives on a daily basis.* Even for the layman, such a system of primary elements, simultaneously mundane and miraculous, has a simple clarity and conceptual elegance that is pleasing without the need to understand the specialized engineering formulas that make the structural connector stand up to rolling earth, howling wind, and rogue wave.

Chapter 9

Place: From East Oakland to San Leandro

I won the coin toss and decided to take the front two and a half acres....

—Barclay

SIMPSON STRONG-TIE WAS EAST Bay born and bred—and the life of the company was to reflect the changes undergone in that community from the early post-war era through the early nineties. By 1960, not a square inch of the old window screen facility in East Oakland was unused. With Simpson Manufacturing growing rapidly, and still very intertwined with Warner Odenthal's roofing business, Barc and Warner started looking together for a new plant location in San Leandro. Sandwiched between Oakland and Hayward, much of San Leandro's agricultural land, dairy farms, and cherry groves had gradually been converted for small industrial uses since the twenties. Between 1940 and 1950, the population of San Leandro doubled. Restrictive covenants barring African Americans from buying houses in San Leandro meant the population was 99.3 percent white by 1960. Its neighbor, Oakland, was 23 percent African American.

At the time Barc and Warner went scouting for new real estate, close to one hundred acres of industrial parcels had recently been annexed by the city of San Leandro. Within this newly incorporated acreage, Barc and Warner decided to purchase a five-acre parcel that backed up against the railroad. With the toss of a coin, Barc won the front 2.5 acres and Warner took the back, and both built new buildings to house their operations. Over the next decade, Simpson Manufacturing and Berkeley Plywood became flourishing businesses within the city that *The Wall Street Journal* called "a national model of small-scale industrial success."

On his 2.5-acre parcel, Barc built a two-story building that fronted Doolittle Drive, a main industrial artery running through San Leandro to

Oakland. It housed everything—sales, accounting, manufacturing, and the warehouse. Next to his own office, Barc built an office for his father, an arrangement that allowed him to enjoy both his father's company and counsel. By that time, Walter had quit driving and would catch the bus, and then walk the considerable distance to the office. True to his original commitment, Walter did not second-guess his son's decisions.

As the thirty or forty people that comprised the SST family in those years settled into their new home, the company was positioned in time and place for explosive growth. From 1960 through the mid-nineties, the two buildings constructed that first year were to house Simpson Manufacturing from just after its inception to beyond the time the company was taken public in 1994. An employee hired by the company in the mid-eighties describes a by-then dilapidated complex crammed helter-skelter with desks and file cabinets, accountants sitting on top of salespeople, sitting on top of product designers, with prototypes of strong-ties strewn across multi-sheet order forms:

There was a railroad behind us, and when the trains would come through, they seemed to crash together. The whole building would shake, and there was this weird chandelier just above the staircase, a chandelier in this really rundown, awful building, and the chandelier would kind of sway. So, you didn't know if there was an earthquake or it was just the trains....One guy in R&D had a kiddie pool in his office, because in the winter the ceiling would leak....Occasionally, you would get nails in your tires because, of course, we had manufacturing there as well....Berkeley Farms was next door to us, and boy did the smell come wafting in from the cows....(Jennifer Price, SST employee, 1991–present; see bio)

The shabbiness of the plant and office facilities in San Leandro reflected Barc's committed frugality, dramatizing his deep and continuing preference for substance over show.

But frugality is only part of the story. Barc's congenital restlessness and need to constantly disrupt the status quo by seeking new opportunities functioned as a counterweight to his native disinclination to spend money on glitz and glamour or the trappings of executive power. He was particularly allergic to the latter, insisting everyone in the company be on a first-name basis with each other in spite of rank, no reserved parking spaces for the brass, and neat but casual dress—even in the gray suit and fedora era, long before Silicon Valley donned blue jeans and T-shirts as *de riguer* dress for salaried and hourly employees alike. So, although the stripped-down surface of things at SST was on the shabby side, Barc was always seeking out new investment opportunities.

What the San Leandro plant did represent—more than frugality—was the early communal spirit of the company, one that was a natural outgrowth of the small number of SST employees, the scrappy conditions, the excitement of discovery, and the early days of slugging it out with the competition. What is remarkable is that the exhilaration of these experiences has extended into the present, not as nostalgia but as present passion among the "old guard" as well as with subsequent generations of Simpson employees who never knew the swinging chandelier, the cows, the squeals of the railroad, or the baby pool catching the drops from a leaking ceiling.

Clearly Barc's initial decision to make the leap into connectors was motivated by his instinct that there was the potential for significant growth in the industry. But what he managed to build was a business that moved way beyond the marketing of widgets—creating instead an animated world of people solving big problems using basic materials. Every product had scores of people behind it. In John Herrera's words: *A Simpson strong-tie is not just a piece of bent metal, but the service, the support, the ethic,* [and] *the passion of the people who designed, cut, tinkered with, packed, stored, and sold the product.* The tensile strength of the final connector was a reflection of their tenacity and originality. Barc's brilliance was to utterly engage those people in a kind of heroic, communal quest.

Chapter 10
People: Giants and Genius

A key element of what made SST different is how Barc treated his people,
allowing them to develop, encouraging their education, realizing the value of the
employee or the person....I think that's the philosophy of Simpson Strong-Tie,
and that's what they're trying to instill across the board. It's just that
appreciation of how valuable your people are.

—Mike Plunk, SST Employee 1972–2013; see bio

G ENERALLY, THE TERM "LEADERSHIP" conjures visions of top-down command, of kings, czars, Caesars, CEOs—of a charismatic capo able to mold people and materials according to a fixed goal and vision. The SST leadership story seems both similar and different from the traditional version. Certainly, Barc brought charisma and native capacity to the task, as well as scrupulous personal integrity, toughness, hard work, willingness to get his hands dirty, a very big personality, and a powerful ego—many of these being common qualities of great leaders. But rarer, perhaps, was the improvisational nature of his leadership, his natural inclination for collaborative ventures carried forward by instinct more than blueprint. For him, the most important part of the leadership equation—and the source of the creativity from which greatness comes—were the people themselves. From the early days, his method was based on a commitment to reciprocity, a belief that power shared begets success much more effectively than power hoarded.

Barclay's striking accomplishment finding the "right" people and then giving them their head was the most vital element in a management style that was essentially nonhierarchical. In the sixties and seventies, the idea of "the horizontal organization" had not been fully articulated in the scholarly business journals, though in the coming decades a whole body of literature was to grow up around this concept. Using this new formulation, certain companies were to start replacing strict job descriptions and vertical decision-making with fluidity of career movement and a largely lateral, project-oriented approach to communication and decision-making. Simpson Strong-Tie became a striking example of what was sometimes known as the "California Business Model" or "flat organization," and a particularly interesting example of its kind given that it was a manufacturing company that might have been expected to embrace a strictly hierarchical organizational chart. It would be fascinating to know to what extent the progressive wind blowing up from what was to become the Silicon Valley—specially from Hewlett-Packard,[3] the most famous of the valley's early *garagiste* enterprises—reached Barclay in the second half of the 1950s.

The way that SST was to turn its particular boundary-crossing style into an extremely and enduringly profitable company was directly linked to its recruitment and retention of remarkable people. There were, of course, some failures in Barclay's approach, but the overwhelming success of the model he created is still driving the management style of the company more than six decades after its founding.

The Originals

They had a lot of family in there, a number of brothers and cousins and uncles and nephews....It's funny. I still remember these people's names. That's how family it was. Ed Hannibal, Ed Johnson...Hal, Laura, Hazel, Rosemary, Ed, Mike, Walter just retired this year. Arlene, Bankston, Breshears. People come and stay. That tells you a lot. This is a home. This is where you come to work for your life.

—John Herrera in 2012 pointing to the 1976 picture of SST Employees
in San Leandro, California

SST SEEMS ALWAYS TO have had a way of attracting larger-than-life characters who went on to leave major imprints on the culture of the company. A picture taken in 1976 of Simpson employees standing in front of the San Leandro plant[4] shows a rogues' gallery of people who were critical to the early success of the company, building the foundation on which its later growth and expansion was based. The business principles they came to embody evolved directly from their and Barclay's experience of collaboratively building the business from scratch.

From its earliest days, SST drew its labor force from the diverse racial and ethnic mixture of the East Bay industrial corridor. Many of the original employees had worked for Barc's father. Predominant among these was a group of Portuguese-American workers whose forebears had emigrated in the late nineteenth century from the Azores to farm the fertile swath of land between the San Leandro hills and the bay. Natural farmers, they created a solid agricultural base of dairies and orchards, and by 1910 made up nearly two-thirds of San Leandro's population.

Sprinkled among SST's bedrock of Portuguese-American employees were others of mixed-ethnic backgrounds who understood the old-world culture through bifocals. Among these was second-wave employee, John Herrera, hired in 1970. A Portuguese/Mexican American, Herrera was San Leandro born and raised, deeply familiar with the history and sensibility of his neighbors. John was in his early twenties with a wife and young child when he was hired into SST. When interviewed in the fall of 2012, he was already a forty-two-year veteran of the company. By the time he finally retired in 2014, he had had a forty-four-year career with Simpson, having risen through the ranks from part-time in the shipping department to vice president of Operations Services—an important member of the home office management team. Explaining the makeup of the SST plant during the late 1970s, he remembers:

> It was kind of a rough and tumble group of people...very ethnic...a lot of Portuguese because it was San Leandro. We recruited locally.... The plant manager was Portuguese as were a lot of other employees, and then Hispanic, Mexican, from up and down Hayward to Oakland. That was the predominance of the crew. We had a few Blacks. Johnny was the first Asian...and he was a plant manager in '76.

Herrera had been recruited by a friend and explains:

> That's how it was done in those early days—when there was an opening, they'd put the word out on the floor, and somebody would bring in a relative. It created a really tight-knit group and was part of the culture not only of San Leandro but of Simpson Strong-Tie. Your parents were born and bred in San Leandro and your children were most likely going to stay there. Barc liked that; he felt close ties among employees could only help strengthen the fabric of the company and enhance loyalty.

In time, both Barc and John Herrera were to realize that this comfortable clannishness also had a darker side.

It was a small operation, Herrera remembers. *We had the one building on 1470 Doolittle Drive, the one that sits right out in front, and there were probably thirty, forty of us, tops....*Seizing the 1976 picture from his office wall, Herrera starts to annotate what is captured in the photo of the SST cast of foundational characters:...*Barc's there, and it says a lot. There's a lot in this picture, if you knew the personalities....*Pointing to Manuel Texeira and his brother, John, he continues:

> *These two guys were incredibly important to Barc. Manuel was the shop foreman, and he carried the business around in his pocket.... He had a little notepad that he wrote things down on. And John, his brother, worked for Barclay forever. John was like a little machine. If his starting time was 7:00 a.m., at 6:59 a.m., he was standing in front of that machine. He turned that machine on, and he would grab a piece of steel and put it in. He was like...an extension of that machine. The machine would be just cranking in his ear. The whistle would blow at break time. He'd stop, walk out to his car, read his cowboy paperback, come back ten minutes later, and do it all again.*

Manuel and John Texeira had been with the Simpson business since before Barc took over the screen company in 1946 and were among the group of factory workers to whom Barc first carried the famous metal joist hanger that Odenthal brought him, and who figured out how to retool the machines to make 25,000 of those pieces according to Odenthal's specifications. Smart and tough, Manuel figured prominently in the early bootstrap history of Simpson Strong-Tie. As a kind of street boss at the plant, Manuel represented the small-town prejudices of San Leandro and it was with him that Barc had to contend when he decided to integrate the plant and the local Sheet Metal Workers' Union shop in the late 1960s. Manuel was a force to reckon with.

When asked how many of the people in the 1976 picture had remained with the company for several years, Herrera listed a full roster. Pointing at Joe Meadows, the first African American to be hired at the San Leandro plant in 1969, Herrera explained that Meadows had retired in 2012, making him a forty-three-year veteran. And there were those in the picture who were still working at SST in the fall of 2012:

Kathy started in '72 I believe. She's still in accounting, payroll....Mike Plunk has been here forty years....Mike Ramponi still works down in the lab here....A lot of these guys had already worked for Simpson for quite some time when I came on board. Roy Caplinger, we called him Cappy, is in here [pointing]. Dave Anderson had been there for a number of years. Hal Lang had started in his teens, I think, late teens, there.

Then, nostalgically,...*but you can see, it wasn't a big crowd. Not a big group....Yes, a lot of fun.* When asked which one he is in the famous picture, Herrera laughs and points to the seventies-looking guy partially visible in the back row,...*the hunk of hair behind.*...John's bell-bottoms are not in view, but Barclay's dramatic sideburns are.

Moving on through the picture, Herrera points at a non-union guy standing at the edge of the group. John smiles proudly as if he were pointing out a celebrity: *That's Tye...Tye Gilb....He was so cool. He was an interesting character.*...Herrera recalls how night-shift workers in the San Leandro plant often heard the back door slam at ten or eleven at night. They learned quickly that it was not a night prowler, but the "madman," as he was admiringly known, tinkering with the prototype for a new SST product.

Hired in 1960, Tyrell Gilb was among the most mythic of SST founding figures. In Herrera's picture, he is the tall guy looking like a Norwegian sea captain, with a shock of flowing white hair. For its raconteurs, the special history and early story of SST is impossible to characterize without explaining the eccentric pairing between Barclay, SST's Salesman in Chief, and Tye Gilb, the company's early resident genius.

When Barc first glimpsed the entrepreneurial possibilities inherent in metal connectors, he realized he needed somebody with technical expertise to help him figure out product designs and applications. Yet, for the first two decades of its existence, SST had no engineers on staff. This is a striking fact in an emerging construction materials company whose primary aim was to replace older methods for supporting and distributing loads with a newer, streamlined system of weight-bearing joinery.

Aside from looking the part of the wild-eyed inventor, Tye filled a critical role in the fledgling company. Like Odenthal, he was trained as an architect, and had both design and construction expertise. Though by modern standards he lacked the very specialized training in structural engineering that would today be essential to the creation of any business involved in the manufacture of products for distributing construction loads in new ways, what Tye did provide Barclay with was a solid threshold level of technical knowledge combined with an unusual capacity for invention and creativity. He brought art as well as science to the early history of the business. Or, perhaps more accurately, Tye Gilb was a version of that Renaissance-type prodigy for whom the distinction between art and science did not exist. Whatever the exact nature and balance of Gilb's gifts, he was definitely the first of many artists that Barc was to recruit and support throughout his parallel careers as an industrialist, art collector, art gallery owner, and board member of important East Bay arts institutions. Though engineers were eventually brought into the company to supplement the skills provided by Gilb, going on to become the dominant group of product designers and testers at Simpson Manufacturing, Barclay's initial choice of an eccentric, lone artist/scientist to lead product development for the first twenty or so years of the business marked the company for life.

A natural inventor like Barc's father, Gilb designed and patented hundreds of products over his thirty-eight-year tenure at SST. Barclay ran the company, but Tye was the technical brains of the outfit. According to Barc, who was always interested in such things, Gilb had an IQ off the charts and a strong personality that made him incapable of accepting anything but loose supervision. Barc seems to have reveled in Gilb's "unmanageability." In keeping with his deepest commitment to finding good people and letting them run, Barc offered Gilb the freedom to experiment and create to the full extent of his capacities.

Herrera and many others who observed the unusual duo firsthand spoke of a *great synergy* between the ingenious technician and the gifted salesman. Both were naturals in their separate realms, and this relationship helped to create the general outlines of a management style based on collaboration rather than hierarchical management that was to be replicated with great success for the next sixty years of the company's history. By rooting the early business in a freewheeling, creative *ethos*, Barclay also seems to have tapped into a mother lode of excitement and inventiveness that has become a distinctive element in the company's identity—a palpable energy that one might not generally associate with a construction product design and manufacturing business.

Ruminating on Tye Gilb's character and the unusual quality of their business relationship, Barclay observed that it is not good management practice to have geniuses at the helm of a company. Rather it is the job of a CEO to find brilliance and let it wander where it will. In his mind, the fate of the organization depended on giving people the freedom to do what they are best at rather than trying to fit them into the confines of a strict job description. Like most rules of thumb, Barc's belief in separating genius from management does not cover all cases, even some he would celebrate. For example, it would not account for the staggering managerial achievements of Barc's lifelong hero, Abraham Lincoln, or even of Steve Jobs, widely considered to be among the dominant geniuses of the digital age, and who, in his second round at Apple, led the company to the double heights of product innovation and market capitalization. Yet certainly in the SST case, Tye Gilb is a dramatic example of the flowering of Barc's conviction about the uses of genius, and one which has left an imprint on the company as clear, quirky, and incomparable as that left by Barc himself.

Tye's creative style shaped the early product line at SST. As an architect, he was familiar with the needs of the construction industry, but, more importantly, his innate inventiveness—granted free rein—allowed him to conceptualize products that would solve specific requirements in new ways. Even before Tom Fitzmyers arrived in 1978—driving the conversion of the construction parts company into a maker of intricately engineered parts—Barc's aptitude as a salesman and Tye's skilled ingenuity had already established SST as an innovative company devoted to technical solutions to basic structural problems.

With his ability to visualize things in three dimensions, Tye could rotate objects in his head, a feat generally performed today with high-tech equipment. His talents were both conceptual and tactile—first in the imagining of an object and then in the physical manipulation of the steel to determine whether the concept could actually be manufactured. As John Herrera recalls, *Part of Tye's brilliance was he would make these things with his hands....*Gilb was famous for scribbling on napkins at Dave's Coffee Shop in Oakland, his lunch hangout, then bringing the napkins back to the factory, where he would grab a saw and the punch press to make a rough mock-up of an imagined part. Like Barc in his roles as chief salesman and CEO, Tye was not a guy to sit in his office dreaming up ideas and sketches to be made by the guys who had been hired to get their hands dirty. Both of them were hands-on in their separate realms of parts and people.

Once Tye had the mock-up of the part, he would test the product, initially using a relatively unsophisticated test press to measure a connector from all directions and in relation to varying degrees of force. In light of SST's accelerating achievements in design and testing over recent decades, the early test press seems primitive in comparison. Yet its use from the earliest days reflects Barc's and Tye's initial insight and lasting conviction that effective testing of products was the most direct way to build trust among their target audiences of engineers, architects, and general contractors. The first test press was superseded by increasingly sophisticated devices, and, in time, Simpson products were to help shape the building codes and specifications they were designed to meet. In this marketing and manufacturing model, product development drove the drafting and enforcement of standards across the industry. Barc's early understanding of this direct linkage was indispensable in building a brand that would make the Simpson Strong-Tie appellation synonymous with a set of engineering standards based on high-quality steel, design, testing, and replicability.

But not everything Tye and Barc touched turned to gold. Ten years in or so, Gilb created a truss connector[5] that seemed at first to do a better job than anything else on the market, so Simpson went into the truss business. But after a while it became apparent that even though the truss connector provided greater strength, it cost too much to produce. So they got out of the truss business and went back to promoting a set of SST connectors that were competitive in cost and performance. Because of its enduring openness to innovation and expansion, SST engaged in more than a few ventures and products that did not succeed, but the company had the continuing momentum of the core connector business to fall back on. Barc observed that the most important thing about making a mistake is admitting it, cutting your losses, and moving forward without regrets. This is an adage that looks simple in its conception, but which is extremely difficult for most people to implement either in their personal or their business lives. To an amazing extent, Barclay was able to do so in both cases.

Of Salesmen and Customers

Barclay has been successful because he's gotten everybody to focus on
understanding the customer and what he needs. Then he's convinced everybody to
be as creative as possible in serving that customer, regardless of what their job is—
from engineer to automatic press operator.... This is the least strategic company
I've ever seen, but the very most tactical. Each and every sale is a good one and
you must go after it. So, they do. They compete every day for
every single additional sale.

—Barry Williams

BARCLAY WAS A POWERFUL counterforce to Tye Gilb's kind of genius. As the company's number one marketer, he believed that the greatest compliment you could pay a person was to call him a salesman. He considered it to be the most honorable of professions. Many would consider SST still, today, to be a salesman's company. In Barc's marketing model, there was little distinction between sales and the constant modification of the product line to meet customer demand. In his own words: *Right from the start, we have worked on building a culture where each one of us realized that his boss was not the person above him at the company; it was the customer.*

From the moment Barclay took over his father's business, he was out pounding the pavement and working the phones. Like his father before him, he was a born salesman, believing that the most effective way to promote a product is to meet personally with the people who are actually going to use it, and, if necessary, to adapt the product to better serve their needs. The corollary to this personal attention to end users was the belief that once a customer gave you his business, you owed him quick and attentive service, especially once the product was in his hands. Over the years, SST was to become famous for being a company set up to receive phone calls from customers—from architects and engineers to building contractors at a job site. A customer can still today make a phone call and get an SST engineer on the line who will walk him through any problem that arises in the installation of company products. *In real time—an actual human voice on the phone.* The voice-to-voice contact is further bolstered by face-to-face contact at the job site and through a wide range of seminars conducted by SST personnel, which target architects, engineers, general contractors, building code specifiers, and enforcers. What is remarkable is that this principle of personal service and response to custom requests has survived into the digital age. The culture of SST was imprinted from the start by its founder's belief that the salesman's art is at the heart of building a profitable business, and that this art must be immediate and direct.

The full-court press marketing strategy goes back to the very earliest days of SST. A few years after first getting into connectors, Barc hired Ray Clarkson, who had flown with him in the Naval Reserve. Like Barc, Ray had been a Navy pilot during the war and was working as a salesman when they met. Convinced that he was made of the right stuff, Barc persuaded him to come to work at SST as the company's first full-time salesman.

Together Barc and Ray handled sales and customer relations, building a larger force as the business expanded. From day one, Barc's aim was to create the most trusted rather than the least expensive product in the industry. He and his growing sales force did this through linking sales directly to end-users, product development, and adaptation. The people Barc and Ray hired for the task were not guys who'd just go into their office with shirts and ties on and make a lot of phone calls. Instead, they'd have a nice shirt and tie in their car at all times, but they'd also have a polo shirt and hard hat that they'd throw on when they went onto a construction site, where they spent much of their time. Going in-person to job sites, lumberyards, and to the engineers and general contractors running the construction jobs, the salesmen were able to observe directly which SST products were selected for various uses, to advise regarding their installation under varying conditions, and to probe project designers, managers, and code enforcers about possible new designs that could accomplish given jobs in a better way. Information gleaned from this hands-on approach could then be applied to modify and expand SST's existing product line to meet unserved needs and to assemble a high level of structural detail to be shared with the people responsible for developing specifications for the industry at large. The goal in these efforts was to have the SST product directly specified in the drafting of blueprints, to provide engineers and builders with a load-bearing element that they could be sure wouldn't fail.

Barclay believed that the key to creating this trust was the use of high-grade raw materials as well as constant testing of the product to make sure it could bear the loads being advertised—a product backed up by empirical proof, not just formulae on paper. Frugal as he was by nature, he realized that to build the Simpson brand, he would need to invest heavily in research and development (R&D) so as to have a product that engineers and construction people throughout the industry would call by name. This combination of thrifty operations linked to a willingness to spend money in the pursuit of reliability is one of Barclay's abiding legacies in business and in his later philanthropy. Over the years, this double-barreled business model resulted in the development of a product that was not the least expensive in the industry, but which engineers trusted over the cheaper commodity spin-offs produced by SST competitors.

By 1960, the business was growing rapidly and Barc made Ray Clarkson sales manager for SST. With characteristic generosity, he credits Clarkson with much of SST's success during the early years, observing: ... *Who could be more important than the salesman: If you don't sell it, forget it. Clarkson did a really good job.* Based on Clarkson's performance, Barc offered him a 25 percent interest in the whole company...*at just a dirt-cheap price.* The contract that Barc drew up for this transaction stipulated that if Clarkson left—either for or against his own will—he was required to sell the 25 percent interest back to Barc for $3 million, which would be *a huge amount of profit for him.*

Another early and key salesman brought on at SST was Hugh Oliphant. During the years he was a salesman and later vice president of Sales and Marketing, there was major growth in both sales and profits. Barc credits him with many of the ideas that determined how the company would go to market and remembers him as the one who really started linking product design and sales to the specification process. Oliphant believed that if they could get Simpson products specified on an increasing number of architects' and engineers' plans, then Simpson would control the market. This turned out to be a shrewd strategy that ultimately set the product apart from its competitors.

Hugh, a large man with a leonine head and Falstaffian girth, had a phrase that became famous with his salespeople, whom he exhorted to build a practice based on *copious quantities of quality control calls*:

> *You need to get out there, and you've got to make constant control calls. Get the product on the plans, get the product to the distributor who can sell it to the job site, and then you've got to go to the job site and make sure they're installing it correctly and are happy with it, and then*

you've got to talk to building officials whose job it is to make sure the product is installed correctly and according to code. We've got to train both our own people and the people who promote and buy from us.
(Kristin Lincoln quoting Oliphant)

The two "T's"—testing and training—became part of the SST fundamental practice that other companies could never quite replicate with the same success.

During Oliphant's years at Simpson, focus on the customer, respect for employees, and an intense work ethic had a passionate proponent. Many at the company still speak of Hugh Oliphant's inspirational leadership and give him *copious quantities* of credit for the success of SST during those years. As John Herrera remembers, *Hugh was an absolute disciple of Barc's, the embodiment of those things that Barclay espoused. He was a hard, hard working guy and...really driven to perform. He definitely embraced Barclay's concepts of selling and the company. He would attack the job.* Barc, too, praises him warmly in his memoirs:

> He did a fantastic job, for way too few years. I'm going to guess it was ten or fifteen. It'd just be very hard to find anybody that good. Then he got cancer and died. He was still young. Aside from his ability as a sales manager and salesman, he was just a first-class guy. He had a lot of influence on our sales force, all of it positive.

The full-cycle approach to marketing and sales espoused by Barc and the salesmen stamped in his image was to profoundly shape SST's approach to product design, leaving a decisive imprint on the identity of the company that would eventually set it apart from its competitors.

Chapter 11
Principles: A Secular Catechism

Barc was an early prophet of a business creed that put people at its center. The ideas were good, great maybe. He was ahead of his time in terms of this sort of progressive orientation toward his people, and then he had more commitment to these ideas than anybody else and he realized that the minute you deviate and people start questioning whether you're actually committed or not, you've lost it all. I think what's more unusual, even today, than the content of his progressive ideas is simply the commitment to upholding them.

—Jennifer Chatman

How the shared values established in San Leandro continue on in the modern company—now occupying state-of-the-art facilities across the globe, with over 3,337[6] employees world-wide—is a story of how belief is transmitted beyond an original mythic place and time. Such imaginative transmission is among the most important components of leadership.

Listening to the personal stories of Simpson people from plant supervisors to upper-level management, one cannot help but wonder at the consistent level of excitement and communal pride in the company, yet this devotion has none of the feeling of creepy groupthink or parroting the boss that might be associated with such consistency. What is impossible to ignore is that there is some kind of collective belief system at the center of the Simpson enterprise—yet one that confers personal freedom along with a profound commitment to shared goals.

Primary Sources

There is only one way to happiness and that is to deny all worry about things that are beyond the power of our will.

—"The Discourses," Epictetus (50–135 AD)

Nearly all men can stand adversity, but if you want to test
a man's character, give him power.

—Abraham Lincoln

Everything can be taken from a man but one thing: the last of human freedoms—
to choose one's attitude in any given set of circumstances, to choose one's own way.

—*Man's Search for Meaning,* Viktor Frankl

Health is not a condition of matter, but of mind.

—Mary Baker Eddy

THE SIXTIES AND SEVENTIES were a formative time for Barc as well as the business. The utopian aspirations of this period marked his thought process side by side with a kind of raw ambition and drive that was less in sync with the times, though utterly consistent with the generations that personally experienced the Depression years and the fascist threat posed by Germany and Japan. Out of this disparate mixture, he built a philosophy that was both personal and focused on joint action.

When, in 1946, Barclay dropped out of Cal to take over his father's business, he had already begun a process of self-education that was to shape him as much as the experiences of war, marriage, raising a family, and building a business. All his life, Barclay was a voracious reader and auto-didact. His eclectic interests ranged from Epictetus, a Greek Stoic (whose philosophical teachings focused on self-knowledge and the importance of distinguishing between the things that we can and cannot effect); to Mary Baker Eddy (founder of the Church of Christian Science, and author of *Science and Health*); to Viktor Frankl (survivor of a Nazi prison camp, where his wife and relatives were exterminated, author of *Man's Search for Meaning,* and promulgator of a therapeutic methodology called "logotherapy," which focuses on the importance of "attitude" in human actions); from the *Bible* to the *Communist Manifesto* (both of which Barc read in between flying surveillance planes and playing poker in Alaska and the Aleutian Islands during the war); from Shakespeare to Michael Connelly; from seventeenth century Dutch painters to contemporary artists; and from theories of business management to early childhood education. His immersion in these subjects and authors shaped his view of the world—but none affected him as intensely and abidingly as Abraham Lincoln. For Barc, who devoured books and speeches about and by him, Lincoln had no peer—as philosopher, humorist, intellectual, communicator, and leader.

Though the stolid teachings of Epictetus probably don't figure prominently on the bookshelves or regular reading lists of most of the world's CEOs (or many other modern beings), Barclay's admiration of Lincoln—as an ethical man and as a leader—is not in itself unique among either the poor or the powerful. In Barclay's case, Lincoln was not simply someone he admired, but the cornerstone of a belief system that he lived by with the kind of unusual consistency generally reserved for the religious among us. Drawn to a *search for meaning* beyond the boundaries of the individual self, Barc was nevertheless unable to accept the suspension of disbelief involved in religious thought. Yet, in Lincoln and a few other of his intellectual heroes, Barc found a passionate secular creed that became inseparable from the way he lived his life. Among Lincoln's fabled virtues, the ones that Barc incorporated most effectively into his business (and his personal life) were the ability to listen and to change his mind (as Lincoln did on slavery); an innate commitment to fairness; a search for—rather than fear of—intelligence and excellence in others; a capacity for collaboration even with potential rivals; and a powerful ego, toughness, tenacity, and strong sense of irony about power and presumption. These beliefs—chopped, diced, and spiced in various ways by the people with whom Barc surrounded himself—became key ingredients in the "secret sauce" of the Simpson Company.

A Theory of Compensation

> *"Tous pour un, un pour tous"*—all for one, one for all.
>
> —D'Artagnan, *The Three Musketeers* by Alexandre Dumas

THE FIRST DECADES AT Simpson Manufacturing were personal and elemental, if not primitive. There was a single automatic press, a single fork-lift, a bunch of guys on the production line, a couple of salesmen, a small plant, and a warehouse, everybody living on top of each other and doing a bit of everything, with an emphasis on ingenuity and frugality—making do with what you had. The company was scrambling, but also swashbuckling in its derring-do. As Barclay produced connectors for Warner's roofing system, he was simultaneously imagining new markets and products, selling and serving customers, and inventing a set of business procedures that suggested a vision far beyond the horizons of either his father's window screen business or his own early achievements with vents and metalworking.

With the incorporation of Simpson Manufacturing in 1956, Barc suddenly and dramatically moved from the limited goals usually associated with piecework to the building of an enterprise whose foundations and philosophy could encompass much larger purposes and profits. At the center of this transformation was Barclay's early design of a multilevel compensation strategy that was unusual for its time—and, as it has turned out, for current times as well. The impulses behind this strategy demonstrate a rare set of convictions regarding how to build a successful business.

In the 1950s and 1960s, there would have been few primers guiding the development of innovative compensation packages for employees of small American manufacturing operations, and certainly not for those below the executive level. The majority of SST employees at the new San Leandro plant in 1960 were in the Oakland Chapter of the Sheet Metal Workers' Union, which opened the way to a fairly standardized rate of hourly pay yet guaranteed nothing but the most limited of benefit packages for its rank-and-file members. The base pay for the nonunionized employees of SST was in line with comparable labor rates for similar work in the area. Salaries were fair, but not princely. Nor did Barc's early experiments with compensation revolve primarily around fixed pay. Rather he focused his strategy on providing employees with low-deductible health-care plans (way before this became a central American political issue), pension benefits, and, more radically, a quarterly profit-sharing system that has few analogues in the way American business was conducted at mid-twentieth century.

Existing models for variable compensation in the fifties and sixties when Barclay first put the key pieces of the SST compensation system in place generally ranged from the Christmas bonus to commissions for salespeople to—in a few "enlightened" cases—per piece productivity pay incentives for industrial assembly line workers. *There were the Lincoln Electrics[7] and a few other companies that were doing some version of variable pay based on production line productivity* (Jennifer Chatman). Yet even in comparison with these relatively progressive—for their time—programs, there was something radical in Barclay's early concept of compensation. This was the conviction that building employee commitment and productivity might best be accomplished through a very direct sharing of the wealth of the entire company on a quarterly basis—and that this short-term compensation vehicle should include people at all levels of the organization.

The most famous element of the SST compensation package is known as cash profit sharing (CPS). As Barclay originally conceived it, CPS involved the sharing of the net operating income of the business on a quarterly basis by salaried as well as hourly employees. In his own words: *The point was to make the company the employees' company as well as mine...that was crucial to their performance and to attracting good people and keeping them. I wanted to make it their company. If their division makes a lot of money, so do they. And again, ... the people...get a percentage. If they have a really good quarter, they can earn a ton of money. A ton. And their salaries are just average....It's worked extremely well over the years* (Barclay). His concept was simple: that everybody be all-in-together, all employees sharing both in the company's upside and downside. In brief, that means that when the business does well, all employees split the profits, and when the company doesn't do well, there is no pool of cash from which to pay CPS, and this part of the compensation package goes away for a quarter or two until the business returns to profitability. According to Jennifer Chatman, *Barc's practices were unusual. I think it's worth saying that in the fifties and sixties this is not what IBM was doing. This is not what GE was doing. These were fairly radical practices, particularly the very, very close contingencies between an individual's productivity and an individual's pay.* Jennifer goes on to observe that it is the extent of the Simpson concept of CPS that was and is unusual—that sharing in the profits was not restricted to executives, nor was it conceived as a simple incentive system for hourly production laborers. Rather, in its original form, the CPS was provided to salaried as well as hourly workers up and down the line. *It was part of Barc's idea early on that you give people a vested interest. It seemed very straightforward to him, even if now things have gotten more complicated* (Jennifer Chatman).

Over the years, CPS has needed lots of tinkering and adjustment. Eventually, as the company grew, in addition to the quarterly CPS pay-outs, Barclay put in place a more standard, longer-term variable compensation element for Simpson employees in the form of private and, ultimately, public stock for performance and/or as "milestone pay" at key employment anniversaries. Yet according to Barry Williams, the Simpson compensation system is still an unusual breed:

> What we have is not a standard profit sharing, but a quarterly profit-shar-ing, performance-based system....I've never seen a quarterly distribution that is in fact as large in financial terms and in breadth of distribution as the Simpson CPS....There is a 20 percent return to shareholders...so no employee benefits until we've made enough money that we show the shareholders that we earned a return on the investment and we've, there-by, earned the right to share....In most other companies, employees who receive variable compensation in addition to their salary earn the larger portion of variable comp on options, restricted stock, [and] longer-term vehicles. The Simpson system is, instead, very oriented to the short-term, to the real-time financial performance of the company, and I've never seen anything like that on so large a scale and on a quarterly basis.

Reflecting on Barc's motivations for setting up CPS originally, Jennifer Chatman probes both the tangible and more elusive sources of his original conception: *I think Barc's view about people is that they should have more control over their fate. That's how he lives his life, and I think he believes others should live their lives that way, so CPS follows that philosophy.* What is indisputable is that more than any other single element in the Simpson compensation formula, the concept of sharing profits across the board on a quarterly basis has created a deep sense of vested interest among the company's employees in both the near- and long-term fate of the business. Certainly, CPS is at the root of SST's motivational system, yet it is not simply an incentivizing tool but seems more in the nature of an ethical precept. At the core of the company's profit-sharing formula is a basic conviction regarding "fairness," a belief that the distribution of the fruits of enterprise should be broad and wide rather than pyramidal.

Freud in the Marketplace: Karl Shultz

> *Barclay told me that, for him, someone's childhood was critical because it really meant they had a good foundation, a good grounding, a sort of moral code, and a basis for an ethical moving forward.*

> —Jennifer Price

CRITICAL TO BARCLAY'S INTELLECTUAL makeup was a deep curiosity about human motivations. Though he was constitutionally incapable of allowing self-investigation to devolve into paralysis, he was committed to finding patterns in human behavior. This took the form of a lasting interest in psychology, which may have been based on an acknowledgment of the mystery of human personality as well as the nearly opposite desire to understand and categorize human behavior in the service of the kind of predictability that might lead to productivity. This latter desire would have been in keeping with the positivistic views of the post-war years of the American century, when industrial psychology was a burgeoning field. Along with this, Barc may—during the Freud-obsessed sixties in America—also have inhaled a contradictory set of psychological precepts based on the idea of an unruly unconscious. What is certain is that he regarded his own childhood as a model for success and happiness, leading him to be deeply curious about other people's beginnings. In response to some or all of these influences, he made a certain form of self-investigation a rite of passage for would-be SST employees up to the threshold of the new millennium.

In 1964, Barclay started to send prospective hires to Karl Schultz, an industrial psychologist. Applicants were asked to undergo a set of IQ, personality, and personal predilection tests widely in use during that era, as well as to participate in a personal interview with Karl, based on questions that he and Barclay had jointly drafted. For the next thirty-five years, Karl provided detailed reports to Barc, and later also to Tom Fitzmyers, on all potential hires before the deal was sealed. This was before such screenings were to be widely deemed guilty of class and other biases. Yet Barc appears not to have been at all suspicious of the possible cultural prejudgments inherent in the tests, not abandoning the mandatory psychological screening until well into the fourth decade after the founding of SST.

Some SST employees who underwent the screening were baffled or bemused:

> *When we first got hired...they made us go and see a guy called Dr. Schultz. He would interview you for three hours. When my family in South Africa heard about this they were floored. In South Africa, if you see a psychologist, it means you're frothing at the mouth and you're ready for the loony bin. It's too late.* (Jennifer Price)

And from Jacinta Pister, hired in 1986:

> *Tom Fitzmyers used to refer to Dr. Schultz as our marriage counselor.*
> *Karl was fantastic. It was really a personality profile. It actually...*
> *put me off at first....It wasn't going to the psychologist so much but*
> *having to take these written tests that were...quite bizarre, I thought.*
> *One of them really truly was the same IQ test I took when I was in*
> *second grade...I remember the pictures. The other part was more of a*
> *psychological profile...I remember my roommate, who was a sociology*
> *graduate, said, "JP, do you really want to work for a company that*
> *makes you do this?" Whatever Karl did, he was looking for people who*
> *had a certain level of intellectual curiosity and IQ. I don't know if there*
> *really was a personality profile, or if it was just, "If you're not too over*
> *the top"—it might have been.* (Jacinta Pister)

It is hard not to wonder what the testing really meant to Barc. In part it appears to bespeak an essentially optimistic conviction that most things are knowable, worthy of open scrutiny and investigation, even people's inner workings. In this, he would have been in sync with much of twentieth-century motivational and inspirational literature, even if at odds with many of the vagaries it was to spawn. Certainly, even a casual survey of the people working at Simpson argues for there having been some kind of systematic selection process at work that favors energy, positivity, personality, and intelligence— but what this form of psychological prescreening had to do with that eludes precise evaluation.

What is without doubt is that Barclay was fascinated by human psychology and personality in and outside the world of business. Briefly, he even considered going back to school to get a PhD in psychology. Among other reasons for this was his thinking that Karl Schultz's reports on the several hundred people hired by SST might provide the basis for a dissertation, where theory and results could be compared. Having operated so thoroughly and successfully on instinct in the building of the business, it is interesting that he was hankering after some more systematic explanation and investigation into the sources of human behavior. Knowing from the start that he didn't have the patience to be a one-on-one therapist, he joined a night class in group therapy given by Cal Extension. His reasoning was that dealing with groups of clients might be productive enough to merit the effort—as a part-time occupation.

To test this idea, he spent a full weekend in group therapy with his classmates. A few weeks later, while reading the front page of the *San Francisco Chronicle*, he recognized the name and face of one of the guys who had participated in the Cal Extension seminar. He had been arrested for murdering his girlfriend. Barc decided to stick with making structural connectors.

Though he abandoned the systematic study of psychology, Barc continued to read about new slants on varying branches of the discipline. Throughout his life, he remained interested in trying to figure out whether a particular person—friend, foe, stranger, politician—was actually what he seemed, or why he did what he did. This interest grew to encompass the fields of early childhood education and development, which became a major focus of his charitable giving during the last three decades of his life. As the years passed, his foundational belief that the circumstances of childhood provided the key to adult character led him to push the programs he supported to serve children from ever earlier age groups. A recurrent component of his charitable giving to such programs was the use of results testing to measure the congruence between theory and practice, idea, and action.

In 1974, after having proposed marriage to his second wife, Sharon Hanley Simpson, he made her take the Schultz test on the airplane flying to a pre-wedding getaway in Cozumel. In this case, it seems to have worked like a charm and a predictor. They were married happily for forty years.

Continuing Education and the Holy Grail

It is impossible for a man to learn what he thinks he already knows.

—Epictetus

IN 1966, TWENTY YEARS after leaving college to answer his father's call, Barc graduated from UC Berkeley. Later, he said he was determined to get his bachelor's degree before his son, John, received his own. And he made it— just. It's hard to say which degree meant more to him. John notes that Barc was also delighted when he went on to receive a PhD. *Without his support and encouragement, I doubt that I would have completed the degree* (John Simpson).

Barc's path to a degree involved a combination of private reading, Cal extension courses, and seminars designed for career businesspeople, including several at Stanford and the UC Berkeley Haas School of Business.

Barclay's capacity for self-schooling was to last a lifetime. It was, in fact, a continuing way of life for him, not simply a series of courses leading to a degree. But, indeed, the absence of a degree did plague him even if its lack had not hampered his career. He wanted entry into the fellowship of learning that linked him backward and forward to first principles. Though drawn to scholarship, Barc never considered that there might be a divide between the realms of thought and action. For him, the excavation and exploration of fundamental precepts was motivated by a belief that thought could engender great deeds.

Barc recalled a number of writings and teachers who—along with Epictetus, Lincoln, and more modern theoretical philosophers—had direct influence on how he conducted his daily life at SST. One of these was an article he read in a 1964 edition of the IBM magazine, *Think*, called "Anger, Guilt, and Executive Action," by Harry Levinson, a professor at the Harvard Business School. The key argument in this article centered on the importance of communicating quickly with an employee who was performing below the standards of the company, giving him or her a reasonable chance to improve. If an employee is unable to make necessary changes, the article argued, it is best to fire him/her quickly rather than let things deteriorate through indirection on the part of the manager. Being straightforward with people seems to have come naturally to Barclay, so it is possible that this article merely confirmed for him something he already knew. From all reports, Barclay took the advice to heart, and as a result there were never many malingerers or malcontents at Simpson Manufacturing. Eccentrics, yes—underperformers, few and far between.

Among the most important influences on Barc's future thought and action was an eight-week intensive course in business management, offered in 1965 by the Stanford Business School for experienced business executives. Barc credits Al Hastorf, one of the professors in this class, with enunciating a principle that was to change forever his approach to decision-making within his own company: *Get the decision down to the lowest level possible.* This adage, which struck Barclay as revelation, ran counter to the dominant practice of top-down management, prevalent in American business during that era: *I listened to that and I thought, ye gods, what a fantastic idea. We have run Simpson Manufacturing that way ever since. It was a revolutionary idea at that time. It builds strong people and makes promoting from within feasible.*

The corollary to this basic precept was that you *hire smart people, then get out of their way*. For Barc, this was the true religion.

Articles of Faith

That's magic to me. Barclay always found new people to buy into his concepts,
and then they become the evangelists, the missionaries of the
secret sauce in the conversion of other people.

—Barry Williams

IN KEEPING WITH HIS interest in inspirational literature—from classical thought through the utopian manifestos of the 1960s and 1970s—Barclay devised a secular catechism for SST known as the "Nine Principles,"[8] which was metaphorically nailed to the door of the company as firmly as Luther's *95 Theses*.

The "Nine Principles" place people at the center of the company's core formula for success, with serving the customer as a coequal precept. Side by side with these two pillars of belief is the important corollary that the business's strength flows from taking the long- rather than short-term view of investments and profits: *Never sacrifice tomorrow for the sake of today*, along with Barc's foundational pledge that the *business is not for sale*, that the owners are in it for the long haul.

A tenet that mirrors Barclay's own life practice exhorts employees to take risks, to embrace innovation and creativity, and to recognize that progress can only be achieved by experimentation and failure along the way (though one should try to *foul up* as little as possible). Perhaps most surprising as a business directive is the principle regarding respect for the contributions of every individual in the company, no matter their position. The corollary to this insistence on the value of the person rather than rank includes the idea that employees should expect to do well financially, but that the company seeks also to provide other kinds of benefits for them and their families. One long-term Simpson employee sees the company as a kind of revolutionary venture, out of sync with standard capitalist practices:

This company has been very successful doing the opposite of what the
American business model has generally done regarding the treatment of

the worker as a commodity who can be easily replaced. Barc's approach
was the opposite. This is not a man who was just out to make a buck....
He's always said, "It's the people. It's the people," and he really believes
that. So, it's the people and...there are families behind these people, and
then all of these families live in communities. It grows from there...I just
hope that it's remembered what and how this man thought, and what his
vision was. (Joseph Way, SST employee, 1993–present; see bio)

Interestingly, Joseph's pejorative use of the word "commodity," whether
conscious or not, recalls Barc's earliest and continuing conviction that the way
to build a successful company was to create a personalized brand that would
embody standards of excellence rather than to mass-produce a commodity
at the lowest cost. For him, the worker was not a necessary evil, but the core
creative element from which the brand was built.

As a business manifesto, the "Nine Principles" is striking in its emphasis
on work at the company being demanding, but also *fun—not a bus stop*, a
place to build a career and a life. In practice, this principle translates into a
view of the business as both a money-making operation and a community of
care, focused on great benefits and pensions; scholarship aid for employees
and their children for education and retraining; and matching funds for
charitable contributions by employees to their favorite causes.

The emphasis on recognizing the particular contributions of individuals
while simultaneously channeling these into community enterprise seems
more in the nature of a personal worldview than simply a set of business
directives. What is particularly striking about the winding road of influences
and instinct that led Barc to build a company out of the inspirational materials
of a deep belief system is that he was able to move from precept to practice.
For it is not simply the *existence* of the precepts that is interesting, but the
consistency with which they were put into practice:

The difference at Simpson is that the organization has made a
commitment to execute these principles...very, very few organizations
have the prolonged discipline, commitment, and continuity to ensure
that such ideas actually mean something. (Jennifer Chatman)

In the language of contemporary organization and management theory,
Chatman describes Simpson Manufacturing as a *strong culture organization*.

She explains that the dynamics and *personality* of organizations can be charted on a matrix that compares levels of *agreement over principles* to the *intensity with which such principles are practiced. What most organizations have, because "culture" is so faddish, are high levels of agreement and low levels of intensity—* what I call "*vacuous beliefs.*" She uses the US Postal Service, whose primary principle is "customer service" (*Who knew?*), as a prime example of this. Then, she explains, there is the reverse case, as represented by many Silicon Valley firms, *where you've got intensity, but no agreement...the marketing and engineering folks going at each other...this is what I call "warring factions."* Of the two examples, she prefers the latter *because intensity is much harder to build than agreement, much harder...intensity requires a high level of trust that people are going to do what they say...* According to Chatman it is both the strength of the beliefs and company leadership's insistence on putting them into daily practice that is the key to Simpson Manufacturing's success:

> *Who you hire, how you socialize and develop people, how you reward people, what kind of beliefs the leaders model, and how they embody these values in every utterance and every behavior...the Simpson track record is impeccable, and that is extremely rare. There's a deliberateness to the practice that permeates pretty much everything they do.*

For Chatman, and many others who work at the company, the core values of the Simpson credo come down to a single word, "integrity"—just as Barc would have it, no blah, blah. It is the structural underpinning, the connector of everything:

> *The leaders of this organization would not stand for a transgression in integrity. They simply would not stand for it. They would do whatever is necessary, whether it required spending money or spending time or firing people. It's not an all-accepting place. It's pretty clear what's expected, and what is definitely not appropriate in the organization.... All organizations speak of this fundamental standard, but Simpson Manufacturing really lives it. You do things the right way. You just do, and that's Barc.*

Barc's creed was highly unusual, yet he was not entirely a lone voice crying in the wilderness. There were a few other firms from the same era, which appear to have understood the importance of core beliefs to the building of a successful enterprise. The most famous of these is, of course, Hewlett-Packard[9]—unlike SST, a household name—located just an hour's drive south of San Leandro:

> The founders developed a management style that came to be known as "The HP Way." In Hewlett's words, The HP Way is "a core ideology... which includes a deep respect for the individual, a dedication to affordable quality and reliability, a commitment to community responsibility, and a view that the company exists to make technical contributions for the advancement and welfare of humanity." The following are the tenets of The HP Way:
>
> 1. We have trust and respect for individuals.
> 2. We focus on a high level of achievement and contribution.
> 3. We conduct our business with uncompromising integrity.
> 4. We achieve our common objectives through teamwork.
> 5. We encourage flexibility and innovation.[10]

What is striking in both cases is that Barc and Hewlett have placed people, integrity, and flexibility at the very heart of their lists of core commandments. At the time SST and HP were getting their start, these ideas were radical and of an intensity that has the feel of religious belief, though in each case the values enunciated were secular and humanist. But like religious belief, these values were clearly inspirational, providing a credo that grounded business on ethical precepts in order to motivate employees. These belief systems shaped the practice and the profitability of both companies.

The graphic representation of Barclay's principles and of the brand built on these foundational practices is a strikingly succinct symbol, consisting of the equal sign with a negating slash through it. No equal:

Chapter 12
Practice: The Making of the Simpson Brand

*We're a recognized industry in America and a major brand. That's one of the
things that Barclay was always proud of—that we make something. We physically
make something that adds value. We're not just shuffling things around.
We're not middlemen. We're making something that's worthwhile....
We all owe Barclay a lot. We're very proud of the company.*

—Mike Plunk

Slugging It Out with the Competition

Joining Simpson at that time was perfect...

—Mike Plunk

THINKING ABOUT THE OLD days, John Herrera describes how a bunch of
them would come to the factory even on the weekends, pulling overtime,
to paint some of the galvanized steel parts: *We'd have a tent from that wall
to out here about four feet deep, and you'd actually physically put the parts on
hanger hooks and drop them in the paint and pick them up and then hang them
up...like doing laundry...it was a family affair, pretty much.*

In the sixties and seventies, all of the shipping from the Northern
California operation of SST could be handled by one guy. Six to ten months
after Herrera came to work at the company, a second full-time guy was hired
into the warehouse, and they continued that way until 1972, when Mike Plunk
was brought on as a part-time packer to back up John. This was before Barc
bought Warner's building and there was little room under the one existing
roof for inventory: *the warehouse, the production, the sales office, everything*
(Mike Plunk). Herrera remembers his wife waking him up at 2:00 a.m. when
she heard rain on the roof. He would jump out of bed to drive up to San

Leandro from Fremont to move boxes inside the warehouse. He thought nothing of it: *Payback.*

Holding up the original F24 Simpson Strong-Tie, John Herrera recalls the era when SST was jockeying for position: *When I came into the industry, we were selling these like hotcakes.* In those days, metal connectors—the foundation part on which Simpson Manufacturing was to eventually base a vast product line—were known as "TECO clips," after the company Barc had first researched when Warner asked him to manufacture the 25,000 joist hangers for his roofing system. As Herrera describes it, *TECO were the big guns...they were the big boys...I mean, often in the seventies, it was like slug it out, man.* There were also a bunch of smaller competing companies, probably around seven or eight in all. Herrera explained: *You might be number one today and number seven tomorrow based on last week's sales. I mean, that was the feel. There was the sense that anything could happen.* But at a certain point, SST pulled ahead. For John Herrera, what ultimately gave them the edge was the quality of the Simpson product: *We won't make a substandard part, and we won't sell a substandard part. We won't sell a part we're not a hundred percent behind....Barc doesn't want his name on it.*

A clear idea of the day-to-day realities that ultimately gave SST the advantage can be heard in the stories of other early Simpson employees who were to devote over forty years of their lives to the company. When Mike Plunk came to work at SST, there was only one automated press, so much of the work was done by hand with punch presses.[11] Since three people worked in the shipping department with only one forklift, Mike was put on the swing shift to squeeze the most utility possible out of the machine. It was a thrifty operation. Plunk remembers that Barclay knew all the people in the warehouse and the guys operating the machines. *Barc was always showing up after standard work hours. He'd come back into Oakland Airport from these business trips...always to the back of the facility. He'd walk through just to see what was going on. It was that very personal, hands-on, direct visual that he wanted. He wanted to see and talk to the people on the floor and find out what was going on. What's selling? Who's it going to?*

Mike's wife was doing janitorial work at the plant. One time, Mike remembers, Barc showed up late at night having forgotten his key to the gates surrounding the plant. A cop stopped him because it was around midnight. *My wife had to go out and verify who he was.*

When Simpson acquired Warner's back building in 1972, doubling the square footage of the original plant, Mike Plunk was given the responsibility of setting up the warehouse. By then he was full-time in shipping and had been made the guy in charge of people on the floor, *a glorified foreman.* He was told to set up a new warehouse from scratch, to go from a very small room to a much larger space where he would have to figure out the layout of racks and stock. *Today, I'm sure that we would bring in consultants and experts. But, in those days, well, you're the one. You run it. You're going to be responsible for it. Figure out how you want to lay it out and let us know what you need.* For Plunk and others, there was exhilaration in the autonomy and creativity possible in the early days:

> *There was much more free rein, much more free spirit…they accepted the oddball….It was truly a group of people getting together and trying to figure out, how do we get this done? There were no rules. Whereas now…the company has become so sophisticated, and the product's so sophisticated…and there's Sarbanes-Oxley.*

Plunk remembers that there was a lot of experimentation and failure—and learning from the failure. As the company grew, Mike was invited to be the supervisor of the warehouse, which took him from a position as an hourly union employee to the salaried ranks of the company, and eventually to other jobs in the home office. He was to work at the company for forty-four years.

Upward mobility was even more dramatically true in John Herrera's forty-four-year career at SST, during which he went from a part-time hourly packer in the shipping department to managing inventory, to designing an early computerized inventory and production system along with a hired computer consultant, to countless ever more responsible jobs within the organization, retiring from Simpson Manufacturing in 2014 as a member of upper-level management. Dramatic, but not unique within the company, Herrera's career trajectory reflected a leadership style at the top that encouraged people to pick up the ball and run with it. The sheer pace of growth encouraged this mobility, but it was also written from the beginning into the culture of the company.

Barc and the rest of the crew worked long hours, and the business was growing rapidly. As early as 1960, even before the Herrera and Plunk era, Barc had started to grow the business, moving into new geographic areas in search of new markets.

Onward to Southern California

>Again, a small family down there, too, in the beginning.

—John Herrera

BY THE MID 1960s, SST was already starting to do substantial business in Southern California. A small customer in Los Angeles, Syd Lyttle, who had also become a friend of Barc's, was running a sheet metal shop in a tough part of town and wasn't very happy with his job. When Barclay suggested that Syd join SST, he jumped at the chance and Barc sold him 10 percent of the entire company at a cheap price. Here again, Barc's belief that business growth and profits are directly linked to giving key players an ownership stake played itself out in simple exchanges of obligation and upside potential: Simpson took over Lyttle's lease and equipment and Syd ran the new branch with a very small crew. Herrera remembers that, initially, there was just a single salesman and a plant foreman in addition to Lyttle. *Recently, one of the employees down in Southern California just did his fortieth year there. I remember working with his father, who was my counterpart in Southern California. So that was kind of fun.*

According to Barc, Syd Lyttle was totally honest, extremely bright, and under his tutelage, the business increased sales and profits at a rapid rate. Their partnership lasted only a few years until Syd died of cancer, but he left behind a branch that was thriving.

On his frequent visits to the LA plant, Barc was known for taking the cheapest flight to LAX, then a bus to the station nearest the plant, from whence, refusing to pay for a cab, he would make the hazardous walk through an economically depressed part of the inner city. Barc's insistence on saving a dime and not allowing himself special luxuries—along with his famously battered, dusty cars—were sources of amusement and wry respect among SST employees, becoming a key element in the emerging culture of the company.

Barclay remembers: *It was exciting to expand and see our Los Angeles branch prosper to the point where a much larger facility was needed.* Through a real estate friend, Barc got a great buy on nineteen acres of land in nearby Brea, California, where he built a new plant facility in an area that was just starting to develop. Barc had paid for the San Leandro real estate out of his own pocket, but, in the LA transaction, he decided to let the company buy the property so that key people at SST wouldn't think *he was milking the company and leave.*

When they moved into the new plant in Brea—in a clever, preemptive move—Barc called the business agent for the Los Angeles area Sheet Metal Workers' Union, telling him they were about to start production in the Brea plant and inviting him to come out and organize them. The union in the San Leandro plant was of the same name, but they operated independently out of an Oakland local. Barc remembered that there was a long silence at the other end of the phone until the LA agent asked some questions to make sure the request was for real; he'd never heard of an owner inviting a union business agent to come organize. Barc enjoyed his amazement. Later, he admitted that he had made the call for purely selfish reasons, since he feared that there were two other *tough and destructive unions* that might try to organize the SST Brea branch. In his mind, the Sheet Metal Workers' Union in San Leandro had done a good job of getting better up-front pay for its people, and in a reasonable manner. In fact, he thought, *A lot of the negotiated changes were things that we should have done ourselves, without any prodding.*

When Barc gave Syd Lyttle a 10 percent interest in SST in exchange for him transforming his metal-working shop into a second production facility for the company, he took the first step of many in making Simpson Manufacturing a transcontinental and, ultimately, global enterprise. Though the Los Angeles expansion did not yet involve crossing state lines, this branching out was the first sign that the connector business might take the company further and further afield.

Integration

Barc knew that it was going to be a challenge. He didn't care. He just thought it was the right thing to do. If that meant a few bumps and lumps, I think he didn't care. That was just part of progress. So that's really cool.

—John Herrera

ABOUT THE SAME TIME as the opening of the new facility in Brea, Barclay decided it was time to take on the integration of the primary manufacturing operation in San Leandro. Diversification of the workforce had not been a problem in LA, but he knew that in Portuguese-American San Leandro there would be strong resistance. According to Barc, the city was known as *one of the most racist in America.* And the unions themselves were part of the problem, in spite of the *pious bleatings of many union leaders during the civil rights protests of the sixties. At that time, the union leaders around the country were mouthing off about how they wouldn't put up with racism. And that, of course, was pure hogwash* (Barclay).

In the Bay Area at this time, Huey Newton and Bobby Seale had founded the Black Panther Party and there was an active chapter of the Congress of Racial Equality (CORE) on the UC Berkeley campus where a number of civil rights groups were emerging as an outgrowth and extension of the Berkeley Free-Speech Movement and anti-war protests. Nationwide, Martin Luther King Jr. had become a household name, and had early on started linking the themes of poverty, racism, and anti-war protest. At the center of the civil rights demonstrations across the country, activists were demanding an end to widespread racial discrimination in hiring.

Undoubtedly influenced by the local and national upheavals, Barc decided to take on integration of the local branch of the Sheet Metal Workers' Union that served the San Leandro plant. He told the plant manager, Manuel Texeira, that the next person he hired must be Black. Manuel's response was, perhaps, predictable: *The men would not accept him, nor would the union.* Barc's response: *Manuel, the next person that you hire has to be Black, and I'll take care of the union.* Barc then called the local's business agent, who answered as Manuel had predicted: *Well, we wouldn't accept it. Absolutely not.* Barc responded that he would call the *San Francisco Chronicle* and the *Oakland Tribune* and *give them the story of the week.* There was a pause and the agent backed down, perhaps thinking that the problem would be resolved at the plant level and that he could make a few calls to seed the clouds. Apparently following orders, Manuel hired an African American, then, a few days later, came and told Barc, *This Black guy just won't work. Fine,* Barc replied, *fire him.* He let Texeira turn and start to leave the office. Then, just as he got to the door, he said, *But hire another Black guy in his place.* On the third try, they hired Joe Meadows, who appears in Herrera's famous 1976 photograph and who retired from SST after over four decades of employment.

Later, in 1982, when Simpson Manufacturing bought the Dura-Vent plant in Vicksburg, Mississippi, they had to integrate that facility as well. *One hundred and nineteen years after the slaves in the rebel states had been emancipated by Abraham Lincoln, we had to "emancipate" our Southern factory,* Barc observed. *Racism does not die easily.*

A young African American named David MacDonald (known as Mac) (SST employee, 1984–2014; see bio) was hired at Simpson in 1984. Born and raised in Oakland, Mac was first hired at the age of twenty-two as a packer in the automatic department, working alongside an experienced packer, taking the newly punched and bent connectors off the machines and putting them into boxes to be shipped. He describes how the company functioned as a mentor for him and others who entered its ranks as unskilled workers, and who were offered a challenging career path if they were willing to seize it: *I know it sounds funny to say, but Simpson has been a big parent to all of us who joined this company. That's why you very seldom hear about someone leaving. The turnover rate is very, very low here.* Over the next three decades, Mac would keep learning new skills and work his way through a wide variety of jobs until in 2004 he became plant manager of Simpson's premier 600,000-square-foot Stockton facility—Branch 20.

Generally, the whiff of "paternalism" would make us reflexively (and justly) skeptical, but it is hard to dismiss the very concrete benefits experienced by Mac as a long-term SST employee, along with the three generations of his family. These benefits included continuing education paid by Simpson for him and scholarships for his children, also paid for by the company. Mac was eligible for these through his own efforts and skills because he excelled at what he did, and because he was not stereotyped into a single role as a piece worker, useful only for his brawn and his willingness to carry out a repeated action. Eager to learn, he moved systematically up through the manufacturing operation at SST:

> *I started learning how to run a machine (press)...and then from there I mastered how to set up the machines, set up the dies, the tools that go inside the machines....Then I became what they call a lead person. That's like directing the workflow in the automatic department.... I became good at working with people, then I became a supervisor.*

Like most people who advanced dramatically through Simpson, Mac is personable, quick, and open. And he seems to have perceived early on that there was real opportunity for him at SST. Before applying for a job, he says he had heard word of mouth that it was *a good company,* but that like most people entering on the ground floor he was initially just looking for a job, trying to support his family. Once in, he started to notice things:

You kind of felt it, you know?...If you did a good job, there were opportunities around the corner waiting. When I started at Simpson, it was still small and you could feel that this was a special company, that it was going to grow, and that there were going to be opportunities. If you came to work and did your job, if you shared and collaborated with people, you started understanding that there was a special feeling about Simpson Strong-Tie, that they were going to be in it for the long-term, the long haul.

When Mac first went to work at the San Leandro plant, the once predominantly Portuguese-American workforce at the company had become more diversified following Barclay's desegregation of union labor in the sixties. By 1984, the automatic department into which Mac was hired included a core group of African Americans, their ranks having swelled since Joe Meadows became SST's first Black employee in 1969; however, though women were well represented in office administrative functions in 1984, there were barely any women on the production line. Gradually, according to Mac, things *started branching out*, as increasing numbers of Hispanics and Filipinos were hired at SST, more accurately reflecting the demographics of the East Bay, and as women were also eventually hired into the ranks of the production line (as well as into engineering, marketing, and upper-level management jobs). Gesturing toward the multi-ethnic, multilingual, and double-gendered work force running the presses in the shiny expanses of the Stockton plant in the second decade of the twenty-first century, Mac exclaimed: *Total melting pot... it's unbelievable how far we've come.*

Commenting on his father's decision to integrate the San Leandro plant and push for racial diversity as the company expanded, John Simpson, Barc's oldest child, observed that he didn't think his father was motivated by any ideological conviction about "affirmative action," *per se*, but more by *a fundamental belief in fairness*—a strong feeling that it was important to give people a chance. As Barc's future philanthropic activities were to prove, fairness was crucial to his evolving philosophy of social change, as was his linked perception that the American playing field was *not* level and that sustained attention and support were needed to even the odds. Increasingly, this was for him both a moral and pragmatic imperative; he came to believe that the prosperity of society at large would depend on the degree to which education and opportunity could be reorganized to arrest the metastasis of the primary wrong.

Strikes

> *Barclay was fiendish about making sure that this group of hourly*
> *unionized labor put some money away for health and welfare, both ends,*
> *both from a retirement standpoint and from a health standpoint,*
> *and this is not a group that was prone to do that.*

—John Herrera

WHEN JOHN HERRERA AND Mike Plunk went to work at SST in the early seventies, the majority of SST employees were hourly and unionized. Base pay was in line with comparable businesses in the area: *The wages were fair. You didn't have to have a lot of education. You just had to work hard. It was a place for people to come and make a living* (John Herrera). In the beginning, Barc negotiated the labor contracts and seems to have been able to keep open lines of communication with the guys on the line. You could count on one hand the number of strikes at the San Leandro plant during its nearly forty years of operation. According to Mike Plunk, the longest strike lasted no more than three days. Contrary to received wisdom on the natural antipathies between management and labor, Plunk claims, *Everybody in the union truly loved Barclay and felt very loyal to him.*

The first strike at the San Leandro facility occurred in 1976 when Barc turned the negotiations over to the branch manager, Ray Clarkson. According to the people who were there at the time, the union's primary concern was that they were talking to Clarkson instead of Barc: *When the first strike came about, everybody was screaming for Barc. He talked to the people who were picketing, and then he went in....He met with the committee, and it was all done like that. He said, "Okay, I'm going to give you this....Let's all go back to work." Just his presence going through there made a difference, and he was that personal* (Mike Plunk).

Apart from wanting to deal directly with Barc, a key issue during this first and the two later strikes at the San Leandro and Brea plants revolved more around the distribution of pay than the rate of pay. The union guys wanted all the money up-front. According to John Herrera, the Sheet Metal Workers'

Union was focused on hourly wages and was not very strong on guaranteeing a benefits package for their workers. Barc's struggle was to convince his union labor that raises in pay needed to be distributed between up-front hourly pay increases and longer-term, nontaxable healthcare spending and pension benefits.

> *Strikes are always about money. But there were times when the stumbling block was not the cash. It was the distribution of it. Barclay said, "Well, I'll give you thirty-five cents, but a nickel needs to go here and a nickel needs to go there for your benefits because you don't pay taxes on those...." Barclay had to literally drum sense into them because they wanted all up-front money. But he would definitely challenge them and make sure that they were putting money away if they could.* (John Herrera)

Many remember the time Barc arrived, driving a forklift, at the picket line surrounding the Brea plant. Following his dramatic entry, he jumped down and walked the line, explaining that back-end money that's not taxed is a good thing, calling on the hourly workers to start building a future for themselves, to think about their pensions. It was a hard sell to guys in their twenties and thirties with young families, but he hammered away at the issue. The ones that listened—now these many years later—are glad they did. Some of them are retiring as millionaires.

A second strike in the late seventies—during a full-force recessionary period—focused directly on the CPS portion of compensation, which didn't get paid to anyone if the company lost money in a given quarter. It came as a shock to the rank-and-file when the quarterly check suddenly went missing, the first time this had happened in all the years the bonus payment formula had been in effect. The guys on the line and in the warehouse had a gripe with this:

> *I worked my tail off this last quarter, and you're telling me because of market conditions, I didn't make any money? You know what? We don't know how it works. We don't like it. We want guarantees.* (John Herrera)

Ironically, what disturbed the guys on the line was the fully democratic nature of the CPS, that its presence or absence in any given quarter applied to everybody, hourly and salaried people alike. If they met their production goals, they didn't want to be penalized if the sales force hadn't done its job, or if there were a recession. They didn't want to be docked if they had met their quotas. To Mike Plunk's way of thinking, *That was probably one of the biggest mistakes the union ever made.*

Barclay's response to the union's complaint was to decide that the CPS was not accomplishing what it was intended to do and that it needed to be fixed in relation to the union guys. *Programs like that have a life, and they've got to be redone over time,* he told Herrera, who was then running the warehouse. Barc commissioned him to come up with a new financial incentive plan for the hourly employees that would give them what they had asked for: a more tangible measurement system that would be calculated on a monthly, rather than a quarterly, basis. The one Herrera designed in 1978 was still being used in some of the SST factories and warehouses in 2012.

The third and last strike in San Leandro occurred in 1986 when twenty-three-year-old David MacDonald had been with Simpson for a little over a year as a packer. Later on, though he didn't remember the exact details of the complaint that had led to the stalemate, what he did remember is that when Barc found out about the stoppage, he came through the gate to where a bunch of the guys were picketing, and said, *Okay, so what's the problem here?* Mac was thrust to the front of the group. He says he already knew that Simpson was a special company, and he wanted to go back to work. He remembers saying to Barc: *This is our company. We want to work. We just want a decent living wage and benefits. We shouldn't be out here striking. We should be in there running a press, making product to service customers.* Barc listened as several guys spoke and said, "Okay, I'll be right back." Mac remembers what happened next:

> He went back behind the gate, and the next thing we knew, we were back to work, probably within a matter of hours....We looked at this man who came out not as some multimillionaire. We looked at him as if he cared. I mean, what owner would come down to a picket line and say, "Okay, what are the real issues here?" and get involved and not let his management team take care of something like that? I think that was just part of Barc's personality. He always wanted to get involved. Before I was hired there, I heard stories about how he used to work out

on the floor, where he actually ran a press and packed boxes. So that
made people feel he was one of us and he knew the working conditions
from start to finish.

In future years, Mac was to find himself on the other side of the fence—
no longer in the union, but part of the team representing the home office in
the negotiation of up to five or six SST labor contracts. The hourly people
could, perhaps, hear issues in a different way from the mouth of someone
who had held many of the same jobs they were filling up and down the
production line—and maybe even imagine themselves on the other side of
the negotiating table.

When SST expanded outside of California, the new manufacturing
facilities in the US—even in strong union states like Ohio—were never
organized. Location decisions for new plants were made on the basis of
markets and transportation concerns; the wage and benefits package offered
by SST appears to have been attractive enough to forestall organizing efforts
among hourly workers. Looking back over the expansion of SST facilities
throughout the US and Canada, Simpson Board Director Barry Williams says
that he believes there was never an anti-union sentiment or strategy among
upper-level management:

> *Under the "all for one and one for all" principle, we make sure that*
> *everybody gets something....Few companies provide the benefits that*
> *we offer. We profit share down. We even give out stock shares. You*
> *get Simpson shares after you've been with the company ten years. You*
> *don't have to buy them. And then there's the extraordinary pension*
> *program....So, the needs served by unions weren't there.*

After sixty years of expansion throughout North America, the unionized
facilities of Simpson Manufacturing remain the original two in California.

Notes for Part II

1 This is the F24 joist hanger, the original piece commissioned by Warner Odenthal.

2 https://www.strongtie.com.

3 Hewlett Packard began their company in a garage in Palo Alto, just as Steve Jobs and Steve Wozniak were to do many years later.

4 Front row, left to right: *Chuck Andrade, warehouse lead man, factory foreman, 1975; Bill Taylor, Tye Gilb's R&D assistant, made prototypes and tested parts, 1975; Joe Steaker, warehouse, 1975; Chuck Duggan, warehouse and part-time R&D, 1971; Tommy Clark, factory, 1973; Barc Simpson; Manuel Texeira, plant foreman, pre-1970; John Texeira, factory, pre-1970; Ray Clarkson.*

    Second row, left to right: *Tye Gilb; Ed Hannibal, assistant controller, 1975; Ev Johnston, controller, one of the initial investors when Simpson began to buy real estate around the US, 1974; Jim Gooch, factory and maintenance, pre-1970; Mike Plunk; Frank Stockman, maintenance supervisor (lost a hand in a freak accident where a wrench fell off his tool trolley and bounced sideways, wedging it in the 600 ton press's foot pedal, and the machine cycled with Frank's hand in the bed of the press), 1974; (name unknown), tool maker, 1974; (name unknown), factory, 1976; Hal Lane, supervisor, tool and die, would succeed Manuel Texeira as plant foreman, pre-1970; Laura Frasier, supervisor, sales office, pre-1970; Ed Davis, factory, would become a plant foreman in 1979, retired after a thirty-plus year career, pre-1970; Hazel Spindler, customer service, pre-1970; Rosemary Heath, customer service, pre-1970; Mike Ramponi, lead man in factory for many years then lead in R&D lab San Leandro and Pleasanton, 1976–current; Kathy Kuwitsky, receptionist, became Simpson's "queen of payroll" for over thirty years, retired, 1972–2015; (name unknown); Walter Burke, factory (never met a press he didn't want to tear apart! Unfortunately, he didn't know how to put them back together and wasn't in maintenance, drove Manuel T., Hal L., Ed D., and every other foreman and lead crazy for over forty years), 1968–2008; John Miguel, factory, 1975; Arlene Conway, Clarkson and Oliphant's secretary, 1974; Dave Bankston, factory, 1975; Barbara Tavares-Andreesen, customer service, pre-1970; John Breshears, factory, long-term lead man in shop, pre-1970; John Ajioka, plant manager, became branch manager of Duravent operation in Vacaville, 1975; John Penpraze, factory, father was warehouse supervisor, 1975.*

    Back row, left to right: *Karl Alvarez, warehouse, 1975; John Herrera, 1970; Bruce Soland, warehouse, 1973, factory, 1975; Steve Frasier, factory (Laura Frasier's son), 1970; Guy Derosier, factory, 1975; Joe Perea, pre-1970; Joe (last name unknown), tool and die, 1973; Dave Anderson, factory, pre-1970; Henry "Joe" Meadows, factory, first Black employee to "stick," retired after forty-plus years, 1969; Jose Pereira, factory; Ronnie Lout, factory, painter, pre-1970 for over forty years; Scott Ziegler, factory, 1975; Jerry Harvey, office, UC Berkeley grad, brought in to ultimately replace Laura F. and bring in some technical support for Tye, left in the early eighties and stayed in the construction business as a customer; Bob Bardwell, factory, 1974; Max Toorop, factory, pre-1970. (Identification and commentary by John Herrera.)*

5 A truss is a framework, typically consisting of rafters, posts, and struts, supporting a roof, bridge, or other structure. It is a structure that consists of two-force members only, where the members are organized so the assemblage as a whole behaves as a single object. A truss connector plate is a metal plate used to connect the prefabricated wood trusses (Wikipedia).

6 2019 Simpson Manufacturing Annual Report. http://www.simpsonmfg.com.

7 Lincoln Electric is a Fortune 1000 American multinational and global manufacturer of welding products, arc welding equipment, welding consumables, plasma and oxy-fuel cutting equipment, and robotic welding systems. Its business model was listed as one of the most studied by the Harvard Business School and has been featured in many case studies by business schools around the world (Wikipedia).

8 Nine Principles of SST (quoted from Barclay's Memoirs):

> **1. ITS FOCUS, ITS OBSESSION, IS ITS CUSTOMERS AND USERS.** We have to deserve the business, and we have to make money for our customers as well as for ourselves.

> **2. ITS VIEW IS LONG RANGE; ITS PEOPLE NEVER SACRIFICE TOMORROW FOR THE SAKE OF TODAY.** So, no matter how much you want the sale, you never exaggerate what our connectors can do in order to get the business. It'll catch up with you.

> **3. IT HAS QUALITY PRODUCTS THAT CONTRIBUTE TO THE QUALITY OF LIFE IN A SIGNIFICANT WAY.** Our connectors do make structures safer—you can be proud to work with a company that can really make a difference in the safety of families and communities.

> **4. IT IS A LEADER IN ITS CORE BUSINESS.** We are the market leader in our connector business and are trusted by construction professionals around the US and Canada as well as Europe, and Asia.

> **5. IT DIGNIFIES THE CONTRIBUTION OF EVERY INDIVIDUAL AT EVERY LEVEL.** No matter what job you do at Simpson, the way you do your job is important from how you answer the telephones to how you work with customers and others. You communicate with and RESPECT others, no matter what their job. We have more respect for a janitor who does a good job than someone with a PhD who does not use their talents to the full.

> **6. ITS PEOPLE ARE EXCITED ABOUT THEIR JOBS AND THE POSSIBILITIES FOR GROWTH, BOTH PERSONAL AND FINANCIAL.** We value our people. You came here for a career, not a bus stop. This is a long-range company, and we are not for sale. Of course, you can and should expect to do well financially, but we have other benefits for you and your family.

> **7. IT ENCOURAGES INNOVATION AND CREATIVITY BY RECOGNIZING THAT SUCCESS SELDOM IS ACHIEVED WITHOUT TAKING RISKS AND MAKING MISTAKES ALONG THE WAY.** If you don't foul up occasionally, you won't make real progress. But try not to mess it up too much.

8. IT FEELS AN OBLIGATION TO THE SYSTEM AND THE COUNTRY THAT SPAWNED IT, AS WELL AS TO HUMANITY IN GENERAL. For example, the Simpson PSB (Put Some Back) Fund supports such diverse causes as college scholarships, tutoring for first graders who are not proficient in reading and/or English, various art museums, and many other educational and cultural providers. And we have the funds to do these things because of the success of Simpson Company. In addition, your company supports such causes as Habitat for Humanity as well as giving out lots of scholarships every year.

9. IT'S A DEMANDING BUT FUN PLACE TO WORK WHERE PEOPLE SHOULD TAKE THEIR RESPONSIBILITIES, BUT NOT THEMSELVES, SERIOUSLY.

9 "Hewlett-Packard" (Wikipedia).

10 Ibid.

11 A punch press is a type of machine press used to cut holes in material (Wikipedia).

PART III

From Artisan Business to Technical Powerhouse

Any time Barc gives a presentation, he's always talking about the future. Whatever we did yesterday really doesn't count. He takes the time to thank us, but there's always this vision forward. There's always this push, looking to the future. Where are we going to go next? What are the next challenges? Where do you want to go? And I find it really, really interesting... he's absolutely focused on the future....Even back in the early days of the company, it was always looking forward.

—John Herrera

One of many dragons and other creatures made from Strong Ties by Joseph Way.
Photo by Joseph Way

Chapter 13
Two-Headed Command: Continuity and Change

They trust each other....It's a very elegant dance between them. Barc is savvy about expressing his view and then backing off....He trusts Tom and Tom's judgment... Tom will solicit Barc's input and honor it, but they disagree often....These two powerful men, who could have completely overblown egos, are able to manage this relationship in a way that I have not seen before, frankly.

—Jennifer Chatman

It was fantastic for me to have fun at the company while getting rich, and at the same time having time to pursue all those other interests, which now included various charitable causes.

—Barclay

We tended to be outliers...we had lots of fun.

—Tom Fitzmyers regarding his and Barc's time on the John Muir Hospital Board, shortly after they met

IN 1978, AT THE age of fifty-seven, Barclay was in his prime, at the height of his powers as a successful business owner. Things were humming personally and publicly, and he continued to swing for the bleachers. As always, restless and exuberant, he was on the verge of reinventing himself. In doing so, he took a step that few business executives would contemplate at his age: he organized his own succession and laid the groundwork for Simpson Manufacturing to move from artisan business to modern company.

Early on, Barclay had proven his nose for finding odd and exceptional people, giving them their head, and letting them run with their strengths. In hiring Tye Gilb in 1960, Barc had hit the jackpot; he did so again in the late seventies when he recruited Tom Fitzmyers, a banker, to take over the daily operations of the company. By objective standards, the selection of Fitzmyers for this role might have seemed a strange choice, both in terms of his training and the extreme difference between his and Barclay's management styles. Yet it appears that the two men used that difference with extraordinary skill in successfully moving the company into new territory. The oddity of the choice and its success is admiringly expressed by Barry Williams, veteran executive of a wide range of businesses and private and public boards of directors, who was both intrigued and impressed by Barclay's intuitive and somewhat eccentric choice of Tom to enter the company, first as head of acquisitions and later as the company's second CEO:

> I wasn't there at the time Tom joined the company, but it's extraordinary—just like Barc and everything he does. I think he had tremendous confidence in Tom. Tom was a banker. Tom loves to tinker and invent things. So he's not just a banker. But I'm saying if you're picking a successor, you sort of look for an operating type, and Barc didn't. He chose Tom…I think the world of Tom. Tom's different from Barclay but an extraordinary person. I can't say that the Barclay "system" or the Tom "system" would work in every company, but in this company, it sure as hell damn well worked and continues to work.

By the time he met Tom Fitzmyers, Barc was the indisputable leader of a company that bore his personal stamp to an extraordinary degree. Yet he pivoted in a moment, ceding much of the fine-grained, daily authority that he had built along with the company itself. He claimed that he was ready to do other things in his life. A few years before meeting Fitzmyers when he was shopping for a loan, Barc's personal life had changed utterly. Happily remarried, he wanted to spend more time with his new wife, Sharon, and his greatly expanded family (she had four young children, ranging in age from five to twelve at the time they were married). Additionally, he had entered local politics as an elected director of BART from Contra Costa County and was contemplating possible bids for elected office beyond BART; and, perhaps most startlingly, he was on the verge of starting a whole new art collecting, exhibition, and sales business with Sharon as partner. Though he had no idea of leaving SST behind, he moved effortlessly into a two-headed management arrangement, which left the daily rough-and-tumble to Tom.

The man Barc selected to co-run his company was an outdoors guy— handsome, masculine, and athletic. Relaxed and low-key rather than restless and charismatic, Tom explained his and Barc's way of working as simple and seamless. As each of them described independently, the deep, dark secret of their successful partnership appears to have been their capacity to listen to each other. Tom: *We just talk about stuff and sort it out that way. We have a huge amount of mutual trust in each other, and it's worked out really well. We don't paper stuff up. We just trust what each other says and, fortunately, we have fairly good memories, so it works out.* Barclay's version of their decades-long collaboration is not dissimilar: *I never have had to wonder whether Tom was shading the truth or withholding some piece of information that would cause me not to agree with him.* The strange nature of their joint process was apparent to people up and down the organization, who seem always to have been acutely aware of their differences as well as their commonalities. As one long-term employee, actively recruited by Tom in 1995, put it: *Barc and Tom have complementary, but very different, management styles. Barc always wants to know what is going to happen today....He'd put your feet to the fire....Tom is different—very comfortable with chaos, and he can tolerate lack of clarity in any given moment and just see how things work out....*(Kristin Lincoln)

In the beginning, Tom didn't know a thing about structural connectors, but then Barc hadn't either and this knowledge gap hadn't stopped him. As Barry Williams suggested, here was someone with a banking background being asked to run an unusual manufacturing company at a time when American business was moving more and more toward the idea of experts and the importance of narrow-gauged, specialized training. Yet, as Williams's comments suggest, Tom Fitzmyers proved to be one of Barc's most talented generalists. He was officially made the second CEO of Simpson Manufacturing in 1983, serving in top leadership roles within the company right up to his retirement in 2017.

Apart from his training as a banker, Tom brought a whole range of less easily defined skills to the job—not least, a high level of curiosity and a love for using his hands. He remembers that as a kid, when the others were out playing baseball in the street, he was making his own radio with a crystal and a cat's whisker. Although he had never aspired to being an engineer, thinking that for him it was too focused on micro detail, he had an innate predisposition for concrete problem solving, and always found engineering fascinating. Tom's view of his contribution to this side of the SST operation highlights a capacity to blend an interest in material details with the ability to pull back and look at things from a broader perspective:

> I've had fun here with the engineering. I've always spent a lot of time in new product development. These guys are all brilliant; I'm not. I just kind of go along. The interesting part about it is that sometimes because you have a different perspective and it's a little bit broader based, then maybe you can help bridge some gaps that others who are so specific aren't as easily able to do.

Tom's predispositions appear to have provided an unusual complement to Barclay's, which tended less toward technology and more toward strategic planning, competitive positioning, and games of chance. What they shared was a capacious curiosity about the larger world, along with honesty, a combination of kindness and toughness, and a great nose for people and talent.

There was only one major problem with the selection of Fitzmyers as the new daily leader of SST and it emerged almost immediately. Ray Clarkson, head salesman and early shareholder in the company, who had been with the business since 1960, believed that the leadership position should have gone to him. According to Barc, *Once Tom was hired, Clarkson started to meddle in management functions for which he had no authority.* After giving him considerable time to adjust to the idea that he would not be heading the company, Barc felt forced to let him go. *I gave him every chance. At least I thought I gave him every chance. Finally, I had to fire him. I hated to do it, but I had to. It really was that simple.* Like his father before him, when he thought it necessary to the well-being of the company, Barc made the hard, impersonal decision to fire an old friend and high performer. Ray, thinking he should get more than the agreed-upon buyout price of $3 million, sued Barc. Ray lost.

～

TOM FITZMYERS WAS HIRED during the recessionary period that spanned the late seventies and early eighties, an economic disruption that took a predictable toll on the construction industry and its attendant businesses. But once the economy started to improve, SST again began growing in leaps and bounds. Tom's fingerprints are all over this next phase of explosive growth for the company.

A mid-eighties decision made by Tom, on his own initiative, symbolizes his interest in technical innovation and experimentation. Based on the conviction that SST had to start doing things differently at the level of basic production, he procured a new kind of press called an Amada, which he instinctively believed would allow the company much greater flexibility in the production of specialized parts. Classified as a turret punch press, an Amada is a numerically controlled, programmable press. Although it was noisy and didn't run as fast as the big presses that banged out parts at the rate of hundreds of strokes per minute, it could do things automatically that were impossible to accomplish with the other presses. Housing up to 300 different tools and 600 dies, the Amada made bending metal more efficient and flexible, so several pieces could be made out of one sheet of steel, cutting down significantly on wasted material costs.

In the Amada, Tom sensed an opportunity—wide-ranging if not yet fully defined—but he could not justify the expenditure of $300,000 on a single piece of equipment. So, he convinced the Amada manufacturer to give the press to SST on consignment. Today, this press and its later generations, have become an important part of SST's "specials" business, a sector of the enterprise aimed at reinforcing the company's commitment to serving the very specific needs of individual customers. Tom's experiment mirrored the kind of future-looking gamble the company had always been good at while moving this capacity in a new direction. His self-declared interest in the engineering side of the business provided critical support for the increasingly important R&D investment decisions he and Barc were to make in the coming years.

THE COMPANY THAT FITZMYERS entered in 1978 was both various and woven tight as steel. The challenge facing leadership in this moment was how to use what worked best in SST's culture while also opening the company up to change and growth. This two-pronged strategy is nowhere so apparent as in the recruitment of an extraordinary group of second-generation employees. Hiring of new people under Barc's and Tom's joint leadership both changed the face of the company and bolstered its indigenous culture of excellence, flexibility, and collaboration. Without disrupting the DNA of the company's early labor force, new hires during the next decades reflected an effort at the top to move the company in the direction of ever greater technical expertise while still encouraging a wide range of talented generalists and salespeople to keep creativity, intensity, and personal service at the heart of the company's practice. For diversity in its most important sense, the second wave of SST employees lived up to the promise and protean powers of its originals:

> What's so interesting to me as I meet employees throughout the organization at all levels and in all functions is there's a certain spark to Simpson employees that I have never seen before....These folks are customer focused, ambitious, high achievers, but also have this unusual characteristic of a willingness to work together. (Jennifer Chatman)

It took a dexterous hand at the controls to maintain this delicate balance, especially as the company grew larger and more diversified in its product line and core identity. Rewarded for ingenuity and their ability to reach across boundaries, SST employees—new and old—continued to maintain and bolster the company's inventiveness and agility, qualities that were key to the evolution of Simpson Manufacturing from a successful artisan business to a highly technical enterprise based on sophisticated engineering and analysis, able to compete nationally and internationally in the twenty-first century. Barc's early instinct that Tom had a *good nose for people* was borne out early and often.

When Fitzmyers took over the daily operations of SST, there were no engineers working in the company. After eighteen years, Tye Gilb, architect, still anchored the technical side of the business right up until 1983 when Chris Patterson was hired as the company's first engineer. In the coming years, under the joint management of Barc and Tom—two archetypal generalists—SST was to build a highly sophisticated engineering department to support and expand the range of Tye Gilb's raw, one-man genius operation. Additions to the staff during this period gave SST the technical clout in the areas of product development and testing for which the company was to become widely known.

At the core of the new group of hires were a couple of extraordinary women engineers—a rare breed in the eighties: Karen Colonias arriving in 1984, the second engineer hired at SST, and Jacinta Pister in 1986. Occupying ever more responsible positions within the expanding business, they were to help shape the company's daily destiny in crucial ways for the next thirty-six-plus years, with Karen rising to become CEO and president of Simpson Manufacturing in 2012, continuing to the present (see bio), while Jacinta has filled the daunting role of Simpson Manufacturing's senior vice president of global manufacturing since 2005 (see bio), coordinating production in fifty-four locations on multiple continents.[1]

The third member of the company's unusual triumvirate of women executives in the upper echelons of Simpson's post-millennial management team was Kristin Lincoln, actively recruited by Tom in 1995 out of a flourishing and secure career at Pacific Bell (now AT&T). When she retired from SST in 2016, she had risen through the ranks to become the company's senior vice president of global marketing (see bio), serving alongside Colonias and Pister in some of the most challenging and influential roles within the company.

Throughout their tenures at SST, this striking threesome did not reflect the traditional profile of upper-level leadership in a construction products company. In fact, they would have stood out as an upper management team in most non-construction businesses as well. Yet their hiring was not the result of a conscious affirmative action policy, nor of a set of non-binding guidelines issued by a human resources department—which didn't even exist at SST until 2013—nor of a dictum from the top of the kind Barc issued in the sixties, when he decided to integrate SST through executive fiat. In each case, Colonias, Pister, and Lincoln offered a level of professional and personal excellence that was recognized and rewarded rather than excluded by the kind of automatic bias, which was often (even generally) a way of life in hiring for a majority of American companies during the years these women joined and rose through the highest ranks at SST.

Colonias the first of the three to be hired, was interviewed by an all-male committee, each of whom had been with the company for many years, when there were not any women in upper-level positions. Yet somehow the foundational culture of the company allowed them to see that Karen Colonias was clearly exceptional, as were Pister, Lincoln, and, undoubtedly, many of the varied group of outstanding men hired into the business during the same years.

From meeting each of these three women, one could extrapolate that the hiring criteria must have revolved around a distinctive set of qualities that included uncommon intelligence, humor, personality, and passion—where the latter word is not used casually. Personality and passion here mean not just enthusiasm, or charisma, or focus, or tenacity—but some kind of intense combination of all of these attributes. These are not sex-linked traits; yet this particular cluster of female excellence at the heart of the company's upper management team does convey important things about the male leadership team that scouted and hired Colonias, Pister, and Lincoln in the eighties and nineties; about what attracted each of the women to the company originally; what made them stay; and, perhaps most importantly, about the institutionalization of certain leadership values within the company's second generation management.

⁓

TELLINGLY, THE FIRST GROUP of Simpson Manufacturing engineers remember drawing inspiration directly from Tye Gilb, thinking of themselves as the beneficiaries and promulgators of the principles of creative investigation and production he had made famous at SST. This sense of intellectual and temperamental lineage is voiced without hesitation by Karen Colonias. Remarkably predisposed to the particular and even peculiar company culture she found at Simpson, we can hear in her words a subtle shift from Barc's and Tye's improvisational style to the rigorous demands of manufacturing efficiency, reliability, and replicability that was to move the company beyond its competition in the eighties and nineties:

> Tye would come up with all of these fantastic ideas, and I would ask him, "Fabulous, but how are we going to make these products?" To which he would respond, "That's not my problem. You guys figure it out." Then, J. J. Lin, a draftsman in the department, would chime in, "I'll think about how we can produce that product." …So, you need both. You need that creative mind, but then you also need the practical production piece…when you can put the two of those together, that's when you'll get unique products that can resolve customers' issues and can earn us the brand name we're looking for. (Karen Colonias)

But getting the balance right in this tradition was not, according to Colonias, easy. She describes how, along with Tom Fitzmyers, her direct boss, she helped to formulate a personality prototype to guide their search for new blood to round out the growing engineering department at SST. They dubbed the model hire as "EWP," which in technical parlance stands for "Engineered Wood Products," but which they recast as "Engineers with Personality"—an apparent oxymoron that was to form the basis of their recruitment strategy:

What I've always said is I could take a salesperson with a great personality and I could teach him or her engineering, but I can't teach an engineer personality. So, we need to be sure that as we hire them, we don't employ engineers who only want to do what they know, who just feel comfortable sitting in their cubicle and working on their computer. We need them to interact with everybody here: our customers, the building officials, the contractors. We need them to travel with our salespeople and enter into an exchange between what they do and what a salesperson does. So, I'm really looking for an outgoing engineering personality...very, very difficult...trying to mesh the culture of the company with the people that we're hiring....This core culture is a key element that Barclay and Tom put in place over a very long time.
(Karen Colonias)

In her wry assessment of engineers as a breed, Karen sounds remarkably like Tye Gilb himself, whose dark imprecations regarding the changing profile of the company are remembered clearly by his assistant, Joseph Way: *Engineers keep hiring engineers here, and engineers by their nature are not creative.* Coming from the older Simpson tradition of table napkin design, Tye apparently found the new emphasis on high-tech machinery and the abstraction it breeds less exciting than the more tactile arts he had practiced with great success in the early years. Nor was he wrong in viewing the arrival of engineers as a challenge to the complex persona—based simultaneously on materiality and imagination—which he had pioneered at the company and out of which unusual mixture he had fashioned something approaching the ideal Simpson personality type.

But it turned out that this constellation of traits could take interesting new forms that Tye may not have imagined, even among some of the new hires schooled as engineers. Just about to turn thirty when she was hired in 1986, Jacinta Pister was trained as a mechanical engineer, with a second degree in business. At the time she got her engineering degree, only about 10 percent of US graduates in engineering were women, a percentage that has changed very little in the succeeding three-plus decades. *It is discouraging.*

I'm trying to encourage my own daughter to stay in math and science. I haven't succeeded with either of my boys, so we'll see if I can get my girl to do it. Like Karen Colonias, Jacinta was as unusual and essential to the evolving identity of Simpson Manufacturing as Tye had been in SST's early history.

Right out of school, Pister had worked as an engineer at Hewlett-Packard, what she refers to as *another friendly, employee-oriented firm.* She describes her younger self as being an assertive, eighties kind of young woman who was intent on ensuring she got the right job for her talents. After Hewlett-Packard, she went back to business school, got an MBA, did a summer at Bank of America, and then went to work in Bechtel's finance and investment group, seeking some more intimate niche within the larger company. Though all her early jobs were with large, well-known corporate entities, she had come out of business school wanting to work for a smaller company. Knowing this, her boss, Barry Williams, later to be a twenty-year member of the Simpson Manufacturing Board of Directors, gave her name to Tom Fitzmyers, for whom he had done some consulting work. When she interviewed with Tom, Jacinta told him she had always chosen her bosses carefully.

In joining SST at that time, Pister had, indeed, fulfilled her wish to work for a small company, and she had also given up the glitz and glamour clearly available to her in the corporate world:

> *I started with SST in '86, in a couple of dumpy little buildings....Our offices were just hodgepodge put together. There were only a few people. No, there was certainly no glamour. I was coming from a high-rise in San Francisco with a view of the Bay Bridge. I had a wonderful office....It really, truly was about the energy and the opportunities at Simpson.*

Ambitious and aware of her own worth, and probably longing for something similar to the Russian roulette stakes taken on by venture capital firms today, she asked Tom for an equity stake in the company. He told her that wasn't immediately possible, but who knew what would happen down the road. Interestingly, she accepted the gamble. Partly, she thinks her decision to take the job at SST may have been a way of getting back to her roots in mechanical engineering.

Pister believes that in hiring her, Tom Fitzmyers also took a gamble. She remembers that he was looking for someone to explore ways to do

things differently at the company and hired her—in the vaguest of terms—
as an analyst:

> *Tom took a chance on me. Who knows what he was really looking
> for, but he knew he wanted somebody who could help him weigh
> various options. I appeared to be analytical, so he said, "What the
> heck? Bring her in...." His energy and enthusiasm and his approach to
> things really appealed to me, and that is a direct extension of Barclay's,
> although they have different styles. They're very different people...
> but complementary.*

Tom saw in her capacity for analysis the road to evaluating possible
innovations that would gradually transform SST from a successful basic
manufacturing company into a modern business of extreme agility and
technical sophistication.

Jacinta remembers that though they did, for instance, do some early market
stratification analysis on products that could be fabricated on the Amada,
it was more instinct than formal data analysis that drove them forward:

> *At the time, coming out of business school, I wanted to run all kinds
> of numbers, but...one of the great things about this place is that we
> don't overdo it. I think that's an important thing. You don't overthink
> because you never can know enough...if you spend forever saying
> "what could go wrong?" you'll never do anything. I learned from Tom
> and Barc that you've got to keep it simple.*

As skilled as she was as an analyst, her capacity as an engineer has also
come into play in major ways throughout her career at SST. She was able to
tinker hands-on with machines, a talent that won her the admiration of both
the engineering staff and people on the line, who had originally worried that
she had been brought on as a kind of efficiency expert, tasked with pruning
jobs. As Tom remarked, admiringly, *She's a tooling guru.*

Like Karen Colonias and many other key Simpson employees, Jacinta has
held a variety of positions at the company over the last three-plus decades,
but all have focused primarily on the perfecting and coordination of the
company's now international manufacturing operations: *In the cleanest, most
clinical terms, I coordinate manufacturing across the globe...which includes
capacity planning, production planning, and inventory control for our global*

operations. At the operational level, this is a job of enormous complexity, involving a constant evaluation of markets in relation to an ever-expanding product line as well as the need to standardize measures, machines, and the metrics of production across enormously varied geographical locations and cultures. In Tom's description, *She is quite simply the big brain who ties together all the people, the markets, and—literally—billions of parts.*

～

TYE GILB'S WORRY THAT SST was skewing away from creativity by hiring engineers should have been somewhat allayed by Barc's hiring of an outright artist to work with Tye during the early nineties. In very concrete terms, this move suggested that the emergence of strict engineering standards at the company need not displace the creative ethic at the heart of the business's original creed. Plucked in 1993 by Barc from his fine arts gallery in Lafayette, California, to become Tye Gilb's assistant, Joseph Way was an artist-fabricator whose range of skills mirrored those that helped put the company on the map during the first twenty years of its existence. Trained in art and design, Way had earned a living both as a drafter in a custom furniture factory and as an abstract painter, becoming one of Barc's and Sharon's lead artists at the Barclay Simpson Fine Arts Gallery in Lafayette starting in 1984.

When in 1993, Sharon and Barc decided to close the gallery, Barc suggested that Joseph try his hand at SST, where he believed his artist's skills might find diverse application. The root idea of a possible marriage between industry and art has an ancient pedigree, but one that has few exemplars in later twentieth-century American business. Perhaps not until Apple Computer tried to emulate the design ideals of the Japanese and Italians in commercial products did US fiscal pragmatism start to open up to the idea that beauty had a place in the marketplace. In taking a chance on Joseph Way, Barc instinctively chose a person whose aesthetic skills and hands-on capabilities did, indeed, have a place in the changing world of Simpson Strong-Tie.

Naturally, Barc steered Joseph to Tye Gilb, whom he knew Way would recognize as a cocreative spirit, and with whom Joseph shared an office for many years. Joseph best explains how his particular talents fit into SST's practice:

> *As an artist, you kind of set up the rules of a game....You create your own problems. Working at SST, there are real problems that are being solved...how to make houses that withstand hurricanes and*

*earthquakes, shelter....So, there are real problems and real solutions
coming out of this place, and that's what I found attractive about
working here.*

Joseph's memories of the company he joined in 1993—whose administrative
and Northern California manufacturing components were still housed in the
original, shabby facility in San Leandro, old and new living side by side—has
a strongly elegiac quality:

*So, I came at a really great time because I got to meet a lot of the
original players—people who are kind of legends in the company. It
was so nice to be here during that period and really get to know them—
especially Tye.*

As Gilb's assistant—in the time-tested manner of a Renaissance
apprentice—Joseph made Tye's prototypes and did all his Auto-CAD
drawings until the maestro finally retired in 1998. Way remembers that Tye
would design something drawn on a piece of graph paper, and Joe would take
the drawing and make a blueprint of it. Very much in the Simpson tradition
of hands-on problem solving and product development, Way would then
glue the blueprint to a piece of steel, cut it out on a band saw, and fold it. In
those days all prototypes were made by hand, a far cry from today when a
3-D printer can turn out a three-dimensional object directly from a drawing.

Eventually Joseph was to have an office in the shiny Pleasanton
headquarters building. Yet many signposts of his unusual pedigree and tenure
at Simpson surround the doorway to his workspace, where a steel menagerie
of fantastical creatures has been fabricated from the industrial symmetries of
joist hangers and their offspring, taking the form of mythic totems bristling
with scales, spikes, horns, powerful tails, huge jaws, and snaggly teeth—like
cave art in the heart of a twenty-first century construction business. Joseph
explains: *I used to sit in front of a carpeted panel where I had attached a few
of the hangers with Velcro; they looked like the heads of dinosaurs to me, so
I used them to make a full-sized giant reptile.* Though many of these unlikely
creatures have been used for various marketing purposes at trade shows, their
elemental power seems to point beyond their utility as a tool in the SST sales
bag of tricks to the fundamental creative urge and practice that brought the
business into being and sustained its rise.

Now into his third decade as an SST employee, having known the old company with its legendary founders still at the helm, and having lived through the metamorphosis of that creative jumble into the more streamlined and technically dictated procedures of the current global company, Joseph Way—perhaps skeptical by nature—says things have already changed in ways that make it hard to predict whether the values that have allowed him to fit into the company so far will be able to prevail over the inevitable corporate drift.

Way's sense of loyalty to Barc is both personal and philosophical, as he wonders how long the founder's imprint can withstand the countervailing forces of time and diffusion. Darkly, he speculated in 2012 as to whether the newer of the employees would even recognize Barc if they saw him in the halls. (Until 2012, they almost definitely would have, since Barc continued to do the new hire orientation sessions right up until the time he officially stepped down from the company.) But, more than simple physical recognition, Joseph is trying to get at some deeper form of acknowledgment:

> I just hope that it's remembered what and how this man thought, and what his vision was, and that they don't start following the leads of some of these consultants, these know-it-alls that say you should do this, you should do that, and turn the company into something it never was, for the worse.

Fueling this statement is Joseph's appreciation for the ways in which Barc recognized Way's idiosyncratic but compelling set of skills and found a way of marrying these with the ideals and practice of the company. For Joseph, Barc's belief that the worker was the key creative force in building the brand was fundamental. What is undoubtable is that an instinct for creative "outliers" was always the foundation of Barc's own ingenious art.

Chapter 14
Entrepreneurship and the Reiterative Process

As long as I was getting sales, making money for the company,
suggesting new ideas, implementing them, I had a free hand.

—Terry Kingsfather

IN ADDITION TO ARCHITECTS, engineers, and artist-fabricators, Barc's prized class of salespeople also remained crucial to the modernization and expansion of the company from the late seventies to the present. Among Tom Fitzmyer's early and most successful protégés is Terry Kingsfather, who was hired to open up new markets for SST in the Northwestern United States. He went on to work at the company for thirty-five years, retiring in 2014 as president of Simpson Manufacturing. Hired in 1979, Terry worked more closely with Tom and Hugh Oliphant than with Barclay, though he was very much aware of Barc's influence behind the scenes. Kingsfather's insights into what it meant to be a salesman at SST echo Barc's original and fundamental belief that a Simpson salesman is the key engine of the company—an independent entrepreneur who is, first and foremost, answerable to the customer:

> *It was like I had my own little business without the expenses or issues*
> *that go along with owning your own business. It's a little different today*
> *because there is so much cross activity between branches, and we need*
> *to be a little careful, but our salesmen in the field in my mind really*
> *direct the company. They're the guys that are out there every single day,*
> *fighting the battle. And that philosophy was passed down...from Barc*
> *and Tom, to all of us—that we're not top-down driven. We take our*
> *direction from our salespeople, who take direction from our customers.*

For Terry, SST offered a level of independence and chance for personal initiative that was different from most jobs in sales:

When we were all growing up, all of us who came up through sales in those early years had a tremendous amount of flexibility to make our own territory. No manager ever came out to me and said, "You're going to do it this way because that's how I do it," or, "Your way is stupid." Nobody ever talked to me like that.

Though it appears that Kingsfather was personally predisposed to independent action—qualities that are undoubtedly at the heart of the mutual attraction between him and SST—he claims that Barc and Tom consciously built a coherent philosophy at the company that encouraged personal initiative and pervaded all aspects of the business: *There was never any fear of stepping outside the boundaries…the best idea always won, whether it originated with a plant worker or at the highest levels* (Terry Kingsfather).

Combined with his own apparent gifts, this approach proved golden for Terry. When he first took over the Northwest territory in 1979, SST was doing about $500,000 worth of annual business in the area; by the time they finally enticed Terry southward to take over major management functions at the headquarters office in Pleasanton in 1997, his territory was doing roughly $9 million in sales a year. *And it was like that all over the country,* Kingsfather claims. Fueled by its philosophy and consistent ability to find the constructive "outliers," SST was on a tear.

One of the most skilled practitioners of the SST's salesman's art, Terry is also one of the company's most articulate explicators of the philosophy that Barc and Tom instilled in their sales force regarding how to bring SST products to market, or, as Terry says, *How we pull through the business.* According to Kingsfather, it is a *soup-to-nuts* process that links product design to specification to installation:

What we try to do is not just sell a product but take it from its inception….We see what the needs are. We develop a new product based on what the industry wants, and we get it code approved. We then take that product to an engineer or an architect and explain what it does and how it will outperform current products and methods. They put it on the plans….We go to everybody—to do-it-yourself companies like Home Depot, to engineers, to home designers, to architects, to the colleges to catch the kids who are graduating in architecture or engineering so that when they come out, they'll get a Simpson binder before they walk out the door....They'll have the Simpson bible long before they have anything else. We also do seminars for those colleges, as well as for working engineers, architects, general contractors, city planners.

Like John Herrera and Mike Plunk, Terry Kingsfather remembers a time before SST had attained its current high level of market share for the connector business in North America—a time when the company was battling a number of tough competitors, all trying to ride the American residential construction boom and to weather its slides.

A lot of companies had the same opportunities we did, but I think if it hadn't been for Barc and Tom pouring money back into R&D and engineering and taking a gamble in hiring salespeople that this would never have happened. They had the foresight to see that specifications were important....It didn't mean that you got the job all of the time, but what it meant was that your product was on the plans.

SST's focus on specifications was of particular concern in the West and South, where earthquakes and hurricanes pushed building codes into the forefront of the new construction and retrofit markets. As Kingsfather pithily puts it: *You know who helped us a lot over the last twenty years, I guess, would be Mother Nature....*According to Kingsfather, many of SST's early competitors—even some that were stronger players than they were in the beginning—went by the wayside through failing to make the same kinds of investments in research and people. Some years back, Warren Buffett—who once wrote to Barc inquiring as to whether he was interested in selling the business, with predictable results—acquired a connector company, which is now producing some competitive, patented products. Kingsfather readily acknowledges that the competition is always out there, but drily observes, *We have a twenty-five-year head start in terms of how we go to market, and our relationships with people.*

In later years, once he joined management, Terry Kingsfather would instruct SST salesmen about the sheer entrepreneurial opportunities available to them through their privileged role within the business: *I always tell these guys I think that the greatest job in the company is being an outside salesman.* What is fascinating is the way Barc and Tom's top salespeople established practices that were to intersect and complement those of its engineers and product designers—and how the engineers, in turn, worked with the salespeople. Here is engineer Karen Colonias's description of her daily work experience at Simpson:

> I came to Simpson...from a more typical engineering role, and... realized very quickly that this company was pretty unique, because I could walk out to the shop floor and see how they're producing things. I could travel with the salesperson in Florida and see how they sell our product and go to the job site versus being told, "Here's the data... design the product." I could actually go to the job site, see the need, design the product, go to the lab, test the product, come back, and reiterate. I could watch the individual pieces being produced, shipped, marketed, and then go back to the job site again. So, I could complete that full loop of the design process, which is pretty unusual.

What Colonias calls a "reiterative" process seems to mirror the full-cycle approach to marketing instilled in SST salesman from Barclay to Ray Clarkson, from Hugh Oliphant to Terry Kingsfather to Laurent Versluysen in Europe. This suggests a continuity between the generalists and the technical people that is rare in any enterprise. It also gives some insight into the degree to which SST's head salesman, its creator, continued to influence the personality and practice of the modern company that was emerging from the rich soil and vision that had brought the business into being during the roiling days of its inception.

Chapter 15
Expansion

It was a foregone conclusion that we were going to grow this business.

—John Herrera

M ANY OF THE INVESTMENT decisions Barc and Tom made throughout the eighties, nineties, and the first many years of the new millennium involved the extension of SST's geographical reach, first by establishing new SST facilities outside of California, then through a global expansion beyond North America.

Like many small companies, the company had uneven success in calibrating its growth. John Herrera remembers that there were some tricky times when SST's sales and expanding customer base started to outpace its production capacity. *There were some really tough spots in the early eighties, because we landed some big accounts and we were hard-pressed to service them.* In 1981, SST opened a warehouse in Texas and one of Herrera's employees from San Leandro went down to start up the new branch. Noting that the San Leandro purchasing agent didn't exactly have the résumé for the job, John says, in SST dialect, *But he made it work.* Once they got to Texas, they hired a welder named Jerry, who recently retired from the Simpson Company after over thirty years.

By 1983, they had already outgrown their first Texas facility and moved that year into a larger plant facility in McKinney. As the first SST expansion outside of California, beyond the direct imprint of Barclay and Tom's very particular leadership styles, the Texas branch is an interesting case study in the way SST prized autonomy over standardization. According to Barry Williams, Texas has a whole different "personality" from the California operations along with its own particular way of getting the job done:

> *In Texas, you see a very singular branch that has gone about things differently. They have their own distribution channel system, which is*

different from that used by the California branches, yet they've applied the "secret sauce" and all the things that have made Simpson great while contributing elements of their own.

Williams goes on to explain that in the early days of the company, the branches were consciously set up as entirely separate units that didn't share sales or inventory. In the view of many, being a branch manager at SST was among the best jobs in the company because you were essentially running your own private business, but with all the protections provided by the company umbrella and reputation. Williams observes, *For a while, the branch managers were the highest paid people in the really good years. They were paid more than headquarters people.*

Barclay's concept, according to Williams, was that this total autonomy allowed the branches to better serve local markets and to adapt service to the particular needs of local customers without the constrictions of having to pass strategic and tactical decisions through a central home office command structure. In this sense, local control was for Barclay a fundamental business principle, a direct outgrowth of his insistence that decision-making should take place at the lowest possible level. At its core, Barc's belief in autonomy was ontological rather than simply operational—a principle grounded first and foremost in his personal psychology, which combined a profound distrust of complex, impersonal reporting structures with a conviction that taking personal responsibility is the engine of a productive life.

By the late eighties, SST's expansion was gaining speed with the company setting up a fourth major branch in 1987 in Columbus, Ohio. Each of the branches, in turn, has subsidiary manufacturing facilities that report directly to the individual branches in such places as Florida, Illinois, and Connecticut. By the time Simpson began to establish an international footprint in 1993, its presence in North America, including facilities in western and eastern Canada, was both deep and broad.

⁓

As the company grew over the next several decades, the issues of autonomy, identity, and acculturation, which came into play when SST expanded beyond the Golden State, were to figure in ever more complex ways. This was especially true when the company crossed the Atlantic into the UK, then into *fortress*

Europe,[2] moving ever eastward, where issues of culture and language were to become increasingly more intricate. The challenges Simpson Manufacturing faced in these expansions across the waves is summarized by Laurent Laurent Versluysen (vice president for European Operations, 1994–2018; see bio): *You cannot ask people to change their roots....Being global is not being big. It's not being international. It's creating links between different markets and cultures....*

In a company built around the practice of horizontal communication, personal networks, and teamwork, the question of what might be *lost in translation* was to become supremely important. In the process of Simpson Manufacturing going international, the company needed to adapt to diverse dialects and customs. Barclay and Tom were to see the company's creed both embraced and altered as the enterprise faced a new set of responsibilities—to a global customer base and labor pool, to regulators, to shareholders.

Though SST had to make some significant adjustments to break into international manufacturing markets, core aspects of Barc's charismatic leadership style remained the same. Versluysen, a Frenchman, captures the essence of this style: *I think Barclay is considered by many to be the soul of the company. I've seen standing ovations when he shows up at meetings...he is very, very human...and, this is felt in such a physical sense....*The choice of the word "physical" is striking in its connotation of felt presence and personal impact on others. To describe better what he means by this choice of words, Laurent tells a story of one of Barclay's first visits to the French plant. *I was impressed. I mean, really, the keeper of Simpson, of the company, coming over to visit us.* Versluysen picked him up at the airport after Barc's very long flight from California. Waving off Laurent's suggestion that he might be jet lagged, Barc insisted, *Let's go straight to the company.* When they arrived at the French plant forty-five minutes later, a sudden unexpected wardrobe adjustment elicited a spasm of Gallic amazement from Laurent:

> *And in the parking lot, Barc decided to change his shirt. It was just in the middle of the parking lot, he got rid of his shirt from his back. He got another shirt—he wanted to wear the one with the Simpson logo on it. I was very surprised...I said, "Do you want to stop somewhere to change your shirt?" He responded, "No, no, don't worry...." He's like me, basically. It's not a monster. It's a human being, and you can talk to him.*

～

SIGNIFICANTLY, EVEN AS INTERNATIONAL acquisitions and expansions moved forward from the early nineties, the company's North American operations continued to grow. Still today, this continental cluster of manufacturing facilities remains the most reliable profit center for the global company. In this regard, Simpson Manufacturing is a particularly interesting twenty-first century American business story—a tale in which location decisions are dictated by the drive to open new markets and better serve customers rather than to outsource manufacturing jobs in search of cheaper labor. In terms of servicing customers, Barry Williams emphasizes that logistical considerations have always been crucial to the Simpson way of doing business:

> So, even if it was cheaper to make our product somewhere else, the logistics are a very important component of our brand. We don't want our customers to have to inventory. We'll make it. We'll store it. We'll get it to you. Again, this is part of the secret sauce. Why can we charge 20 percent more than anybody else? It's because we make a better product and we'll provide you all the information you need to use it, we'll hold the inventory, and we'll get it to you the day after you order it.

In discussing Simpson's expansion overseas in relation to its continuing strength in the US, Barry Williams points out some distinctions between Simpson Manufacturing and the fate of other basic American manufacturing operations during the second decade of the twenty-first century:

> I think we're an exception to what's going on in most manufacturing businesses, because we don't make commodity products, per se. We take a commodity product and make it highly specialized and better. So, what's allowed us to keep jobs here is the fact that we're making a precisely engineered product that can support US technological input and US labor costs. We do buy some products internationally. But they tend to be mostly the commodity products—like nails. Also, our product has such a small cost—it's like a three- or four-dollar product—even if you make it cheaper in China, you couldn't ship it cheaply. Our product's one where you try to manufacture it near where you can use it.

Williams's nuanced distinction that *Simpson has a higher proportion of non-commodity products than most basic manufacturing companies* does not disqualify the company as an interesting example of an American business that still makes a physical product, which has continued to expand in the US even as it started to grow beyond its own national borders—meaning that jobs at home have not been jeopardized by extra-territorial expansion. Simpson Manufacturing never had any plans to flee American shores.

Chapter 16
Transmitting the Creed

The people here are just phenomenal. I think everybody will tell you that we have a lot of friendships in the company, that people are not just your business associates. Everyone is working on the same thing, which is a rare human experience. Everybody wants to be part of something. The pride people have knowing our products save lives is in everybody's DNA. If a Simpson product is going into a school, it just has to work. There's just no deviating from that line.

—Kristin Lincoln

As SST began to expand, the company's small workforce naturally increased, both in California and in its growing number of outlying facilities. The new employees hired from 1981 going forward—even those brought into the original cramped San Leandro warehouse and home office— were a second generation of hires who had no personal experience of the first twenty-eight-plus years of the company's idiosyncratic beginnings. Nor, for those outside of Northern California, did they have any day-to-day experience of Barclay and Tom's joint leadership style. It is remarkable, then, that the sense of family and of a shared, nearly genetically driven creed, apparent in the first phase of SST development, is still manifest in the company's recent history—even following dramatic, international growth and the transition of the company from a privately held business to a publicly traded enterprise in 1994.

A prime example of the way in which the Simpson creed was absorbed and promulgated by the second wave of SST hires is provided by Kristin Lincoln, the third member of the company's striking trio of female leaders who were essential to the growth of the business from the early eighties through the second decade of the twenty-first century. Unlike Karen Colonias and Jacinta Pister, Lincoln was not an engineer, but more of the generalist stamp pioneered so successfully by Barc and Tom. A graduate of Stanford Business School, which she attended with support from SST while she was working for the company, Lincoln is a shrewd observer of the fundamental leadership principles that she believes make Simpson Manufacturing an unusual and significant story within current American business.

Like John Herrera, she sees Barc as having always been a risk-taker, a tendency bolstered during the second phase of the business's development by Tom's interest in engineering and his recognition of the need for experimentation and change. In Lincoln's view, the willingness to invest is directly linked to the Simpson belief in taking the long view:

> One of Barc's key leadership traits was being willing **to invest in unproven things** [author's emphasis], *for example investing in R&D before he knew there was a market for what he was investigating....He was investing for the long term. There's a lot hanging on whether or not these strong-ties hold up or not. It really matters whether buildings fall down or stand. That is a long-term perspective and one of the things that makes this story interesting—American business isn't necessarily famous for long-term investment strategies.*

Like Joseph Way, Lincoln believes that another key quality that separates SST from many other American companies is having a founder who believed that taking care of his employees was essential to the company's fundamental mission along with the recognition that behind every employee there is a community. Kristin believes that not many companies build their businesses based on these irreducible humanistic principles or are as consistently profitable as Simpson Manufacturing has been over a period of sixty years—in spite of the challenges involved in riding the cyclical tides of the construction business.

In this view, an interest in human resources—in the lowercase, fundamental sense—has always been part of the core culture of SST and is directly reflected in the idea and reality of the Simpson Manufacturing brand. For Lincoln, the company's tangible commitments to recruiting excellence, to treating its people well, and to setting the highest standards for product development and testing have, in the end, created a mutually reenforcing, *symbiotic* relationship between the SST brand, the people responsible for it, and the customers they serve:

A Simpson Strong-Tie is significantly more expensive than connectors produced by its competitors. That's because it involves the top in R&D, the best quality steel, the highest quality people. That's what makes it a brand. A brand is all of the perceptions that a customer has about what you provide them and whether they're willing to pay more or not for the trust that comes with the product....It doesn't matter what role you have in the company. What matters to people is that we do things right, period. We do it the right way. We do it the ethical way. (Kristin Lincoln)

This concise statement could have been written by Barclay as a company manifesto sixty years before, when he first imagined the SST business model. The consistency of vision is itself striking, as is the level of undiluted, passionate commitment to the goal and the daily—in Lincoln's words—*ethical* practice. For her, the result of this form of branding is that the customer wants to do business with a company that honors this practice, completing, as she says, a *beautiful circle of life.* Such convictions suggest that Barc and Tom succeeded to an uncanny extent in transmitting a set of values to the people to whom they were gradually passing the baton.

Notes for Part III

1 See 2019 Simpson Manufacturing Annual Report for a full list of current facilities of the company. https://www.simpsonmfg.com.

2 Laurent Versluysen remembers a picture sent to him, possibly by Barc himself. It was of a big elephant and Europe was pictured as a fortress with a small door. The elephant couldn't move through the door.

PART IV
Sharon and the Double Family

This is a fun guy....

—Sharon Hanley Simpson; see bio

Barclay and Sharon, early eighties in front of the gallery.

Chapter 17
Courtship

I didn't have time to think about getting remarried.

—Sharon

I was married young, raised three children…I was looking for a good time.

—Barclay

IN AUGUST OF 1973, Sharon Hanley was living in Orange County, divorced for less than a year, with four children ranging in age from six to eleven[1]: *I couldn't believe I was living in Orange County. I had a bumper sticker that said, "Good Neighbors Come in All Colors"; it was lily white and very right wing. Not a good place to raise kids. I wanted to move north but didn't have the money and didn't want to disrupt the kids' schools, Cub Scouts, and stuff… after everything else.* She and her ex-husband had had to sell their house to settle the divorce and she and the kids were living in a condominium. Her ex-husband, Phil, immediately moved in with his girlfriend in Westwood, at some remove from the daily life of his four children and ex-wife. Sharon worked in a doctor's office at low pay to support her family.

She remembers not being interested in anything except casual dating. From childhood, she had enjoyed dancing and was open to a fun evening on the dance floor, but not much else. Her marriage had been rough, and life was complicated enough, working and raising the kids. Lizzie, one of the twins (and Sharon's look-alike), recalls, *Mom had men all over her the minute she was separated, you can imagine.* But Sharon wasn't looking.

In February 1971, Barclay Simpson, aged fifty, left his wife, Joan, and moved into a rented apartment in the Watergate Apartments in Emeryville. As he had long (privately) planned, this move came shortly after his youngest child, Jean Devine Simpson (Jeannie), left for her freshman year in college.

John Barclay Simpson, the oldest of their three children, had left home at sixteen to attend private school and was well-launched on what was to be a highly successful academic career. Having graduated from UC Berkeley, Anne Katheryn Simpson (Annie), the second of Barclay's and Joan's three children, was newly engaged to Bob Gattis, also recently graduated from UC Berkeley. When Barclay left, Annie was still at Berkeley, and she and Bob moved in with Joan for the months leading up to their wedding the following June of 1971.[2]

Having been married since he was twenty-four, Barclay was interested in making up for lost time. Jeannie remembers: *He was quite the dating-crazy man for a while there.* After twenty-six years of a difficult marriage in which Joan's alcoholism was a nearly daily difficulty in their lives, he was not looking for long-term commitments.

Though Barclay had certainly experienced a sense of freedom and adventure in his business life, his emotional life—albeit rich in child-rearing and active friendships—had for many years involved major constraints and intractable problems, which did not lend themselves to willpower or solution. Constitutionally, viscerally at odds with the kind of ambiguity or guilt that leads to repetition and paralysis, Barclay could not tolerate an emotional life dominated by an illness that had remained incurable. The decision to leave Joan reveals crucial aspects of Barclay's innate personality as well as the founding principles of his deeply held, and not entirely sunny worldview. Exuberant by nature, Barclay's apparent optimism and physical joyfulness were grounded in a full acknowledgment of the dark, the implacable, and the irreversible. But that knowledge was itself a point of departure for how he chose to live. The rigorous concept of acceptance espoused by the classical Stoics braced his personal philosophy of life, as epitomized by Epictetus's directive: *There is only one way to happiness and that is to deny all worry about things that are beyond the power of our will.* For Barclay, this perception was neither a negation of tragedy nor a call to passive acquiescence, but a form of clear-eyed acceptance of the state of things that made action in the world possible and essential. The key to a useful life was a refusal to wallow or be transfixed by the mud and the murk. These beliefs are given voice in his cryptic, unadorned accounts of his brother's death by suicide and his decision to leave his wife of so many years.

In the midst of Barc's immersion in the wild world of 1970s dating, some close friends kept mentioning a thirty-five-year-old woman they knew—beautiful, smart, kind, recently divorced—with four kids in Southern California. The first part sounded good, but the second part really didn't fit what Barclay was looking for—and, besides, he wasn't looking.

Sharon's goal was to raise her children and pursue an orderly life: *I couldn't envision getting remarried—because it had been so awful before.* Meanwhile, her ex-sister-in-law and her husband kept saying, *We've got this guy. He comes down to Brea and Newport Beach…you should meet him.* Sharon wasn't interested. *But they kept bugging me, so finally, I said okay….*

The four of them were to meet at a restaurant. There was a staircase, Sharon explains: *All I remember were these plaid legs walking down the stairs. He came over to the table, and his first line to me was, "Stand up." So I did, and he said, "Oh, my God, I thought you'd be ten feet tall from the way they're talking,"* which was a cute thing. Later he took her dancing, though it is not clear whether he knew of her prowess, or whether that would have stopped him. *Of course, he couldn't dance his way out of a paper bag. He had no rhythm at all. But he was so fun.*

He took her home in a Buick Riviera—what his daughters called *the pig car—but it had the biggest trunk,* he tried to explain. Once they arrived at Sharon's apartment, he got out of the car, saying, *I have something for you.* Then he disappeared to the rear. As the minutes ticked by, Sharon's thinking, *I've got to get four kids off to school and go to work in the morning. Finally, I get out and walk to the back of the car. All I can see is this plaid butt attached to a body that is deep in the trunk, fishing through rolls of toilet paper, golf clubs, and sweaty workout clothes. It's clear he's been pretty much living out of this ugly car and its big trunk. At the bottom of the mess is a stockpile of books, which I can't help noticing all have the same title. He hands me a copy of* The Little Prince, *saying with a flourish, "Especially for you." I respond, "And all the others." I couldn't stop laughing.*

Barc calls to say he enjoyed the evening. Sharon says she is about to take the kids for a visit to her parents' house in La Selva Beach, near Santa Cruz. Barc suggests he come down. But Sharon says, *No,* not wanting *to mix it up with the children and all that.* Not easily deterred, he writes her a three-page letter on binder paper. *It was hilarious. It gave me options for his next visit to Newport Beach: we could take all the kids to Shoe City and get them sneakers; and/or we could go to a baseball game, where I could: a) order a hot dog with mustard; b) order a hot dog without mustard; c) order a hot dog with* onions. *Very romantic! I read the letter to my mother and we were on the floor laughing....I have a collection of his letters in a shoebox. I don't know whether I will ever be able to read them again.*

They began to see each other intermittently in Southern California. In mid-fall, Sharon flew up to San Francisco for a job interview with Equitable Life that her father had set up for her. She was only making $600 a month at the doctor's office, which didn't go far with four children. Barc picked her up at the airport and she spent the night at his place in Emeryville the night before the interview. *My father hit the roof...he was furious because Barc was only five years younger than he was...how could I as a mother of four....* Sharon replied, *Well, Daddy, I think you should meet him.* Heading directly into the iceberg, Sharon apparently thought that her father would be placated by encountering Barc in the flesh. They met for breakfast at a little diner, perhaps an important opening crack, but the iceberg didn't dissolve easily.

In early December, lying in bed before sleep, Sharon is reading an article in *Sunset Magazine* about Cozumel and the Yucatan Peninsula when Barc calls to tell her he is off to the Yucatan for a few weeks. Amazed, Sharon says, *You won't believe this. I am reading this article about the Yucatan this very moment.* He says, *Why don't you come with me?* The children were to be with Phil over the holidays, and she was to have gone to her parents for Christmas. Thinking about her father's reaction, she hesitates, waffles, tries to explain. Barc says, *You're thirty-five. Do you have to call your father?* Sharon responds, *I do. I'm that kind of kid. I do. I have to have their approval.* When she does call home, her mother takes the phone from her fuming husband and tells her, *Darling, go and have a good time.* Sharon is shaking, but very excited.

Barc had already been in Cozumel for two weeks when she flew down to meet him. She remembers jungle, a hidden Halley's Comet, and extremely simple accommodations. No bling, glamour, or glitz: *We had an incredible week. It was very primitive then. No restaurants or cruises or dive ships. We stayed at Señor Rodriquez's house, an adobe block thing...how did Barc find that place? But it was fine with me. Señor Rodriquez slept in the living room on the couch, and we had the bedroom....Every night, Barc insisted that we get up at three in the morning, risk waking up Señor Rodriquez as we collected our bikes from the living room, then we rode out into the jungle, looking for Halley's Comet, which was supposed to be passing overhead. We never saw it, but we saw lots of fireflies.*

What must Señor Rodriquez have made of them?

There was a miraculous quality to this odd courtship: *We never got sick, we drank beer, went to the open markets, and ate tortillas, never got sick....* The pearly, pink conch shells could be found in clusters on the beach…and Halley's Comet, which they finally saw out the window of the plane on their way home, must have, indeed, been overhead, surveilling them as they rode through the buggy jungle every morning before dawn.

In January, Barc returned to Southern California with an unvarnished proposal: *I think we need to make a plan. Plan Abel is that we don't date anybody else. Plan Baker is that we date other people, but we don't sleep with them. He skipped Plan C and went to Plan Dog, which was that we not see each other again.* They decided on Plan Abel.

Sharon and Barc's new dating career was filled with limitations, even apart from the geographical distance, which sometimes made them feel as though they had chosen "Plan Dog." Sharon explains, *It was a little hard for him to get used to, but I wouldn't let him spend the night when the kids were around. I didn't want that for them until we decided what we were going to do.* In spite of whatever frustration he may have had regarding "the house rules," when he did finally meet them following the December Cozumel trip, he put himself out with the kids. Sharon remembers that he never forced himself on them, but was very down-to-earth and personal, telling them to *"Call me Barc." Since they had always called adults "Mr." or "Mrs." this was a big thing for the kids.*

Julie, Sharon's second child, was nine when Barc came into their life: *I remember when I first met him. I was in the little hallway of our apartment playing jacks and I feel this energy coming up the walk. There's a knock on the door and I open it. It's this guy wearing plaid bell-bottoms. He says, "Hi, I'm Barc Simpson and I'm here to see your mom." He shakes my hand, says, "What are you doing?" He sits right down and plays jacks. To me that's the quintessential Barclay, curious and enthusiastic. Doesn't matter who you are, he wants to know who you are and what you think about things. I'll never forget it.*

In February of that year, Sharon accepted the job at Equitable Life and got ready to move the whole caravan northward. With her father's help she had found a lease-with-option-to-buy condominium in Walnut Creek—1,400 square feet for the five of them. Barclay offered to help with the logistics, driving down in the famous Buick because Sharon didn't have a car that was reliable enough to make the journey north. Barc said he would stay at the home of the Picketts, old friends of his, and that they could all get together there for dinner the night before the trip. When Sharon walked into their house, she realized she also knew the Picketts because their son was in her son, Jeff's, Cub Scout troop. It felt good, she said, to know that some of Barc's closest friends were people she already liked and admired. Julie remembers that Mrs. Pickett made *an incredible picnic* for all of them, which softened some of the strangeness of the move: *I remember thinking, "If Barc has friends like these…he's not all bad." I was still saying, "Who is this guy, he's a foreigner to us, really nice, but who is this guy?"*

Sharon remembers that just outside of LA, they stopped at a diner at the top of the Grapevine: *Jeff took his juice or something and poured it on Amy's egg, and she let out an ear-shattering wail, and I looked at Barc and thought, "Well, welcome to the real world."* But, apparently, the Grapevine diner incident didn't dissuade Barc—albeit newly single, newly free, and prosperous at the height of the sexual-cultural revolution. There was still time to bail. But the ragtag band continued the drive north with him at the wheel.

During Easter of that year, the kids being with Phil for the week, Barc and Sharon went to his house in Tahoe. Sharon remembers becoming conscious at about 5:30 a.m., and finding Barc, ever an early riser, already fully awake, though she was longing for a little more lolling and snoozing. *I've got a great idea*, he said without preamble, *why don't we get married?* The great idea came complete with deadline details: *I'll give you until 5:00 p.m. tonight to give me an answer, and if you say "no," don't worry, I won't jump off a bridge, but I don't think we should see each other anymore.*

He was staking everything on the roll of the dice, but he was neither cautious nor confused. He knew what he wanted, maybe had known since Cozumel—or even before, perhaps while digging around among the dirty clothes in the Riviera's trunk. Though cunning, Barc was never one to let overly complex strategy get in the way of action. When he intuited value, he was always looking for the shortest way between two points. This restless will to action didn't always pay off in business or in his personal life—but, mostly, magnificently, it paid off in spades. In this case, his gamble won him forty years of drawing to an inside straight. Neither Sharon nor Barc could ever remember how long it took her to give him an answer—but she did make the deadline.

Leaving Tahoe soon after, they met Sharon's parents in San Jose to tell them the news: *My mother was thrilled. My father was stoic rather than vociferous. He said, "Well, congratulations."* Once back in the car with Sharon, Barc remarked, *That was a chilly response.* Sharon nodded. But they had definitely crossed the Rubicon.

⌣

ONWARD TOWARD THE PRIZE. Barc's oldest son, John, was planning to come out from Philadelphia to present a paper at UC Berkeley—so, Barc organized a "Movie Night" at the Walnut Creek condominium with Sharon's kids and his own three. He spliced together both their family movies, projecting jumpy shots of four young kids, interspersed with post-war images from the fifties and sixties of his own three children, now fully grown. Lots of hilarity. Then a big hand-drawn "Intermission" sign signaled a change in the action as Barc began to make public announcements as they used to do at the Grand Lake Theater of his own childhood: *The church women's auxiliary was to meet the following Tuesday, the Boy Scout's Merit Badge Award Ceremony was scheduled for the twenty-fifth, and…* [one beat pause] *the marriage of Barclay and Sharon is calendared for June eighth in La Selva Beach.* Sudden total silence. Everyone looking at each other. Then big commotion and pass the popcorn.

As promised, they were married on June 8, 1974, in Sharon's mother's little church in La Selva, followed by a reception in her and her husband's backyard. Sharon's parents kept the four younger children with them and Barc and Sharon took off for two nights in Carmel, accompanied by John, Annie, Jeannie, and their various spouses. Sharon laughs, *It was quite a honeymoon.*

⌣

EVERYTHING HAD MOVED SO quickly—massive changes of place, housing, consort, family—and finances. Sharon had been struggling financially for years. From the moment she met Barc, he had told her they were on a "budget." She recounts: *This is what I loved, because with my first husband there was never a budget. I didn't know if he was going to bring money home or not. He'd spend it on just crazy things. How different with Barc. I remember the secure feeling of knowing the rent will be paid. I will have money for groceries. I'll have money to pay PG&E. It was an incredible feeling….*

Courting and marrying Sharon hadn't made a dent in Barc's instinctive frugality. He didn't woo her with glamour, jewelry, or stories of wealth and comfort. Based on his own living conditions, car, clothes, and daily habits when she met him, not to mention their odd vacation in Cozumel, Sharon had no way of knowing that she and Barc were to become not only rich, but major East Bay philanthropists. What she understood instead was that she and the children were, after years of turbulence and insecurity, "protected"— that she was going to be able to pay the bills. This knowledge was not a thing apart, but simply a measure of Barc's overall solidity. It read safety, not wealth.

However, on at least one special occasion, there was a break in the pattern of welcome predictability: *Just before we got married, Barc gave me a check for $500, and he said, "I want you to go out and buy as many things as you want and only for you." And I can remember looking at that $500 and thinking, "This is a million dollars." I had never seen a check for $500...I couldn't believe it....*But it didn't change the fundamental, secure fact: *...I knew we were on a budget, and we were.*

Letting go of the fear and insecurity was a big change for Sharon—and for the children: *Gradually the kids settled into the change...they came to realize that when Barc said something, he meant it, but that no matter what, he wasn't going to yell, never going to hit them or me, that there'd be no temper tantrums in the new house. It took them awhile to come down off of the tension. It took me awhile, too.* But not Barc. According to Sharon, Barc's reaction to having been in a very difficult and lengthy first marriage was nowhere apparent. *If I hadn't brought it up, I probably wouldn't have had an idea of what happened. Barc started day one with us as if it were a clean slate. Barc is like that....It's his philosophy, and it's innate in him.*

For his three older children, it may have been more of a balancing act.

Chapter 18
The Double Family

The family hangs together because Barc and Sharon are absolute.

—Jeannie Simpson; see bio

MOVIE NIGHT" WAS THE beginning of what Jeannie was to call *the double family,* an entity whose dynamics were to fluctuate over time. The seven "children" had met each other before the evening in which Barc broke the news of the wedding, but, according to John (see bio), *It was still a big surprise. I had met Sharon, liked her a lot. But it happened very quickly. It was a big surprise.*

The fall-out from the "big surprise" was, predictably, always partially linked to how each of Barc's original three children managed over time to digest their own childhoods in relation to those of his "new" family. As John, Annie (see bio), and Jeannie would all agree, *Barc really got it right the second time around.* All expressed pleasure and wonderment at the depth, happiness, and durability of Sharon and Barc's marriage over a period of forty years. Yet this realization couldn't help but be complicated by their mixed memories of their own parents' marriage, their sense of their own childhoods, and their father's decision to leave their mother, who, in time, was to die—too young—of her illness. They were lucky, as Annie observed, that their father lived so long, allowing all of his children to know him over many different stages of their own lives and his, to have a chance to make sense of their childhoods over time, and to know their father as adults.

John, the oldest, after a somewhat difficult early adolescence, left home for good at sixteen, growing to productive maturity outside the boundaries of his original family. Barc and Joan's middle child, Annie, has double-edged memories of her primary family. *I thought it was weird that I had parents who never argued,* she remembers, but stops short of commenting on the nature of this civility, or whether she experienced it as a sign of their closeness or disaffection. She recalls her father as absent—*he was always at work*—and, yet, also as a pervasive, extremely influential presence, *a great listener, a teacher*, who believed deeply in *fairness*, yet was a strict disciplinarian who didn't particularly think it necessary to pilot his children through moments of emotional difficulty. During the first three years of high school, Anne recounts that she abruptly went from being an A and B student to getting by with Cs and Ds, as she put on forty to fifty pounds. *It was a difficult time for me…and I was strictly on my own.* She remembers noticing how other parents seemed to be hands-on with their children while she was pretty much left to her own devils and devices. *My father believed you pretty much had to handle things on your own.* So she did. In her senior year, she decided to lose the weight and get good grades and managed deftly to reverse her downward trend. It is hard to imagine that this transformation wouldn't have caught her parents' attention, though she doesn't recall any particular response from them. Or not until Barc enthusiastically helped her with her application to his much-beloved UC Berkeley.

She, more than any of the other of her siblings, inherited both her parents' love of Cal, which provided Annie with what she describes as one of the happiest times of her life. *I was primed by both my parents to love the school, and I did.* In a counterpoint story to the one about her unremarked decline during high school, Annie has a distinct memory of her father taking real trouble to reassure her in a moment of anxiety in her freshman year. On the day she was to go for interviews at the sorority of her choice, Barc appears to have left work (a rare occurrence), to have searched for and found her VW bug parked somewhere on the streets of Berkeley, and to have left her a note that she has still. It read: *"Don't be scared. Any sorority that gets you as a member is lucky. Love, Dad."* It was such a sweet, personal gesture. I wasn't used to that. I knew it was something special.

Annie recounts that it only dawned on her slowly what it was that Barc had achieved in building Simpson Manufacturing. She says she was already in college before she started to understand, after hearing someone talking with admiration about the Simpson Company. Stories about her father integrating the plant in the sixties against tough opposition, his insistence on sharing the profits of the business, and providing his employees with rich benefits started to permeate her consciousness in a new way. *He was always at work....He really knew how to run a company.*

As she grew up, Annie heard repeatedly from her father that *guilt was a wasted emotion.* Late in his life, she recounts, she asked him whether there was anything he felt guilty about. It's hard not to wonder whether she was referring to her mother. But what he responded was, *Yes, I wish I had spent more time with my brother.* Against his own strict rejection of useless regret, he seemed still to have been wondering if there were some action he could have taken to prevent the suicide. There are very few other examples offered by family, friends, colleagues, or employees of Barc deviating from his cherished philosophy of not looking back.

Whatever questions Annie may have harbored, her admiration—and love—for Barclay emerge palpably, echoing repeatedly in her statements regarding his capacity to focus his attention in profound and personal ways: *He was a great listener...a really great listener...he always heard you out...even when he was just biding his time to disagree..."Yes, sweetheart, but..."*

Youngest of the three children, Jeannie recalls the rumbling fears and feelings of her childhood in more explicit terms: *There were a lot of storms in our family. My mother was alcoholic for most of my childhood and my father made up his mind early that he'd stay with her for the children. I knew there was a problem but thought love could solve it. He never spoke with us about it. I remember once sitting in a parking lot with my father and I said to him, "When are you going to leave?"*

This must have been a painful moment for Barclay as well as Jeannie. Jeannie didn't mention whether he offered an answer or explanation. But, later, to a non-family member, Barclay made no attempt to "explain" his actions or soften the facts as he saw them: *I realized, after many attempts, that things were not going to change. So, I made a decision, and then waited until my children all left home.*

Though Jeannie seems always to have been aware of strain and pain within her family and admits having had a *very difficult time when my father left my mother,* she describes Barc in intimate, physical, and joyful terms: *I grew up with not a normal family life, but I grew up with a hugely supportive father. He was always fun. My earliest memory of him is when we were in the pool at Orinda Country Club. He was throwing me in the air. I can tell you exactly where we were standing in the pool. I must have been three. He always had a real presence for me even when he wasn't home. There was a power about him, and that power came from just his being. There can be a huge storm and he's not going to be blown over. He's grounded.*

Predictably, the merging of the two families was experienced differently by each of the two clusters and by each of the kids individually, as well as being fluid over time. For one thing, there was a major difference in age between the seven children. Both Annie and Jeannie remember, *In the beginning it was really fun and easy.* They and their husbands took the kids to San Francisco dives and restaurants, opening up a miraculous world for the new kids in the family. Annie's husband, Bob, became a major male force in their lives, developing a particularly close relationship with Julie, who recounted how, at family dinners, she and Bob would always switch the name cards so that they could sit together.

The early ease with which one group of siblings accepted the other rose and fell, shifting over the years. Sharon's Lizzie, who was only seven at the time Sharon and Barc were married, echoes Annie and Jeannie's recollections of the initial period: *Having the other family was fun for us. They loved my mom. They were fun-loving. Different music. Jeannie and Annie and their husbands were a blast. They did cute stuff with us. They were young and hip, would take us to the city to a funky little restaurant. I loved having them around. It got complicated as we got older.* Jeannie confirms this, separately from Lizzie: *Our father and Sharon shared the philosophy of his children and her children always being "our" children. At times this pissed me off. I thought, you know, the three of us are totally different than the four of them. Each group has some serious strengths, and each has some serious problems. Sometimes I didn't feel like being grouped together. In the beginning it was really fun and easy. It didn't become difficult until we all got older....*

Though the intramural and extramural differences fluctuated over time, there are certain commonalities of perception among the seven children that have given this "double family" a discernible, roughly coherent identity as a single family. Overwhelmingly, these shared perceptions have to do with what Sharon and Barc meant to each other, how they reflected each other's values, and the way they, but particularly Barclay, were changed over time through their palpable love for each other. This is perhaps a rarer story than the one involving the vicissitudes of their children's reactions to the new totality.

Jeannie reflects movingly on what the sudden change meant to her personally as well as on the effects of Barc and Sharon's relationship in their own lives:

> *I was just young enough so that I loved Sharon from the get-go. She has an extraordinary capacity and graciousness. She was so loving, open, and I really needed that. I was still looking for some woman to be a mentor in my life. Sharon changed my life. She taught me how to be a loving, kind person. That was not an outward part of my father's personality and my own mother did not have the ability to do that. I will adore Sharon forever.*

Jeannie considers herself very fortunate in this relationship and also comments on how the somewhat frightening nature of Barclay's bluntness and disciplinarian rigidity, which she remembers from her childhood, evolved over time:

> *My father was always fun, but there was also a fear factor around him. He was tough when I was growing up. There were rules and you didn't break them, and if you did there were consequences. He's always been tougher on his three kids than her four kids. Once he married Sharon, he slowly softened because he felt so much love. She made him happy. The family hangs together because Barc and Sharon are absolute.*

As Lizzie comments, there is a way in which Barclay—so busy and often absent from the family while he was building the business throughout his twenties, thirties, and forties—got a second chance in helping to raise Sharon's four kids: *It was so different for us; it was like he had had a dress rehearsal, but now had a partner who could take his good qualities as a father and enhance them. Without Mom he would have given us so much, but the two together gave us so much more. He was happy, enjoying his life with Mom, so was very present. I feel really lucky.*

Julie remembers Barc's advent in their lives as a dramatic moment of transformation:

> *Our real father was a damaged guy. I'm so grateful I wasn't raised by him. Up until I was ten or so I was filled with a physical "joie de vivre," being a gymnast and ballerina, always moving around doing cartwheels, dancing—but psychologically I was terrorized. I never*

knew when my father was going to blow up. I was terrified growing up. Then this guy comes up the front steps and all of a sudden it's fireworks and sunshine and happiness.

Independently of Julie, Lizzie reinforces these perceptions, while also alluding to what Jeannie had called "the fear factor" around Barc: *This man moved in who was the polar opposite of the man we had as a father prior. Barc moved in and the TV moved out. Our lives changed radically. Barc was much stricter than we were used to, but he was so happy and the positive energy coming out of both our parents made the structure and guidance great. I loved it.* A quintessential story for Lizzie is the time early on when she broke a glass on the kitchen floor and froze in place waiting for the explosion of rage she had come to expect in such moments from her own father: *The first time I broke a glass, I did a terrified retreat, trying to escape the inevitable eruption. None came. Barc looked at the mess on the floor, and said, "Lamb, where does Mom keep the broom?" That was it. I was in shock. He didn't clean it up because it wasn't his thing, but I did it gladly.*

Amy, Lizzie's twin, tells a similar early story of her own. She was *very close* to her own father, but remembers being drawn to "Pa," as she called Barclay, from the moment she met him. She wanted to be with him as much as possible. Knowing he got out of bed early every morning to meet friends for their dawn jog around the Lafayette Reservoir, she intrepidly asked him if she could come, too. *Yes, Lamb* (he called all the girls "Lamb," says Sharon), *but only if you're ready with the right shoes and clothes when it's time to leave. I won't wait. I leave at 5:00 a.m. If you are here at 5:01 a.m., I'll be gone.* Proudly, Amy met him at the door very early the next morning, and for many mornings afterward. Explaining that he and his friends ran faster than she did, Barc would leave her on a bench in the dark to wait for his return. Resourceful, Amy recalls that she would often run in the opposite direction to meet him on the trail as he circled back. (Inevitably, the day came when Amy could outrun Barc and all his friends, lapping them on her turns around the reservoir.) Then she'd go with the men to the coffee shop and listen to their talk. *Pa was very attentive to me….I worshipped him….He let us live.*

One morning, Amy remembers, their usual pattern was broken. Generally, Barc left his car unlocked in the parking lot. It was a horrible, gold sedan, the one known as "pig car number two," strewn as it always was with a strange mixture of dirty gym clothes, squash and tennis rackets, old food wrappers, and a bunched-up tuxedo. He was ready for everything. Amy explains that Barc normally just dropped the keys on the floor. *That's because nobody would steal your car,* Sharon observed. This particular morning, Barc had put Amy in charge of the keys and, in her haste to keep up with him, she managed to lock them inside the car. When they returned from the reservoir, Barc went to open the car door, and Amy, suddenly horrified, realized what she had done. She froze and stared at him, long bangs over big eyes, waiting for the rage to strike. He looked at her, then said, *I guess we're going to get a little more exercise this morning than we planned on.* She knew he had meetings and tensed, waiting for anger or a lecture. But instead they just set off, side by side, chatting the whole two miles to the house of a good friend. An hour later, armed with a clothes hanger, Barc and Amy—now coconspirators in a great adventure—picked the car lock and drove home to tell Sharon their morning's tale. Sharon remembers Amy running into the house upon their triumphant return: *I just remember this little girl with big brown eyes running in and saying, "Mom! Mom!" and telling me the whole story.*

Amy loved physical activity and was interested in business. "Pa" and she played tennis and golf together, and he backed her financially when in her twenties she decided to open a restaurant in Tahoe. She says she was able to pay him back in three years. Amy says Barc loved it that she always had a job, and she claims he told her, *Of all the seven children, you are the only one I would have hired into my business.* But what stood out most for her was how much he loved her mother—and the way in which his treatment of her children reflected this passion: *He really showed up in our lives. He always meant what he said and did what he meant. He made time for us.*

But not all of Sharon's children experienced the radical change in their lives in the same way. Jeff Gainsborough, the oldest of Sharon's kids who would have been eleven at the time Barc arrived on the scene, recalls a long, *tumultuous* adjustment to his own parents' divorce, to Barc and Sharon's lightning courtship and marriage, and to the deep-rooted differences between his blood father and Barc. Jeff's response was one of prolonged *resistance*, what he remembers as *a decades-long struggle with his own father*, occurring side by side with his repeated *testing* of Barclay, whose rationality and calmness was a constant reminder of his own father's anger and unpredictability. It was, by Jeff's account, to take years for him to accept that his blood father was *not capable* of giving him the emotional reflection he was so stubbornly seeking. He began, he recounts, to feel sorry for himself for the absence of the father-son relationship he craved. These feelings were compounded by what Jeff judges to have been a series of *horrible* failures in business and love. But suddenly *a light went on in my mind.* In the lowest moment of anguish and self-judgment, Jeff abruptly realized that all those years he had had a father—one who showed up at every football game, every track meet, who gave him an intense love of history and physical challenge, who couldn't be pushed around by his sullenness and need for confrontation, who taught him why good manners count, how to turn stubbornness into tenacity, one who said that it wasn't failure that mattered, but whether you got up again. At the age of forty-seven, Jeff asked Barclay to adopt him.

Jeff and his wife, Klubo, made it to Sharon and Barc's house a few days before Barclay's death in early November 2014, where the whole family had gathered for the last days. Jeff was in time to have essential conversations with Barc, who was mentally and emotionally lucid, and apparently very moved by his adopted son's appearance at his bedside. Jeff and Klubo had to leave before the end. *I never knew Jeff loved me,* Barc told Sharon afterward.

Chapter 19
After the Wedding: The Crowded Condo, Winnie in DC, and Rolling in the Snow

Barc taught me that you could have fun learning.

—Julie Simpson

IMMEDIATELY FOLLOWING HIS AND Sharon's wedding, Barclay moved into the 1,400-square-foot condo in Walnut Creek, overnight shedding his independent bachelor life to live with four young children and a new wife in a constrained space. The Grapevine incident became emblematic of his new daily reality. Perhaps it felt like an ongoing reprise of his and Sharon's week with Señor Rodriquez in Cozumel—except the noise level was much higher. The six of them were to live on top of each other in this condo for five years, right up until Julie's sixteenth birthday.

As all the kids remember, Barc's moving in with them immediately meant a major change in the furniture: TV out the door, replaced by a massive dictionary next to the dining room table. Lizzie remembers: *We loved that dictionary.* Julie, independently, echoes her: *We had dinner together just about every night, all six of us. He'd sometimes insert a word into the conversation and ask if anyone knew what it meant. If we didn't, dinner would stop, someone would go to the dictionary that stood on a stand nearby, they'd look it up, and come back and tell the whole table what it meant and use it in a sentence.* To this day, both Lizzie and Julie have a dictionary on a stand displayed prominently in their houses, a certain kind of value-laden memorial and portrait sculpture for both of them.

In addition to the dictionary dinners, Lizzie talks of how conversation, stories, books, and language, in general, were part of their daily fare: *We've always talked more about psychology, art, or philosophy than politics. Barc used to be really into poetry. He gave me such a love of language. He had a book in his* hand at all times. I loved reading. I didn't miss the TV. He let me know there was just too much out there. We read a lot together. I remember being injured once and he read The Swiss Family Robinson to me. He'd pick out classics. And he was a storyteller in his own right: We got to pick the characters and he'd create the story. We could literally say, "My character is a garbage can with ears." The big kids had recurring characters, but we got to pick new characters every time. He was so good at it. He was silly in a lot of ways. He'd go to a business meeting with a hat with a ponytail on it.

For Sharon, one of the most striking things about Barc was his ability to compartmentalize things: It could be a stressful time in the business, as it was, for instance, during the Ray Clarkson lawsuit, and when Barc was also president of the BART Board of Directors,[3] but the minute Barc walked through the door at night, he was immediately engaged with what was going on with the family, what everybody did that day, helping with homework. This capacity to separate things into those about which you could do something at any moment and those you couldn't helped her a lot, Sharon says, even if she experienced a major period of exhaustion after six months of being married to Barc, until she learned a new way of parsing and pacing events and emotions.

Then there were the "family councils," as Julie recounts them, a telling snapshot of Barclay's particular style of leadership and decision making: We had regular, obligatory family council meetings where everyone got one vote and Barc got six. He loved to hear what we all thought, but then he made the decisions. There was a suggestion box. With Barc there was not a lot of psychology going on, but he did think everyone should have a voice, very fair, very business-like. At least you felt you had a voice, but it was clear who the boss was. Yet Mom could say anything to him. He was so secure. And then they'd always laugh.

One of the common threads in these stories—including Jeannie's striking memory of her father's power of being—is Barclay's physicality and capacity for adventure, a trait that Jeff picked up and transformed into extreme sports. Lizzie recounts, As a kid I loved it—the spontaneity and travel—even if it drove my mother a little bit crazy….The first time we went skiing at Tahoe, we hiked up the mountain. I was seven years old. Barc put me on his shoulders and skied down the mountain. My Mom was having a heart attack, but for me, it was the most exciting thing. He had that childlike fearlessness. When, at twenty-five, I jumped out of an airplane, he made me think things like that were okay. It was *in my nature. My mom was horrified, but my dad thought it was the best thing. He wanted to jump out of an airplane.*

In 1975, the summer following the June they were married, Barc and Sharon decided to take all of Sharon's kids on a cross-country trip in a Winnebago—a space even more intimate and intense than the Walnut Creek condo. The plan was to stay in public campgrounds, and they took off without having made any reservations or even defined the exact route they were to travel—in Barclay's words, *We just headed east.* Predictably perhaps, a few days out, one of the drains overflowed, as Barclay remarked cheerily, resulting in a *disgusting mess. But otherwise, we had few mishaps.*

In Lizzie's words:

> *We had no reservations, just pulled over by the side of the road and slept. We found hot springs and I remember once Barc lowered Julie down into the hot springs by a rope, my mother standing by worrying that there might be a whirlpool down there or it might be too hot.... When we got to Washington, DC, in the middle of the night we pulled the Winnebago into a construction site right smack in the middle of the city* [as in the Washington Mall, then undergoing reconstruction]. *We just parked and slept. When the workmen started coming to work at 6:00 a.m., we looked out and at the exact right moment jumped out of the camper and took off for a day of sight-seeing, leaving "the Winnie" where we'd parked it the night before. It looked like part of the construction stuff. We did things like that, which as kids we thought were awesome. Barc wasn't worried about things.*

And, apparently, this included not being afraid of authority. The mall parking space turned out to be so convenient, they stayed there for the several days they were in DC as Barc and Sharon showed the kids what they considered to be the extraordinary monuments of *the greatest country in the history of the world* (Barclay).

In addition to Yellowstone, the Chicago Museum of Science and Industry, and DC, the Winnebago also made the pilgrimage to the old, rocky farm in northern Vermont where John and Janett Simpson had staked a claim when they arrived from Scotland in 1830, ultimately producing twelve children who were to fan out over the sprawling continent—as far as Oakland, California. Well over a hundred years later, aging Simpson aunts still held the family farm, tending its cemetery and welcoming new generations of Simpson offspring when they unexpectedly arrived out of the blue in an ungainly Winnebago, in a kind of reverse covered wagon migration back to origins.

In Philadelphia, they went to Liberty Hall and met up with John Simpson, his wife Diane, and children Matt and Lissa, who were living in Philadelphia, while John was completing a two-year post-doc at the University of Pennsylvania. They got to see John's laboratory before the expanded family entourage and other friends set out again, headed ever eastward to the Atlantic Ocean for swimming and July Fourth festivities. It is hard not to wonder what John, a veteran of beautiful summers and winters in a series of family condos in Lake Tahoe, made of the Winnebago transcontinental journey, or its bulging new brood. But he, as much as anybody, understood Barclay's elastic powers.

On September 25, 2014, a bit more than a month before Barc's death, John wrote a letter of appreciation to his father following a trip back to Lake Tahoe with his second wife, Katherine, after having been away from the lake for nearly ten years. The letter, which is signed, "Love, Johnny," is full of reminiscences of times spent with his father at Lake Tahoe, alone and in company, that highlight Barc's exuberance and ability to find fun and adventure wherever he went:

> As we crossed the summit of the grade en route to Kings Beach…I recalled one wintertime adventure where you and I had to put chains on the family station wagon in order to get up the last quarter of a mile or so. That ancient Pontiac [yet another of Barc's long-suffering cars] just wouldn't go in the snow, even that little distance, and you and I laughingly…rolled about in the snow while we fought the tire chains. We did make it up and over, and you managed with your good nature and unfailing optimism to make an odious, uncomfortable, and annoying task into something fun.

To an extraordinary extent, these words echo Jeff, Julie, Lizzie, and Amy's descriptions of Barc's capacity to transform daily life and its trials into raw entertainment. In John's words, it is also possible to hear Jeannie's memories of Barc "being present" in her life in spite of the family pain in which she and he were embroiled, or Annie finding the hand-scrawled note in her VW bug.

John Simpson, Barclay's Scottish-born grandfather

Jannett Simpson, Barclay's Scottish-born grandmother

Barclay as a Navy pilot in WWII

The OS2U Kingfisher—Barclay's WWII Fighter Jet

Barc in Cozumel, 1973

Sharon in Cozumel, 1973

Sharon Hanley Simpson,
at the time Barclay and
she first met

Barc and Sharon with Marilyn and Tom Fitzmyers hiking in Lake Tahoe

Barclay and Sharon at the Barclay Simpson Fine Arts Gallery in Lafayette, California, for the opening of the Rembrandt Show in the late 1980s

Ringing the gong at the
New York Stock Exchange
in spring 1994

Barclay and Sharon at the Ribbon Cutting Ceremony and Dedication of the Memorial
Athletic Stadium and the Simpson Center for Student-Athlete High Performance

UC Chancellor Robert Birgeneau and Barclay cutting the ribbon at the Dedication Ceremony

UC Chancellor Robert Birgeneau placing the Berkeley Medal around Barclay's neck

Barclay and Chancellor Birgeneau
enjoying the fruits of their joint labors.

Barclay addressing the assembled crowd after receiving
the Berkeley Medal, January 2013. *Photo by Peg Skorpinski*

John concludes with a reminiscence about him and Barc playing golf in the very early mornings, with a clear statement of what it meant to him to be the center of Barc's focus in those moments: *I just loved playing that silly game with the father whom I so adored, and whose full attention I had on those early morning jaunts.* In this small memory shard, John puts his finger on the essential core of Barc's charisma as a businessman, as a philanthropist, as a friend: the capacity to be fully present with other human beings. This is both a fundamental act of respect and an art based on genuine interest in the world outside of the self. Though immediately recognizable, this trait is both rare and elusive in spite of being the indispensable precondition of leadership— and fatherhood.

Chapter 20
Special Projects, Pruning, and Housing a Marriage

Working for Barc at SST was a mixed blessing.

—Sharon

A LIFELONG ENEMY OF nepotism, Barc, as a matter of principle, never employed any of his children at SST. Yet, shortly after they were married, he did offer Sharon a job as his "special projects assistant" at the company, never having had a secretary before or after her rather brief tenure in this anomalous position. Breaking with tradition, he asked her to come work at the Simpson Company, just in the mornings, so she could continue to be available to the kids in the afternoons. He suggested she set up an educational program, follow stock trends, and handle other special tasks for him. Sharon said, *Sure*, but in the doing, she found the transition from beautiful, loving wife to employee a bit fraught. Barc was famously blunt, and Sharon found that her feelings got hurt when he would say, *I don't think you should be doing it that way*, or, *Where's the...?*

One of her solutions to this dilemma was to find tasks for which Barc had no understanding or expertise. She took to pruning the evergreen pears just outside the office windows, climbing up in the trees with a handsaw and clippers: *Nobody had pruned these trees for a long time, and they needed it....* But this elicited a major complaint from Ray Clarkson. He was aghast at the vision of the president of the company's wife climbing like a skilled, armed monkey through the trees. Barc thought it was great. *Just get it done.* Sharon thought it was great, too—*getting it done, and I knew how.* In this and many other ways, she gave new meaning to the term "special assistant" while also becoming a favorite among SST's colorful band of employees. She remembers, *I got to know the employees, and I loved the whole atmosphere. Everybody was so equal—just as they say.* In spite of the positives, working for Barc—unlike being married to him—turned out to be a short-term engagement.

Since the Walnut Creek condo was a bit tight around the edges, Barc and Sharon went house-hunting, found a piece of property in Orinda, and started interviewing architects. Barc placed the project in Sharon's hands. She had never built anything before, but she started to accumulate pictures and ideas of what she liked. They interviewed approximately twelve architects and never quite found the right chemistry until someone recommended architects Myra and Ron Brocchini[3] through whom they also eventually hired the contractor Andy Paisal.

Sharon loved working with Ron, Myra, and Andy. She remembers spending five hours at a time with them at the kitchen table of the condo, being cross-examined regarding the use and flow of every room, materials, door handles, the whole myriad of details involved in building a house. A hands-on project manager, she was delighted by the creative challenges of designing a house that was both beautiful and functional for a daily family of six and the principal gathering spot for the larger family and countless friends. Both Sharon and Barc loved to entertain, and this house was to become a major center of East Bay hospitality for business, artistic, philanthropic, and university groups over many decades.

What is remarkable about the house that Sharon and Barclay built between 1976 and 1980 is its close connection to the layered, vertical site on which it sits, the movement of light throughout the house, the sense of a permeable barrier between inside and outside in which walls devolve into windows, making terraced gardens visible from shifting angles. Even now, nearly forty years after they moved in, the house has a feeling of newness and modernity. According to Julie Simpson, many of the basic design features of the house—*the shingles, the split levels, the extensive use of redwood and douglas fir*, and the way in which building forms adhere to the landscape— were, *like so many Northern California custom homes built in the seventies and eighties, likely influenced by the Sea Ranch development* and its spin-offs, which flourished on the Northern California coast from the 1960s onward. She remembers Myra explaining how *the entry of the house was based conceptually on the drama created by cathedrals*, an effect achieved by the rapid transition between a low-ceilinged area just inside the front door and a sudden opening upward into two-story height in the living room where a burst of natural light through multiple windows enhances the impact of the sudden expansion. Julie loved Myra's description of the inspiration behind the design of the entrance to the house, loved the fact *that spirituality has a place even in design—allowing such a human need to be satisfied—even in a house owned by a Stoic,* she joked.

The house has both elegance and informality, pleasing in its simplicity of form, in its restraint, in its essential modesty. Though designed during a period when Barc and Sharon had barely begun collecting art, the interior of the house was, in time, to become one of the preeminent art gallery spaces in the East Bay. A reflection of the radical juxtaposition of negative and positive spaces that was part of California-style modernism in those years, the interior of the house seems perfectly made for art—boisterously, variously, ingeniously displayed, with Steinlen posters looming gorgeously on a wall near the long dining room table; a jewel-colored, contemporary ceramic vase rising vertically from the grand piano in the living room; and light installations tumbling down a staircase to the playroom on the ground floor. The way in which this diverse collection is contained and displayed on the walls of a family house gives a sense of vitality and intimacy rather than the cold professionalism that might be the goal in many collectors' mansions or museums. As Jonathan Moscone (see bio), an intimate of the Simpson family, comments, *Rarely have I seen such an extraordinary art collection so domestically presented.*

The grounds of the house echo the profusion of color, texture, and surprise of its interiors. In addition to being a natural dancer, Sharon is a gardener of uncommon ability—her inspired skill translated into visible passion in the gardens that clasp and adorn the property. Tumbling over steep terraces in the back of the house, the gardens lap at the surrounding hard-scape patios and staircases before cascading downward into a series of flowing spaces—some hidden, some revealed—with gates, stone walls, and pergolas, full of successively blooming flowers, shrubs, ornamental grasses, and outdoor sculpture, selected by Barc and Sharon over decades of collecting. This mingling of topography, vegetation, architecture, and art is dramatized throughout the property and exterior of the house in surprising details, including wrought-iron entry gates, adorned with abstract, painted forms and a wooden front door, sculpted out of raised shapes and colors, both by Stan Dann. Most striking, perhaps—anchoring its own separate garden area—is the looming Simpson Man, standing guard over the property, a replica of Michelangelo's "David," fabricated from Simpson Strong-Ties by Igino Pellizzari.

The house and grounds are an extraordinary snapshot of a marriage—of shared aspirations and delight; pleasure in materials rather than luxury or pristine, clipped edges; exuberance and Sharon's skilled hand everywhere. When the Stan Dann gate swings open to let you into the inner sanctum of the property, it is immediately evident that Sharon is yet another—albeit the primary—example of Barc's compelling interest in and attraction to artists of various kinds. What is also clear is the extent to which she was an inspired companion and collaborator in his restless, eager explorations through the new worlds to come.

Notes for Part IV

1 Jeff, 3/7/62; Julie, 12/17/63; Amy and Lizzie, 9/16/66.

2 John, 6/8/47; Anne, 7/21/49; Jean, 6/30/52.

3 Of Wong, Brocchini, and Associates.

PART V

Other Passions

I was ready to try my hand at other things.

—Barclay

*1978: Police officers, Sunne McPeak (in back), Barc, Mike Healy
in front of the Caldecott Tunnel.*

Chapter 21
Bay Area Rapid Transit District (BART)

Showing up on BART platforms at rush hours and answering questions, had to get some votes. Trying to beat out thirteen other candidates, some of them well-known, was a full-time day-and-night job for the month before the election.

—Barclay

EVER RESTLESS, BARC WAS by the mid-seventies on the lookout for community projects that might benefit from his prodigious energy and core belief in the power of goodwill and good attitude to move mountains.

Barc recounted that his first lesson in "practical politics" happened during his tenure on the board of trustees of the John Muir Hospital in Contra Costa County. Early on, he was elected chair of the nominating committee with the direction to fill two new board seats as well as to vote on term extensions for certain trustees, including the president. In customary style, Barc assessed the status quo in relation to fairness as well as fiscal efficiency and concluded that though the hospital was used by many African Americans and young people, neither group was represented on the board of trustees. He went out looking, and alongside members of his committee, interviewed several candidates, agreeing unanimously on a lawyer from Orinda and a recent graduate of Pepperdine University. These two candidates were then invited to dinner with the full board, followed soon after by an official board meeting in which the nominating committee made its recommendations. Barc's summary of the proceedings is curt and cold, a lesson learned: *For the first time in history, the recommendations of the nominating committee were turned down, and some other members put up a slate of their own. It did not include either of our nominees, nor did it include the current president, who had supported the committee's two nominees. He was replaced as president and dropped from the board.*

After this experience, Barc was to spend five more years on the John Muir Board, where he also met Tom Fitzmyers when they both served on the finance committee. Barc was never asked again to serve on the nominating committee, though he was elected chair of the building committee, which succeeded in constructing the first major addition to the hospital, on budget and on time—an unusual achievement in such an enterprise. He credits it with helping him get elected to the BART Board of Directors in 1976, where he served until 1988.

Barc attributes his twelve years in elected public office to the encouragement of Mac Nielson, *a valued friend for many years*, whom he first met at UC Berkeley in 1946. Nielson had been an officer on a submarine in World War II, and, like Barc, came back to college to get a master's degree in business. Nielson was active in the Contra Costa County Republican Party. Though Barclay was a registered Democrat, he switched parties when he decided to run for the BART Board of Directors based on Nielsen's ability to assemble significant party support for his candidacy. The position of BART Director was theoretically nonpartisan; nevertheless, each of the major parties wished to place a member of their own in the office. In Barclay, who was largely unknown in public and political circles, the Republican Party would be getting an apolitical candidate who had in the past and was to continue to vote for Democratic and Independent candidates at the state and national level throughout the rest of his life.

The switch of party affiliation in order to run for office is indicative of Barc's essentially pragmatic and nonideological predispositions. Though elected community service interested him, the kind of maneuvering involved in politics was not congenial to his "call it as you see it" nature. While canny and certainly capable of strategy, Barc probably didn't have the necessary chameleon-like qualities characteristic of most long-term politicians, or any real taste for partisanship. One of his strongest supporters throughout his BART tenure was to be Sunne McPeak, a rising star in the Contra Costa County Democratic Party. In politics, as in everything else, Barclay was essentially an "independent," basing his judgment on the qualities of individual people. Brains, the ability to get things done, the capacity to work well with other people, and an instinct for fairness were the irreducible characteristics that attracted him and formed the basis for his decision-making and his affiliations, both professional and personal.

What appealed to Barclay about running for the BART Board was the fact that BART was, at that time, getting lots of bad press for performance, as well as for expense account irregularities in high places. In addition, there were labor problems and lagging ridership numbers, all of which threatened to sink the still relatively young rapid transit system. Drawn to the challenge and backed by Nielsen's party resources, Barc, the least known of the fourteen candidates running that year from Contra Costa County, began to speak to anyone who would listen: BART passengers on platforms, businesspeople, VIPs, and social organizations of various kinds. Campaign strategy sessions took place at the Walnut Creek condo kitchen table and his small army of young children handed out brochures on street corners, giving special meaning to the concept of a grassroots candidacy. For a month prior to the November 11 election, Barc remembered that he was largely absent from Simpson Manufacturing as he spun from one event to another, selling himself as a businessman who would use his proven skills to right the ship. On election night, the kids had all fallen asleep long before Barc's narrow win was announced. He was a publicly elected official.

The day after election night, the calls poured in—some complimentary, but most from people *wanting something.* The board was due to elect a new president, a job which was rotated on a yearly basis. During the coming week, after meeting with various members of the board, he quickly came to realize that there were two opposed factions. When Arthur Shartsis (partner in Shartsis Friese LLP, BART Board Director, District 3; see bio), the only other newly elected director, joined one of these, making it a four-to-four split within the body, Barc suddenly found himself the crucial swing vote. Playing his cards deftly, he managed to end his first BART board meeting with the president's gavel in his hand, on a five-four vote, that landed him—*the lesser of evils candidate*—in the leadership position over warring blocs. Essentially a straight shooter, Barc was also a skilled poker player, fully capable of sleight of hand.

Mike Healy, BART's Director of Media and Public Affairs from 1971–2000 (see bio), confirmed that Barclay's surprise election caused controversy with a few of his codirectors; however, most of his colleagues didn't have a problem with Barc in spite of his having jumped the pecking order. Joan Van Horn, BART's Legislative Analyst from 1973–2004 (see bio), suggests that there was a qualitative difference between Barclay and some of his colleagues on the

board, several of whom appeared tethered to *small-town, parochial interests.*
He brought a more objective view, was less beholden to local political forces,
and had the day-to-day experience of managing a competitive business with
a diverse labor pool. He was used to balancing competing forces and listening
to both sides. For Healy, Barc's concrete experience and temperament served
the BART Board particularly well at this point in its troubled history: *He was
a no-nonsense guy...who took a hard-nosed view of things...he immediately
wanted to see the performance indices, wanted to understand how the financial
structure of the district worked...he had a lot of questions.*

As evidence of this, the first thing Barc did as president of the board was
to meet repeatedly with Frank Herringer, General Manager of BART, and
other key staff to determine whether he would support the GM or *pursue
his ouster.* As Art Shartsis—who closely witnessed Barclay's behavior over
a period of decades—observed: *It was an essential part of Barc's business
philosophy; if somebody wasn't doing a good job, he got rid of them. That was
it. Absolutely matter-of-fact, nothing personal. That's what he did.* So it was
natural that he would go immediately to the top of an organization that was
failing repeatedly.

According to Healy, Herringer had been *brought in to save BART*
following the "Fremont Flyer" incident in 1972, when one of the trains flew
off the track, a dramatic instance of the many performance malfunctions that
plagued BART in the early days. A business school graduate from the East
Coast, Herringer had worked in the Nixon White House, done a stint in a
business consulting firm, and held prominent positions in Washington DC's
Urban Mass Transit Administration (UMTA) before being recruited to take
over the role of general manager at BART, a position that he accepted with
the caveat that he would only serve for three years. At the age of thirty-two,
Herringer was the highest-paid public employee in the state of California,
an issue that would contribute to the public debate over BART salaries
throughout the early stages of the district's operating history.

Believing that he had been elected in order to get to the bottom of BART's
recurrent failures, Barc immediately wanted to hear Herringer's version of the
story and *to assess his character.* Neither overawed by Herringer's credentials
nor embarrassed by his own ignorance of transportation engineering issues,
Barclay would have been both a blunt interrogator and a good listener,
ready to ask difficult questions and to seek clarification on matters he didn't

understand. Character and performance assessment was territory that Barc knew well; his conclusion in this case was that Herringer had the qualities of a talented manager, who could master both the technical and personnel problems plaguing BART. Used to working closely with Simpson Company managers and staff, Barc dug into the details, coming out of these early meetings convinced that one of his key roles should be to keep the board off of Herringer's back *so that he could get the job done.* It appears that he found Herringer a congenial spirit, a businessman at heart who, after completing the three-year term he had promised to serve, left BART in January of 1979 to join Transamerica Corporation as vice president and assistant to the chairman, rising through the ranks to become CEO and chairman of the board, while also serving on other corporate boards including Charles Schwab, Inc. and Amgen, Inc.

Though Barclay only overlapped with Herringer for a few months, and though there is no record of how the GM regarded the newly elected director, Simpson was to become a key ally of and support to Herringer's successor, Keith Bernard, who served first as BART's manager of the budget and then, starting in 1979, as general manager, a position he held throughout Barc's twelve-year tenure on the BART Board. An admirer of Barclay, Bernard spoke of him as *a born problem solver, collegial in his instincts, and largely able to operate above the fray of the petty politics and power squabbles* that were common on the board. One reason Bernard may have liked Barclay was because he was actually a "working" director, willing to get his hands dirty in the details. For instance, as Healy remembers, Barc almost immediately began to burrow into the murky world of how bids were solicited and awarded at BART. Such details would have caught Barclay's attention because they represented the intersection of core concerns regarding technical competency, financial management, and fairness. These were issues that had absorbed him during the whole of his business life—yet, in his new public role, were to play out against a backdrop of political considerations that made the evaluation of fundamental values and objectives more intricate and less transparent. It is hard to know whether, initially, Barc was fully aware of the challenge of applying rigorous business procedures to a highly politicized organization operating in the heart of a region as complex as the San Francisco Bay Area. Indeed, when he emerged a few days after his election as the president of the BART Board, Barclay found himself already in the midst of political eddies of many kinds.

Ignoring early allegiances, Barc appointed Arthur Shartsis—a member of the *Gang of Four* who had contested his election to the BART presidency—as chairman of the administration committee, along with Bob Allen, who had also voted against him. Together with this *Team of Rivals*[1], Barc began to look into the BART expense account scandal that had been unearthed by the Alameda County grand jury, arousing the passions of the press. Ultimately, they assembled the proof necessary to go to the grand jury, which was eager to indict, and to talk them out of prosecuting the malefactor on the grounds that it would further damage the faltering BART District. They got the Alameda County District Attorney to waive their prerogatives.

During the early weeks of the investigation, relations between Art and Barc started to shift dramatically, as each recognized a complimentary mind and spirit in the other. As Shartsis puts it:

> *Barc and I were untethered to the history of the district. Barc had then a reasonably successful business. It wasn't Simpson Manufacturing as we know it now, but it was a successful business. And I had a law firm that was only two years old, so I was pretty young and brash. We both had the same view that you had to run things like a business. As a transit agency, there were obviously social and political aspects that had to be taken into account, but, basically, you had to make the thing work.*

Barc's version of his and Shartsis' mutual recognition of each other is similar to Art's, with some characteristic Barc touches:

> *A real plus from this whole process* [of looking into the expense account scandal] *was that Art and I stopped acting like two tomcats on the back fence and realized that our objectives, and the methods we used to achieve them, could be quite similar despite his being a lawyer. Besides, we both went to Cal.*

One of the early and ongoing outcomes of Barc and Art's collaboration at BART was Barclay's decision to hire Shartsis's then fledging law firm to represent SST in the lawsuit launched by Ray Clarkson. This suit could have caused major problems for SST and must have been a source of financial and personal anxiety for Barc considering his long-term friendship and professional collaboration with Ray during the early days of the business. Barc appears to have made a "snap" judgment in selecting the young and little-known Shartsis law firm to represent him in this important matter. The choice was undoubtedly based on his instincts regarding Art's native intelligence and character rather than on any systematic analysis of whether Art had the right connections or the experience to guide him through the particulars of the case. Like so many of his employment decisions, Barc's quick perception in this instance bore fruit as the Shartsis firm did succeed in helping SST prevail in the Clarkson suit, the first of many legal matters that Barc was to outsource to Shartsis's firm in the coming years. In this professional *cum* friendship relationship with Art, Barc seems to have been able to overcome his innate dislike of the legal profession to the long-term benefit of both of them.

For a transit district, the main product is ridership, and Barc, the businessman and salesman par excellence, set out early in his tenure to get Bay Area commuters out of their cars. With his characteristic enthusiasm, he talked Mike Healy and Sunne McPeak, County Supervisor, to engage with him in a bit of guerilla theater. Doffing sandwich board signs exhorting drivers stuck in traffic to "Take BART Next Time," the three warriors convened at 6:00 a.m. at the congested western entrance to the Caldecott Tunnel. As an example of concrete action, it was pure Barclay.

Regretfully, the highway patrol arrived within minutes to close down the renegade exploit before pollsters could establish its efficacy—though it did accomplish the goal of getting BART into the papers for reasons other than technical failure or corruption. For the next many years, Sunne McPeak often used the incident in the opening lines of her political speeches, claiming that BART worthies Barc Simpson and Mike Healy had nearly gotten her arrested for standing in traffic before she could become a well-known champion of transportation issues throughout the Bay Area.

If resolving the expense account scandal was to characterize Barclay's first weeks as a BART director, the labor contract negotiations that started in late 1979 were to put him and Art Shartsis squarely back in the limelight. In September of that year, after a number of work stoppages during August, BART management entered into tense negotiations with the Service Employees International Union (SEIU), which ultimately resulted in one of the longest-running and most contentious strikes in BART's history.[2] Part of what is interesting about this chapter of Barc and Art's joint efforts is that neither of them fits the profile or predispositions of the classic big business "union buster." Barc had the experience of having negotiated effectively and fairly—as reported by many of the SST rank-and-file members—with the unions operating within his own business. Art had grown up in a staunchly Democratic family and represented the most liberal cities (excluding San Francisco) within the overall BART District. Neither had an ideological problem with the rights of labor.

Their problem had to do with the fiscal sustainability of the district under the existing conditions of the labor contract then in force, which paid salaries and benefits that were in the ninety-ninth percentile relative to other local and national transit districts. As a long-term standard, Barc and Art believed that such labor rates were unsustainable for a public system, and certainly for one that was wobbling so visibly in the early years. Moreover, as Shartsis points out, BART also had very highly paid executive staff, creating a certain queasy-making self-interest within management to let labor rates rise, which would then trigger a rise in upper-level compensation. Simpson and Shartsis' first move was to freeze executive pay to send out the message that the linkage between management and labor rates was to be sundered. By late August 1979, wild cat strikes and work stoppages involving the BART police one day and mid-level management the next were becoming regular events, creating enormous instability throughout the system.

Shartsis says he and Barc were of a single mind in relation to the unsustainability of BART compensation packages going forward, and together they launched a multi-pronged information campaign to explain the economics behind establishing new standards, with special emphasis on the Cost-of-Living Adjustments (COLA). Ultimately, Simpson and Shartsis succeeded in getting a majority of directors to vote for Barc's recommendation that the board would establish a compensation target for everyone working in the district at the seventy-fifth percentile of local and national pay scales for comparable work.

Immediately following the board's vote, SEIU led one of the biggest strikes in BART's history, including accusations of "lock out" and "strike" from both sides. In their attempt to get the board to hold the line and not hamstring BART management by entering into direct negotiations with the unions, as they had done in the past, Simpson and Shartsis became targets for the union's ire:

On the front or back page of the San Francisco Examiner *was the five-column picture of Paul Varacalli, secretary of the SEIU, with a headline that read "We've got to get rid of Shartsis and Simpson."* (Arthur Shartsis)

The union picketed SST, though they never went to Shartsis's house in Berkeley, even though Art had bought a large coffee urn so as to offer hospitality to the picketers. Jokingly, he expressed disappointment that he gave a party and was spurned by the invitees, who overlooked his cordial welcome. Ultimately, the district was able to resolve the strike through a clever formula that gave modest wage gains, altered the rules governing the Public Employee Retirement System (PERS) contributions, and made serious modifications to the COLA provisions of the new contract. This issued in a long period of labor stability at BART: *From 1979 until 1988, we had complete labor peace. Once you had a fair and firm position, you're fine* (Arthur Shartsis).

In the years following the strike, Simpson and Shartsis were to remain allies throughout their lengthy tenures as BART directors. Among their joint projects was their successful campaign to get the district to make the hard decision to raise fares, one that the board, with its fingers ever in the wind, had largely dodged. Given their commitment to instilling business practices that might guarantee BART a sustainable future, Barc and Art believed that fare increases were the natural and necessary corollary to improving operating performance.

Another fundamental change Barc and Art pursued through the administration committee was to alter existing unattainable performance goals and objectives established at the time BART adherents were struggling to sell rapid transit to the populace at large. According to Shartsis, many of these original objectives were technically impossible from an engineering standpoint:

The best example would be that they had projected train speeds and frequencies that were faster than the coefficient of friction. They did it for political reasons....The trouble is trains couldn't stop and start that fast.

Barc, who was always taking continuing education classes at UC Berkeley's Hass School of Business, was originally an advocate of the then-popular idea of "management by objective," which was the official assessment tool for BART's regular and very public judgment of its own performance. For historical reasons, use of this methodology inevitably doomed the district to failure. Such certain and recurring declarations of unmet goals didn't augur well for the public's perception of management or the long-term sustainability of heavy rail transit in the Bay Area. Once Barc saw the fatal circularity, he shifted quickly from theory to practice. Shartsis again recalls their unanimity:

> *Barclay and I were of a single mind. We declared the old goals dead and set new goals. So, early on, it was Barclay coming and saying, "We've got to be more businesslike," and me saying, "Look, what is it that we can achieve because we can't achieve the goals as they are currently stated."*

Shartsis believes his and Barc's collaboration was transformative for the district:

> *During those first four years, we changed the district, created the modern system that exists today....Barclay was fabulous, just fabulous. There was almost nothing that we disagreed upon. The rest of the directors were much more interested in public events, whereas Barc and I didn't care about that. We were just trying to fix this thing.*

As these fundamental changes were put into action, the two of them turned their efforts toward the often-contentious business of getting the primary rail-lines extended beyond their original geography. This effort included promoting extending lines to Warm Springs, south of Fremont; to Pittsburg-Bay Point, east of Concord; and to the San Francisco International Airport.

This latter extension was both controversial and highly visible in the eye of the public. Located in San Mateo County, which had voted down the original BART Bond Measure that levied a half-cent sales tax in participating counties, the airport extension was considered a crucial but forbidden destination under state law, pending the completion of the projected lines in the original BART locations, one of which was held up in court. Barc's comment on the ensuing political battles demonstrates his characteristic disapproval of narrow-gauged interests:

> *The BART extension to San Francisco Airport was delayed several years because of individual directors squabbling about extensions to their districts, as well as a lack of the necessary funds.*

For Barc this issue might have involved a delicate balancing act, yet he seems not to have shrunk from the controversy. Accustomed to taking the long-term view, he was convinced early on that BART must go to the airport, even though that extension was not geographically located in his own Contra Costa County District, and to that end worked hard to help shape the political compromise and funding solutions that would allow for regional growth without jeopardizing state law and local politics. Philosophically, he believed these to be congruent rather than oppositional goals.

Barc spent much of his third term as a BART director working on the airport extension. Often the favorite BART spokesman because of his charm, hardheadedness, and rationality, he was regularly drafted into service by Keith Bernard, Larry Dahms of the Metropolitan Transportation Commission (MTC), Mike Healy, and Joan Van Horn to meet with state legislators, local politicians, businesspeople, and such power brokers as Dean Lescher, head of the *Contra Costa Times*.

> *The main reason that I had run for a third term was to help to get the airport extension together, so I volunteered for a job nobody else wanted as chair of a committee to negotiate with San Mateo County for funds for the extension. After quite a few meetings, it turned out that they really wanted the extension, and signed up to contribute $200 million.* (Barclay)

A final political minuet among various board members deprived Barc from being the guy to announce this important early deal to the press—*talk about sleazy politics!*—yet he was nevertheless *excited* to have been directly involved at a key juncture in the shaping of a funding pact that significantly advanced the possibility that the airport extension might actually be built. *Happy* to leave the BART Board shortly afterward when his term was up, Barc sums up his foray into affairs of state as follows: *Thinking back, my years at BART were better than a master's degree in politics. I'm certainly not happy with everything that I learned, but the time was well spent.*

During his last term at BART, Barc briefly explored the possibility of running for state legislative office. But the feelers he put out didn't convince him such a run was winnable. Having been impatient with local politics at the BART level, it is hard to understand what it was that made him consider continuing in politics given his compulsion for transparency and calling the cards as he saw them. He thought of himself as a realist, but he also had a nearly romantic belief in the possibility of accomplishing great things through the power of will and concerted communal action. Politics seems a strange field in which to exercise such gifts.

Chapter 22
Art Collecting and the Gallery

The Hogarth print turned out to be a fake, and that's what triggered Barc's interest.
It was like a mystery, like a detective story to him.

—Sharon

THE SEVENTIES WERE FULL of changes for Barc. After so many years of marriage, childrearing, and building a profitable business from scratch, he was hungry to pursue and cultivate other interests. When he met Sharon and made a whole new set of commitments to marriage and childrearing, his desire to branch out appears to have been stimulated rather than damped down.

Among other explorations, he began to take humanities courses at Diablo Valley Community College, near the Walnut Creek condominium, where he dove into a night class on the works of Charles Dickens. In setting the scene for Dickens's novels, the professor showed etchings and dry-point prints by William Hogarth, an eighteenth-century renegade, realist artist whose incisive caricatures were full of the kind of social critique for which Dickens became famous over a century later. Both artists had fathers who spent time in debtors' prison, which contributed to their satiric, sometimes dark style of portraiture; and each were intent on pulling off the gauzy screen hiding the many ills of English life, including debt, disease, and great disparities of wealth.

Barc was immediately drawn to the Hogarth engravings, which *depicted the seamy side of British urban life at a time when most artists were creating landscapes, or portraits of the aristocracy* (Barclay). Returning home from the Hogarth class, he told Sharon how taken he was with the engravings he had just seen. The next day, she began calling around to San Francisco galleries trying to track down a Hogarth print to give Barc for Christmas. Both credited her purchase of Hogarth's sepia ink engraving, "The Laughing Audience" of 1733, as the beginning of their joint career of active art collecting.

The only problem was that the engraving turned out—in spite of the authenticating certificate from the top-end San Francisco gallery that had sold Sharon the print—to be a fake. This fact emerged the following year when, looking to buy another Hogarth, Barc entered what he called *the number one print gallery on Bond Street*, in London: *A rather elderly lady with a green eyeshade led me to the area where they had a plethora of Hogarth engravings. I mentioned that I already owned an original of "The Laughing Audience," and it was done in sepia ink. She looked puzzled and said, "I don't think that he ever did anything in sepia."* To prove her point, the woman showed Barclay the *Catalogue Raisonné* of Hogarth prints, which confirmed the absence of any print resembling Sharon's thoughtful Christmas gift. Barc bought what he now realized was his first Hogarth print from the woman along with the *Catalogue Raisonné*. When he returned home and was able to compare the official version of the print to his own Hogarth, Barc could see with his own eyes the shrieking differences. He vowed to do his own "authenticating" in the future. But there was a lot to know.

Barc called the Hogarth episode *intriguing and awakening*, and one that was to catapult him into a concentrated period of study and self-training in the specialized fields of art authentication and valuation, along with the supporting skills involved in framing, mounting shows, and sales. The Hogarth *Catalogue Raisonné* became the first founding element in what was to become Barc's and Sharon's distinguished art library, which one expert, many years later, was to call *priceless*.

On the surface, Barc's new avocation seemed a long way from his day job of building a business based on bent metal parts, though some of the elements of his avocation as a collector mirrored the principles and even the materials that had shaped SST. Just as Barc had focused his mind on the technical attributes and possible applications of metal joist hangers, he now took on the vast intricacies involved in creating complex images and effects from incised metal plates. As had also been true in the business, he wanted to master the knowledge that would allow him to rely on his own judgment, not just be the guy who wrote the checks or who hired skilled intermediaries and "experts" to build a collection based on someone else's taste and criteria. For Barc, collecting art was never simply a pastime, but a deeply pleasurable labor, different in kind from that which had given rise to the business, yet consistent in method and degree of dedication.

One of the immediate outcomes of the Hogarth experience was that Barc began spending three weeks every summer taking courses in art history, literature, and philosophy at Cambridge University in England. A born auto-didact with an astoundingly good memory, Barc found enormous pleasure in the Cambridge classes, which offered him an entrée into the liberal education which had been truncated by war, marriage, child-rearing, and business. Once hooked intellectually, Barc bore into his subject, reading voraciously, taking additional specialized classes, calling experts when he didn't understand some technique, and wheedling entrance into the print room of the British Museum, generally only granted to those with the right academic or professional credentials.

On his yearly trips to Cambridge, he spent untold hours in London galleries and auctions. On one of these trips, Barc purchased a Rembrandt etching at a Sotheby's auction, the first of many of the master's prints he was to buy over the years. Characteristically, he was interested in procuring the best, and many print experts rated Rembrandt as the greatest etcher of all time. Certainly he has been the most copied of artists, subject to various forms of sophisticated replication. Intrigued by his rare skill, his documentary as well as visionary imagery, Barc entered into what he described as *a time-consuming love affair*, putting together an important collection of Rembrandt prints over the years.

In the course of collecting, he assembled a world-class library on Rembrandt, learning to decode the complexities and various "states"[3] of the prints, all of which affected value. As with Hogarth and Dickens, Barc was drawn to the vicissitudes of Rembrandt's personal life, loves, and economic fortunes:

> *It turned out that the most prolific source of information on Rembrandt's activities and personality were the Amsterdam court records of the time. He constantly was suing or being sued, and when that wasn't the case, he was in court for some other reason.* (Barclay)

After years of study, Barc felt comfortable in claiming that while he was not really a Rembrandt expert, he did come to understand the level of risk when bidding on a particular print.

Through his immersion in Hogarth and Rembrandt prints, Barclay entered a world of technical and aesthetic intricacies that roused his deepest interests: *Original prints, mainly engravings, etchings, dry points, and lithographs, have become a passion of mine.* Partly, he was interested in top-level art prints because this focus allowed him to work with excellence without spending the sums of money required to purchase paintings by the acknowledged greats. Explaining that canvases by such masters as Picasso, Toulouse-Lautrec, Rembrandt, and Whistler were too expensive for the art budget he allowed himself, Barc was able through print collecting to be in the company of genius without breaking the bank. Ultimately, this focus and immersion allowed him to assemble quality print collections by Hogarth, Rembrandt, and Whistler, which he was able to display in one-man shows at his soon-to-be opened gallery in Lafayette, California, as well as at the UC Berkeley Art Museum.

Though he started with well-established masters, Barc also soon began collecting and extolling the qualities of such other only slightly less-celebrated artists as Martin Lewis, Samuel Palmer, A. T. Steinlen, Victor Pasmore, and others.

The intellectual challenge was clearly a major motivation for someone who had always been hungry for knowledge. Yet it seems likely that other desires also came into play. In hiring Sharon to work at SST, Barc had clearly been looking for a joint enterprise that would allow the two of them another path for sharing their lives. Though Sharon claims to have enjoyed her time at SST, her experience as a "special assistant" to Barc, tracking stock charts and pruning had not been an overwhelming success. So perhaps the fake Hogarth episode was a stroke of luck in Barc and Sharon's early marriage. In Sharon's case, art collecting and, later, running the gallery, used both her aesthetic and rare social gifts. She was a natural with artists, drawing them to the gallery and promoting their works with potential buyers, a born saleswoman in her own right. She had both an eye and a presence congenial to the celebration of beauty. Whatever the initial spark, the pleasures of art collecting and the eventual ardent promotion of art and artists were to become central to the ongoing adventure of Barc and Sharon's life together.

At the beginning, they bought a print here and a painting there, with no inkling that this kind of casual collecting might lead to a business. An early stage in Barc and Sharon's adventures in art involved a house exchange with a

UK family in Epsom, England, less than twenty miles outside of London, for six weeks in 1977.

During the Epsom trip, Barc and Sharon purchased a lot of new art, most of which could not possibly fit into the already bulging Walnut Creek condo. Sharon remembers one night at the dinner table in Epsom, after a day in London book shops and galleries, turning to Barc and asking, *What are we doing? We've bought up all this art...where are we going to put it?* With Ron and Myra, they had already designed the new house under construction in Orinda around walls that were to hold certain paintings. But there was a limit to the available display space in what certainly was not a mansion.

Barc promptly answered, *Well, let's open our own art gallery!* Sharon says this was classic Barc—*Well, let's just do it!* Her own reaction was more tempered, *Oh, dear....Well, honey, let's get into the new house first and get the kids out of high school and all of that....*But once the idea was out in the open, as far as Barc was concerned, the train was on the tracks: *So, of course, we opened the art gallery within twelve months after we moved into the house—the three girls were still in high school* (Sharon).

The Barclay Simpson Fine Arts Gallery premiered officially in 1981, immediately following an ambitious camping trip around Europe in a VW pop-up van that housed Barc, Sharon, and their three younger daughters, once more on the rambling road, stopping at art galleries and famous museums along the route. In the interim between Epsom and the VW pilgrimage, Barc had commissioned Ron and Myra to design a gallery in the large, squarish industrial building along Mount Diablo Boulevard in Lafayette, California, that had originally been built by Barc's father to house Bill's drapery business, complete with a large showroom on the ground floor and a downstairs basement area where the seamstresses worked. When Bill died, Barc's father left the building to Barc. Though they expanded the footprint, the basic architecture of the building was not altered greatly. It fronted on the busy boulevard, adjacent to a fertilizer company, and was both car- and pedestrian-friendly. Although definitely an example of a certain kind of industrial-inspired minimalism, the new space had none of the exposed brick designer quality of trendy San Francisco art galleries. Certainly anomalous, it was the only bird of its feather at that time in Contra Costa County.

While the gallery was being built, Barc and Sharon had taken a framing course in San Francisco in line with their decision to create a frame shop in the downstairs area. In addition, they set up a mini workshop in the garage of the new house in Orinda. In the garage and the new gallery, Barc and Sharon did most of the framing for their opening show and a few subsequent ones, later hiring Jim Reed to run the frame shop and to take over the task of framing for gallery shows. Sharon recalls: *We had so much fun doing the framing. It was cut and paste and saw all day long, like kids in a toy shop.*

That opening show was, in Sharon's words, *a very eclectic mix,* with prints by well-known artists such as Rembrandt, Whistler, Picasso, Miro, Toulouse-Lautrec, and Chagall, along with a handful of landscape paintings by nineteenth-century British artists. In years to come, once they had better honed their approach to marketing and when the collection itself had expanded in depth, they were to do one-man print shows of Toulouse-Lautrec, Whistler, and Rembrandt, complete with catalogues of documentation, which reflected Barc's careful scholarship and personal preferences. Yet, at the first gallery opening, the approach was still heterogeneous, a mix of quality and genre, aimed at a possibly multi-layered clientele. Barc's assessment was low-key but positive: *The show was up for several weeks. We sold enough pieces to make it profitable, and we had quite a bit more similar inventory. It appeared that a mix of original prints by big-name artists and a few oil paintings by lesser-known artists of various periods could result in a profitable gallery even in a small town such as Lafayette.* What was an unqualified success, by all accounts, in this first opening and in the many to follow was the level of hospitality and ebullience, which made the gallery openings a calling card for a growing group of collectors and non who shared a taste for culture and fun, commingled.

Sharon describes some of the homely details of that first opening, many of which were to become hallmarks of what was to follow: *The girls worked behind the bar. We didn't even think about them not being twenty-one, pouring wine, passing cheese. Mother and I made the hors d'oeuvres for that show and everyone afterward for thirteen years.* An artist in her own right, Muriel had designed and sewed the banner attached to the exterior of the building advertising the show—a labor she was to perform for all the shows to come. Pre- and post-show vacuuming was done by Sharon, who also worked the floor as hostess and head art salesman, the latest of Barclay's cherished breed, and by far the best looking. Whether she was dealing with experts or neophytes, her enthusiasm, warmth, and goodwill proved to be the bedrock of the gallery's allure and success—which, from the beginning, was antithetical to the sophisticated haughtiness of a big city art space.

When we started it was just the two of us….It was a mom-and-pop operation (Sharon). In time, the gallery was to pull in some unusual collaborators, a small but varied collection of people whose personal gifts and inclinations were to shape the enterprise, along with collectors and clients—and the artists themselves. Casual in its early days, the gallery was yet intended to be a fully professional venture, not simply a plaything for amateurs. Barclay never had an inclination for dabbling. He was all-in with the gallery. By the time they closed it in March of 1994, they represented a roster of artists from several parts of the world, in addition to the US, *in particular India, Britain, Germany, France, and Italy* (Barc).

When Barc became an art collector, he also became a scholar of the discipline out of fascination with the art object itself—its material presence and its technical sleights of hand—as well as from a canny desire not to be tricked. As Sharon said, it was a kind of detective story that drew him, a desire to follow the trail and understand the hidden clues. The gallery was critically important to him because it involved him and Sharon in a joint enterprise, but also because he genuinely saw it as a new business opportunity where he might apply many of the marketing and sales tools refined at SST. For Barclay, any venture he gave himself to needed to be wedded to a mission, either of profit or improvement—and increasingly this was to mean social improvement.

The gallery played an important interim step in Barc's progress from businessman to benefactor—though this distinction suggests some kind of absolute choice between profit and philanthropy that never existed for him. Barc's classically profitable ventures and those aimed at social "revenues" were to run concurrently, not as alternatives to each other, but as coventures with overlapping methods. Certainly, Barc wanted the gallery to make money. Yet, because it also provided other deeply personal pleasures, some of the "profit" was built in before a prospective client ever showed up. There is no question that Barc was more flexible in his oversight of gallery finances than he had ever been with SST. Still, he believed the clearest way to objectively judge the efficacy of any enterprise—whether it was selling structural connectors or getting the BART trains to run efficiently—was the application of strict business principles linked to the idea of profit, however broadly defined.

Making a "profit" was a manifestation of irrefutable value and seriousness, not simply an interest in making money per se.

A recurring question related to the idea of profit was the age-old query as to whether buying art is a good investment. Though a seller of art, Barc's answer, he said, was always a blunt *no*:

> *Just like shooting craps at a casino, one can get lucky. If so, pick up your winnings and go home. Art is somewhat similar. The odds are against you. If you are buying from a gallery, the commissions are substantial, as are those of auction houses....The great Spanish artist, Goya, is a prime example. I love his prints, and years ago started to accumulate them thinking that they were way underpriced. Perhaps they were.... They still are. The works of Toulouse-Lautrec, on the other hand, have appreciated quite a bit over the years...but the return in the last ten years still doesn't match most popular stock averages. By now, I have had over thirty-five years of experience buying art as a dealer, and also as an individual. Once in a while, despite knowing better, I think I see a chance to buy a painting or print at a bargain price. Seldom has such a purchase turned out to be as good an investment as a relatively safe money market fund. So, buy a particular piece of art because you love it, not as an investment.*

The message here may cast light on the mixed "profits" to emerge from Barc and Sharon's joint art venture.

Among their early collaborators was Lynda Dann (see bio), daughter of the Bay Area artist Stan Dann. She was twenty-three years old at the time she knocked, uninvited, on the door of the gallery. An artist in her own right, she was a graduate of art school and had ventured into sales, marketing her father's work, a venture which awakened some native skills, but ultimately proved too challenging on the personal side. She was desperate for money and something she could sink her teeth into. Having noticed the unlikely presence of a fine arts gallery facing the main boulevard in Lafayette across the street from where she had been selling ostrich-skin high heels, she gathered together her résumé and her courage and knocked on the big front door. By chance, both Barc and Sharon were there at the time, so she was able to ask both of them if they were hiring—and, after giving it a bit of thought, they decided they were.

This rather happenstance beginning was to blossom into one of the great friendships of Lynda, Sharon, and Barc's lives. It was also to have an impact on the way the gallery developed over the eight years Dann worked in a part-time position there, first as filer and general factotum, then, quite quickly, as one of the Simpsons' prized salespeople, and finally as an artist whose work was shown in three separate shows.

When Lynda joined the gallery in 1984, she was not given any strictly defined job description: *They didn't try to fit me into a slot...if I had a reasonable idea about how to do something in a new or different way, they just said, "Great, do it."* The result was that, in spite of her youth and relative inexperience, she says she was *never intimidated*, but felt she could be herself. *Maybe it was the way they were with people—so open and interested—but also just the energy they had for what they were doing.* For Lynda the passion Barc and Sharon had for the art itself was crucial. *They would fall in love with a piece of art and buy it on the spot. No cooling-off period....*But also crucial to Dann was the way *they tapped into the best part of me...I was able to have fun at the gallery...we had so much fun.*

Dann remembers there was a lot of unevenness in taste and quality in the gallery at the time she arrived. One of her first unsolicited comments was about the arrangement of the mats used for framing. They came in all sizes, colors, and materials, consistent with what Lynda called *Barc's unconventional ideas about framing.* Having done a short stint as an employee in Barbara Anderson Gallery and Framing in Berkeley, one of the Bay Area's most respected framing shops, Lynda had learned a lot from her employer's exacting and minimalist aesthetic. By forceful suggestion, she succeeded in standardizing the Lafayette gallery's mat sizes and simplifying colors and textures. In this, she showed both temerity and a capacity for the kind of attention to detail necessary to building any kind of quality brand. These would have been qualities to catch Barc's attention.

Lynda was to expand her aesthetic critique to the gallery's assorted inventory, which by that time was being augmented through purchases of mixed lots from independent brokers. She remembers one show with a cat theme, in which spectacular posters by Steinlen, selling for $15,000 to $20,000 each, shared space with a very commercial kitten rolling a ball of yarn. Following the show, she called Barc and Sharon, saying direly that they had to have a meeting. Lynda remembers that Sharon was worried, thinking

Lynda was pregnant and about to announce her departure from the gallery. Instead, Dann declared that they must stop trying to be all things to all people—had to stop mixing old masters and quality contemporary art with merely commercial pieces. In short, she was preaching the establishment of a brand based on recognizable standards of excellence. The Simpsons listened.

But that was a bit later on. In the early days, Lynda's first major suggestion to Barc and Sharon was that they include the art of a friend of hers from art school named Amrit in their upcoming Christmas show. Lynda had consciously put her own painting on the back burner when she went to work at the gallery, but she was interested in promoting the work of living as well as dead artists. After seeing examples of Amrit's unusual painted scarves, Barc and Sharon told Lynda to run with the idea. Which she did, carefully framing the work in simple, modernist frames, then actively promoting the striking results to clients who showed up at the opening. The sales were significant. In the new year, Barc called her into his office and announced he wanted to move her into sales and altered her compensation to a salary plus commission basis.

Naturally, as a Barc-driven enterprise, the gallery focused intensively on sales. In Sharon, Barc had a natural salesperson, whose warmth and personable style provided Lynda a perfect *role model,* she claims; however, Barc was a stern mentor. Once, overhearing Barc making a sales pitch to a client, Dann entered the conversation uninvited, interjecting some observation or piece of expertise. Barc's withering look froze her in her tracks. Later, he called her into the office and dressed her down ferociously: *Don't ever, ever, ever do that again. Never interrupt me when I am promoting a sale.* Struck dumb, she crept out of his office, wondering how they were to get through her blunder. But the next time she saw Barclay, it was as if nothing had happened. He had said what was on his mind and he never held a grudge. If he had thought her incompetent, he would have fired her. But a misstep was just that—not a life sentence.

Dann observed that the key to sales is finding out what the client *desires,* then working to find a way to match that longing or *need* with an object. This investigation may involve getting to the bottom of an innate yearning, or, simply, finding out the size of their living room wall or the color of their furnishings. This was in spite of Barc's oft-repeated (and sound) admonition to whomever would listen *not to buy art to go with the interior decorating.*

Together, Sharon and Lynda made an extraordinarily appealing duo as they worked the floor during openings. Lynda remembers:

> *Selling at gallery openings was really fun for me. It was a people experience in which the challenge was to figure out who was the person in front of me, how can I engage with them, how can I figure out what they want, what their house is like, what might grab them.*

Whatever the secret to art sales, the fact was that Barc and Sharon were generally able to get 100+ people to the gallery openings, which, remarkably, happened every five to six weeks, an extraordinarily tight schedule for an art gallery with such a small staff. In Lynda's words, the gallery became a fixture in the community. They would advertise in *Diablo Magazine* while the openings were reviewed regularly by Carol Fowler of the *Contra Costa Times* as well as journalists from the social pages of other publications. These openings became real *events*, both cultural and entertaining, for the local populace, who were not as likely to make the trip to the big metropolis on a Thursday night. In regular attendance were friends from BART, SST, and some regular clients from Contra Costa County's social set and extensive mid- to high-income population. In Lynda Dann's words, over the years Barc and Sharon succeeded in creating a *community* around the gallery.

What Lynda Dann remembers best are the hilarious times she and Sharon would have after the openings were over, when everybody including Barc had gone home. They would crack a bottle of champagne and start hamming it up: *I would redraw my lipstick line and start playing the diva, Sharon was a song and dance person and could do fabulous routines, we would end up on the floor convulsed for hours. She was my best friend, a mother, a cabaret dancer....* For Sharon, Lynda was like another daughter, but also a best friend. Lynda recounts that the most compelling part of her sales job—taking various works of art to a client's house for trial hanging and selection, a task which she loved—would only come fully alive when she got back to the gallery and could give Sharon a blow-by-blow description of exactly how the visit and the sale had gone. For each of them, this intense friendship stands out as an important emblem of what the gallery came to mean.

Another important development was when Barc succeeded in recruiting the artist Joseph Way to the gallery. Born and bred in Brooklyn during the fifties, Way graduated from the Pratt Institute in New York and after getting his degree in art and design went to work as a drafter in a small custom furniture factory. Near the end of the seventies, he migrated to Northern California with his young family, hoping to make it as an artist. An abstract painter working in watercolor and gold leaf whose distinctive style had started by the early eighties to catch the eyes of collectors, Joseph first met Barc and Sharon over dinner one night at the home of a Kaiser doctor who had been collecting his work privately.

Following this first encounter, Barc called Joseph immediately and suggested that they discuss the possibility of the Barclay Simpson Fine Arts Gallery taking him on as one of their artists. Ironically, Way—a classic struggling painter with a family to support—had just gotten an offer from a big gallery in San Francisco and was weighing his options. What tipped the scale for him toward the relatively unestablished gallery was knowing that Barc was the man in charge. At the other gallery, all selections of artists had to pass through the ranks. There was not a single hand on the tiller. Later, he said, *It was one of the best decisions I ever made.*

Represented by Barc and Sharon until they closed the doors of the gallery in spring 1994, Joseph describes them as *the greatest people to work for.* In Way's experience, gallery owners were notoriously in the business of taking advantage of their artists; but he recounts how Barclay came at the relationship from an entirely different perspective, telling him, *I'm going to make a name in this business by being honest.* Predictably, Barc also curated the interests of his clients, basing sales on an attempt at full transparency. When, for instance, a collector was considering buying one of his high-end artists, he would invite them to do the kind of personal investigation that he, himself, had learned to undertake following the fake Hogarth print episode:

> Visitors to our Rembrandt show could examine the thirty-three prints on the walls and in our catalogue to find specific details on any particular one. Unlike the auction houses, we made a particular effort to show the potential buyer the complexity, and often the uncertainty, in dating a particular piece, as well as how substantial an effect that date could have on the price. Anyone wanting to do personal research was welcome to use our rather complete library on Rembrandt's prints.

Ultimately this library was to be left to the Berkeley Art Museum (BAMPFA).

In the end, the reputation of the Barclay Simpson Fine Arts Gallery came to be based primarily on the founders' professional and personal involvement in the careers of the living artists they represented. Barc and Sharon gave rein to their artists rather than trying to shape them to meet the marketplace. Way recounts that Barclay, unlike most gallery owners he knew, never told him what to produce. If pieces were selling, he never said, *Keep doing that. We're selling well.* Rather, Barc and Sharon always encouraged him to explore new ideas that interested him—a strategy which, along with honesty, had borne fruit at Simpson Strong-Tie. During the many years Barc and Sharon showed Joseph's work, Barclay rarely mentioned Simpson Manufacturing and certainly never explained anything about the company except to say that he sold bent metal. It was not until Joseph met an engineer at his wife's Lamaze class that he got some sense of Barc's day job. When he mentioned to the engineer that he was with the Barclay Simpson Fine Arts Gallery, but that the owner made his living doing something with connectors, the guy looked amazed: *Simpson as in Simpson Strong-Tie? Oh, jeez, that's like the guy who invented the paper clip.* This was interesting news to Joseph but didn't figure in his relationship with Barc and Sharon until close to the time the gallery closed.

A Brooklyn kid, Joseph liked Barc's toughness as much as his graciousness. He recounts an instance when, while dropping off a painting at the gallery, he heard Barclay on the phone with an artist who was giving Sharon trouble about something: *He just ripped this guy to shreds...up one side and down the other...which made me respect him more. Barc's not a pushover...you don't mess with him.* The admiration was mutual. In awe of Way's talent, Barclay told him and others repeatedly that the quality of his work gave the gallery credibility. Being an outlier in the art world, both in terms of location and his general attitudes toward artists, Barc was aware that he and Sharon were operating as renegades in a highly stratified and exclusive business. Yet it was not a position that gave him pause. Over the thirteen years they were open, they showed and sold everything from Whistler to Way; from Rembrandt to Rapisardi[4]; from Steinlen to unknown student artists, trying to make their way in a tough world. Their pleasure was in diversity.

After the gallery had been operating for a year, Barc and Sharon hosted a party following an opening at their house in Orinda, inviting artists as well as clients who had purchased works of around $2,000 and up. There were ninety-nine invitees. Sharon describes the enthusiasm for the event as *a sort of small-town deal.* In the coming years, they did many such parties for their artists and collectors both—and always when artists would come to openings from far away: *If someone was coming from Maine, or Graham Clarke from England, or Martini from Milan, we would have a dinner back at the house and invite people who had purchased their work already, or who we thought were potential buyers.* And it paid off, according to Sharon. People would actually show up later and say, *You know, I think I would really like to purchase a "Sandro Martini."* Thinking back, Sharon muses, *It was a ton of work...we tried to do it all. Barc wrote an annual newsletter, summing up the year. He was reading some of those the other day. He got the biggest kick out of it...a lot of work, but we had so much fun working together. I guess I would have done anything with him, because I just trusted that we would figure it out.*

Lynda Dann remembers that Barc, Sharon, and Joseph were hanging the artist's first Simpson Gallery show the day she came looking for a job. For her, their getting Joseph Way was an important moment for the gallery. In representing a contemporary artist of Way's stature, Dann feels that the emphasis moved importantly from dead artists to live ones, from scholarship and collecting to Sharon and Barc becoming deeply involved in promoting the careers of individual artists, many of whom they came to know intimately and abidingly, even after the gallery closed. Passion for prints, paintings, and sculpture was complimented by Barc and Sharon's interest in people on all sides of the enterprise of art—and it was this that Dann feels gave the gallery its extreme vitality and significance: *I have never before or since been in an art gallery that had this kind of energy and comprehensive concern for the people.*

Though they had done much of their early collecting in the UK and Europe and through well-known auctioneers, as time went on Sharon and Barc's focus became much more Bay Area-oriented. If the advent of Joseph Way was an early sign of this shift, the major pivot took place when Barc and Sharon became directly involved with the California College of the Arts (CCA), located in Oakland, with some facilities in San Francisco. In 1986, Barc joined the board of directors, a position he held until his death in 2014. During all of this period and beyond, Sharon was also to be very involved in CCA activities and initiatives.

Among the most imaginative of these initiatives was what became known as the CCA Barclay Simpson Award, begun in 1987, which provided direct cash payments in the amount of $2,000 to $5,000 to each of up to four CCA graduating MFA students to use in any way they wished to help launch their careers. The winners of the award were selected by a three-person jury, and they were also guaranteed an exhibition of their work. For the years that the Simpson Gallery was open, these exhibitions became a recurring part of the gallery's repertoire of shows and also opened up its original "business plan" to the mission of helping young, contemporary artists get exposure. Some of the CCA Award Show artists went on to seek and be granted professional representation by the Simpson Gallery. As the gallery became better known within the East Bay art world, many local artists came knocking on the door with their collection of slides seeking representation, including some rank amateurs without a professional résumé. Lynda Dann remembered, *We would work our asses off to get them real visibility, and suddenly young artists who had never earned a dime were making substantial amounts of money.* At least in the good times.

A key part of Barc and Sharon's marketing strategy was the purchase of booths at the international art fairs in London (twice) and Los Angeles (five times), where, according to Barclay, they *did quite well* and where they came into contact with artists and dealers from many parts of the world. Sharon's memories of these demanding events give some sense of the mixture of anxiety, hilarity, and constant packing and schlepping involved in trying to be a full-service operation on a shoestring. Particularly memorable was one of their return trips to the Bay Area:

> We were in Beverly Hills, dropping off a painting that had been purchased at the fair. It was raining. I went up to the front door of a tall apartment building but was asked to please go around to the service entrance. We unloaded in the rain, carried the canvas up a flight of stairs, came down again, and I started to readjust the load in the back of the truck, with Barc upfront in the cab. I was readjusting enormous canvases when the entire shelfing system came down on my head...I'm yelling, "Barc, Barc, Barc"...until he opens the slat between the cab and back, and he says, "Oh, Jesus," hurries around, and digs me out...and we end up having to repack everything.

They were late getting started on the trip home. By then it was pouring rain. They made it over the summit of the Grapevine (made famous in their prenuptial migration northward). It started to snow while they were still on the northern flank of the mountain, so they pulled into a one-horse motel at around 11:00 p.m. and parked the truck loaded with art as close as possible to the door to their room.

> We got into the room where we crawled into a single bed. We remembered reading that if you're freezing, you should get naked in a small space together and trap the double body heat....We wrapped ourselves around each other and waited for daylight.

At the crack of dawn, they left the motel behind and pulled the van into the parking lot of a greasy spoon coffee shop, maybe a Denny's, alongside of serious, transcontinental haulers. The coffee shop was full of truckers. They started to eat their breakfast, retelling each other the most nightmarish parts of the previous days' exploits. But their conversation was suddenly drowned out:

> I just remember this trucker yelling into a phone, "Well, the oil has all froze up." Barc and I looked at each other and we just fell apart. Our whole lives, we have had the best laughs...we learned that in Cozumel....We laughed and laughed.

Joseph Way's memories of the way in which Barc and Sharon approached the LA art fairs recall the frugality, but also the other side of the coin: *Whatever Barc does is done intensely and five star*. In open contrast to the general snobbery of the art business, Barc and Sharon would create, in Joseph's words, *very friendly spaces for people*. Unlike the other vendors at the fair, they would set up their booth area with couches, which would draw people in to relax, talk, and look at art, enticing them into what Joseph called *the Simpson Gallery web. Once Sharon and her coworkers started talking to people, they did great. With the shows, too, everything was just top-of-the-line, whatever he did. The graphics, the opening parties...he never skimped on anything.* Here, again, Barclay's style is full of contrasts: frugal in the extreme in the insistence that he and Sharon, with a few assistants, pack and port the art, driving through snow and fog in a rented truck—yet elegant and welcoming when it came to feting the artists and potential buyers. You save a buck to spend a buck. Joseph Way says both artists and potential buyers were often shocked when Barc would pick them up in his Ford Taurus rather than a silver Mercedes.

If the gallery had been largely born out of Sharon and Barc's adventures in collecting, their passion for the work of art itself gradually grew into a shared vocation focused on promoting the careers of living artists. In Barc's words:

> We thought that a few of them had considerable talent. While it is impossible to chat with Rembrandt except in one's imagination, it was fun to get to know some of these young artists. To put it simply, they charmed us! So, in a relatively short space of time we were having shows for young unknown artists, and the big-name prints stayed in storage.

Interspersed with their shows of contemporary art, they did continue to have the occasional one-man and group shows featuring Rembrandt, Whistler, Toulouse-Lautrec, and other masters of various genres. Yet the ballast had shifted. According to Barc, it was a choice that had a direct financial impact:

> During our most active period as a gallery, showing relatively unknown artists, we never made a profit. I am convinced that if we had continued to show the kinds of works that were in our first show, we could have made money. But we would not have had the enjoyment of getting to know and becoming friends with a group of talented and interesting young people. In a few cases, we were able to sell enough of an artist's work to enable her or him to pay the rent and put bread on the table. And quite a few of our artists were then able to get shows in other parts of the country, both while our gallery was still active and long afterward.

For Barc and Sharon, this shift toward helping young artists build a professional résumé involved rethinking their original goals. Increasingly the gallery was becoming a nonprofit venture in which the overall experience trumped financial considerations. In Sharon's words:

> It was a lot of work, but it was really fun. And we have these relationships now. Every summer—even after the gallery closed—we would have a barbecue garden party for the artists. We would write to them in Europe and the East Coast…if you're planning a trip, and it might coincide, here's the "Save the Date" announcement. And, often, we'd be surprised by their showing up.

For several years, Joseph Way was the Simpson Gallery's best-selling artist. But with the national recession of the early nineties, even his sales started to dry up, just as the gallery's deficit began to grow. Knowing that tough times would eliminate much of the discretionary income people used to buy art, Barclay began to think they could no longer provide their artists with the kind of rewarding representation for which they had contracted. This moment in the gallery's history coincided with one of the most painful periods in Joseph Way's life, when his wife and one of his sons became mortally ill with a rare disease. Around the time the family crisis first hit, Way had decided that he needed to seek out more regular and remunerative employment than an artist at his level could hope for, especially in dreary economic times. Barclay offered to help him find a place in another gallery. When Joe declined the help, saying he needed to try something new, he received a package from Barclay containing an SST products catalogue with the following message: *Please go through the catalogue with the idea of seeing if such a prosaic set of products, compared to painting, could arouse your creative juices.* What touched Joseph was not only Barc's personal concern for him and his family, but also that he would have a *vision* of what a watercolor painter might have to bring to Simpson Strong-Tie. After undergoing a series of interviews and a probationary period, Way was hired at Simpson Manufacturing in early 1994, where he continues to work to the present day.

Also, in 1994, Sharon and Barc stopped mounting regular shows and keeping steady gallery hours. They continued to collect art they loved, and to make major contributions of time and money to art institutions in the Bay Area, with special focus on the Berkeley Art Museum, California College of the Arts, and the Oakland Museum. A thirteen-year undertaking, the Barclay Simpson Fine Arts Gallery was a quest, a community, a base for young artists—and a window into the strange materials out of which a miraculous forty-year marriage was made.

Notes for Part V

1 *Team of Rivals: The Political Genius of Abraham Lincoln* by Doris Kearns Goodwin, 2005.

2 For a full account of the BART strike mentioned here, see *BART: The Dramatic History of the Bay Area Rapid Transit System*, Michael Healy, November 2016.

3 In printmaking, a state is a different form of a print, caused by a deliberate and permanent change to a matrix such as a copper plate (for engravings, etc.) or woodblock (for woodcut).

4 A testy Italian sculptor whose studio near Florence housed a pair of life-sized bronze horses, an ironic reference to the famous pair on Venice's San Marco Square.

PART VI
Put Something Back: Conviction in Action

As a philanthropist, Barclay is extremely consistent; there is a spirit inside him that makes him sparkle, and you know that there is kindness behind what he is doing. Sharon reflects and shares that. Together they are a tour de force.

—Roselyne (Cissie) Swig, community leader, philanthropist, and original and long-term member of the Berkeley Art Museum Board of Directors; see bio

Julayne Virgil, current CEO of Girls Inc, with some of the girls enrolled in its programs, Oakland, California.

Chapter 23
Motives and Methods of Philanthropy

What you can extrapolate from Barc's form of giving is how instrumentally he thinks about his philanthropy, that he sees the opportunity to use his resources to catalyze opportunity at an important moment for individuals and institutions.

—Larry Rinder, director and chief curator of the Berkeley Art Museum and Pacific Film Archive, 2008–2020; see bio

He teaches people as he goes. And I think the reason people can learn from Barclay is because he is so clear about what he is doing.

—Cissie Swig

When I think about Barc and leadership, I think of the Mozart effect, young students who listen to Mozart before taking a test do better than those who don't. Well, those people who work for and with Barc learn more about leadership than those who don't.

—Earl (Budd) Cheit, Simpson board member from 1994–2014, dean emeritus of the UC Berkeley Haas School of Business; see bio

IN FALL OF 2013, an intimate group gathered at Barc and Sharon's home in Orinda to celebrate the recently completed oral history of Barclay Simpson by Neil Henry for the Bancroft Library at UC Berkeley. Among the dignitaries assembled were Henry and other Bancroft staff, Chancellor Birgeneau (Chancellor UC Berkeley, 2004–2013; see bio), Jennifer Cutting (UC Berkeley Development Office; see bio), various Berkeley Museum board members and staff, Arthur Shartsis Esq., several of Barc and Sharon's children, and a handful of Barc's friends from his UC days. Barc welcomed everyone, thanking Neil Henry and the university for allowing him to be a participant in the Bancroft Library's oral history project.

Then, without a polite transition, and with emphatic cadence, he made a simple statement: *The most important issue in the world today is the education of low-income kids.* He paused, looking around at the august, assembled group. *I'm going to say that one more time.* And he did, slowly, deliberately. *The most important issue in the world today is the education of low-income kids.* Then he thanked everybody for being there and walked back into the gathering. There was complete silence as the intensity of his words continued to hang in the air.

Though positive in principle and practice, Barclay was always aware of the forces of darkness that were lapping at the edge of the community, threatening the sense of a social contract. In moments like the one described above, the darkness just beneath the unfailingly sunny surface of his disposition would show itself not as despair but as an insistent belief that we must understand our own direct connection to those sharing our space and time on earth, and that the inequality of others diminishes all of us. No casual tilter at windmills, he systematically wielded a cudgel against pretense and complacency. The urgent pressure of his moral conviction backed up by action was impossible for those in his audience to forget or discard.

～

"MONEY IS A KIND of poetry," says Wallace Stevens—*by which he means money is a metaphor for something. What did money mean to Barclay?* (Joseph Di Prisco, Board of Directors, Cal Shakes, 2007–2012; see bio.) In building the business, money seems to have meant many things to Barc, at different times and simultaneously: competing, risking, losing, winning, growing, reinvesting—loving the game, and sharing the profits. A multivalent metaphor, money was to Barc a sign of seriousness, conviction, work, community—and riches for many, not just a few. *Money to Barclay is to do something, to make something happen,* says Jonathan Moscone, Artistic Director of Cal Shakes, 2000–2010 (see bio). Giving us more poetry to ponder: *He doesn't live in a feeling state about money....*In personal, concrete terms, money meant to Barc building a beautiful, though not palatial, family house; collecting art he loved; and taking care of his large family. What it didn't mean was luxury mansions, first-class airline seats, limousines from the airport, or expensive vacations, clothes, jewelry, boats, or cars. As metaphors go, Barc's perennial dusty black Ford Taurus says it all—engine and image perfectly conjoined to character.

Though being a gifted entrepreneur is not necessarily the same as being a productive philanthropist, there seems, in Barclay's case, to have been important overlaps in motive and methods between building a business and building nonprofit organizations. Signs of what money meant to Barclay were clear long before he started giving it away. Materially speaking, the one made the other possible; yet there appears also to have been a strong psychological linkage and continuity between both undertakings, a style of leadership that was clear, consistent, oriented toward outcomes, generous, and exemplary. In business and philanthropy, getting results mattered intensely to him. For Jonathan Moscone, Barc's straightforwardness about giving had to do with the fact that he earned his money rather than inherited it. Whatever the truth of this particular explanation, recipients of Simpson donations speak repeatedly of Barc and Sharon's ease and grace in giving. In Barc's case, this may have come from the confidence of having built a successful business from scratch, or it may have emerged from the even deeper sources of his being—from his awareness of his luckiness in life, his love of the world, and his deep belief in equity in the social sense of the word.

Over lunch with Barc back in the early nineties, Peggy White, Executive Director of the Diablo Regional Arts Association (DRAA) (see bio), the nonprofit component of the Lesher Center for the Arts in Walnut Creek, shared her idea of starting a program to bring in kids from Title I schools to see high-quality performances at the Lesher Arts Center—*something that would wow and inspire them, something that would make them leave feeling awed and amazed.* According to White, this was a pivotal moment in her relationship with Barclay:

> *A spark went off with Barc and me that day. I told him I grew up in Atlanta where I went to the Northside High School Performing Arts Programs. That's the only place there wasn't racial tension. That was when Lester Maddox was governor. It was really hard. I remember just how powerful the arts were in bridging cultural differences.*

Barc was so enthralled by Peggy's concept about involving kids from Title I schools in Lesher Center programs that he wrote a check on the spot, ultimately providing two years of seed funding to get her idea off the ground and to work out the knots. When he handed her the check across the deli table, White was flabbergasted and overjoyed:

*I'd never had that happen, where someone got so thoroughly behind
your idea, believed in it so much. But I also didn't feel pressure. I felt
encouragement. I felt like he just wanted to see it happen. There wasn't
a stress factor. He said, "Just go do it. Just go do it. Go out and get the
kids that need it the most—the younger, the better."*

Focused on schoolchildren and some of their parents, who are not likely
to have had many other opportunities to see high-quality theatrical and
musical performances, the "Arts Access School Time"[1] program, as it came
to be called, had some growing pains, but is now running full-force all these
years later. Peggy remembers a time several busloads of junior high students
from Richmond arrived at the Lesher Center. The novelty of the situation
and typical teenage group mentality made them raucous as they entered the
impressive theater. But soon after the curtain rose on the first act of *To Kill
a Mockingbird*, the kids were mesmerized, sitting on the edge of their seats
for the entire show. At the end of the performance there was silence as the
stunned teenagers made their way back to the buses.

To me, this is an example of what Barc and Sharon wanted to see happen,
says Peggy. When Barc wrote her the first check so spontaneously over the
lunch table, he had told her it was only for two years, to get the program off
the ground, so that it could find long-term corporate sponsorship. *I think
Barclay knew that corporate funders would like the program, but I hadn't
realized how important the curriculum component was. Barc must have
known, because he kept steering us in the right direction.* Over a quarter
of a century after Barc provided the initial funding, DRAA's Access to
the Arts program has a solid corporate and foundation base, including
annual funds from the California Arts Council; JPMorgan Chase;
Chevron; Kaiser Permanente, Diablo Service Area; Lesher Foundation;
T. J. Long Foundation; National Endowment for the Arts; Target; and
Wells Fargo. The seed money, the *heart* money, helped make that possible,
according to White.

Jonathan Moscone, in his own particular idiom, echoes Peggy's
experience of Simpson's philanthropic methods with a telling image: *Barc's
like acupuncture. He hits a certain nerve. He feels very strongly that that's where
you hit, and the rest will happen, and I think he's right about that.* Moscone
further explains what he means by recounting an early discussion he had

with Barclay regarding his need for funds to initiate California Shakespeare Theater's Artistic Engagement program[2]:

> *The least complex conversation that I've ever had about money was with Barc. I said to him, "I need this." It was a three-sentence conversation. He asked me three questions. And I answered, and he said, "Great." It wasn't just that he said yes that made it great. It was the fact that there was no anxiety in the conversation. And, usually, everyone has anxiety about money—the givers and the givees. I didn't feel afraid of him after that.*

The kind of directness described here is a form of radical transparency that was to characterize Barclay's philanthropy, as it always had his entrepreneurship. Many noticed.

Cissie Swig, as a continuous member of the Berkeley Art Museum Board of Directors from the 1960s onward, had ample time to observe Barclay close-up. She watched and worked with him through his roles as president of the museum board, then chairman, and as the primary donor to the new museum who made foundational grants to BAMPFA in a total amount of $77.3 million between 1989 and 2016. Throughout the long struggle to build a new home for the museum, and through other generous donations that Barclay and Sharon made to such institutions as the Contemporary Jewish Museum in San Francisco and San Francisco Museum of Modern Art (SF MOMA), Cissie Swig had a ringside seat from which to watch and judge Barclay's rare leadership style as a philanthropist: *He has a very pragmatic way of analyzing his giving—and then, he's very loyal. But at the same time his expectations—and rightly so—are high. There will be performance. I really enjoy watching his philanthropy, because there is something very honest, very clear, in some ways quite original. He doesn't give with lots of strings attached.*

An extremely distinguished donor in her own right, Swig knows what she is looking at when it comes to support of the arts and the complexities of community giving. Like Barclay, she is concise in her understanding and expression, but eloquent on the subject of what made Barc special in the philanthropic arena. Her observations recall Peggy White's sense of being listened to and then encouraged. For Swig, this style is both inspirational and instructive for the people working in the institutions Barc supported:

He is interested in the project. He wants it to flourish, he wants it to succeed—and there's no bravado, which is extraordinary in itself. His gift is a statement of encouragement and of acknowledgment to whomever and whatever institution he is supporting. That has to bolster the confidence and the drive of recipients. That is so rare! No posturing, no exercise of power for its own sake. He uses force differently.

Cissy Swig recounts that she grew up in the Midwest, where people were straightforward, plain-speaking, and thinks that may be why she responded to Barclay immediately on meeting him. *He asks incisive questions, and expects quality answers, no fooling around. But he also takes such joy in the enterprise. He genuinely enjoys what he's doing, which I think is wonderful.... His philanthropy is just like that. And he's so kind. That's his legacy; it's an example.*

Cissie Swig's canny description of Barc's motives and methods of giving—both in terms of the capital provided and his active efforts to inspire staff and potential donors alike—were made dramatically concrete in the institutions he chose as causes. When Barc gave, he gave generously at a level that would enable an organization to move forward, not merely stay afloat. In many instances, he stepped in when an organization was at a critical leverage point, saving it from stillbirth, making possible its continuance and expansion. This happened early on with the seed money he provided to the "Young Entrepreneurs at Haas" (YEAH) program and to the "Access to the Arts" initiative at the Diablo Regional Arts Association. With the Berkeley Art Museum and Girls Inc., Barc and Sharon's contributions were utterly transformative, critical to the growth of these institutions, and essential to the definition of their missions.

Chapter 24
The PSB Fund

*The Simpson PSB Fund aims to create a world where all children and youth
have the opportunity to reach their full potential through non-formal
and formal education, art enrichment and the opportunity to live in
healthy and safe families and communities.*

—PSB Website[3]

IN 1988, WHILE BARC was still the chairman of Simpson Manufacturing and the owner of an active art gallery, he and Sharon set up the Simpson PSB (Put Some Back) Fund, aimed at providing support to education and arts programs with particular emphasis on literarcy and guaranteeing greater access to the arts for children from low-income backgrounds. Though the fund is not geographically restricted, the vast majority of its contributions to date have been to institutions and causes in the East Bay, a distinguishing fact for Bay Area philanthropists, who have often channeled their giving to nationally visible causes and cultural institutions in famous San Francisco. In keeping with this East Bay focus, the fund's major financial commitments— in addition to thousands of hours of Barc and Sharon's personal time—have been to Barclay's beloved UC Berkeley, with nearly $115 million donated between 1965 and 2016; to the California College of the Arts, where Barc and Sharon became the most prolific donors in the history of the college; to the Oakland Museum of California; to the Diablo Regional Arts Association; to Barclay's much-cherished Girls Inc. of Alameda County; and to the California Shakespeare Theater of Orinda, where Sharon served on the board for twenty-five years and has a major building named for her. Contributions outside of California include a $5 million gift to support the University of Washington's Humanities Center (named for Barc's father, Walter Simpson), a donation that helped attract additional private gifts, transforming the fledgling facility into what Barc's son, John Simpson, calls one of the preeminent humanities centers in the country. During Barc and Sharon's extremely prolific philanthropic career, they have given over $200 million dollars to support passions as ferociously compelling to Barclay as those that had gone into building Simpson Strong-Tie.

Barclay's decisive movement into significant charitable giving in the eighties was provided with a particularly sound material foundation once Simpson Manufacturing was taken public in 1994. In that year, he sold two million shares of company stock, with proceeds going directly into the PSB Fund. Additional stock sales of this kind were made on behalf of the fund in subsequent years.

During this period, he began actively encouraging company employees, many of whom had benefited significantly from the initial public offering (IPO), to follow his example by making charitable giving a priority in their own lives. To light the fuse, a Matching Gifts program was established by which the company would match financial contributions employees made to charities of their choice. As a company, Simpson Manufacturing became a national sponsor for Habitat for Humanity, contributing $250,000 a year for several years and encouraging employees to provide volunteer labor. Obviously, such charitable donations resulted in certain kinds of tax deductions for the company and for the employees who participated, but they also demonstrated a concrete belief in "putting some back" into the community, a creed that emanated from the company's top leadership. This form of "exemplary" philanthropy was to become a major cornerstone of all of Barclay's giving over the years, in which he combined making substantial foundation grants himself and actively exhorting others, through his example, to step up to the plate on their own. Commenting on Barclay's leadership through example, Barry Williams explains the way in which the "virtuous" cycle was fueled:

> Barclay took the company public not to make a whole lot of money himself—he already had plenty of money. He wanted to reward his employees who held company stock, he put some in trust for his kids, and the rest he started giving away. And this has had a tremendous impact on his employees who thereby saw what somebody who's made a lot of money chooses to do with it. It's part of the respect they have

for Barclay that he could have a heck of a lot more if he wanted to, but he's giving it away.

From the time of its inception, the PSB Fund was always run jointly by Sharon and Barc *with no staff, no meetings, just simple, the way Barc liked it* (Sharon).

Chapter 25
The Art of Giving to the Arts

It is art that makes life, makes interest, makes importance, for our consideration and application of these things, and I know of no substitute whatever for the force and beauty of its process.

—Henry James; lines often quoted by Barclay, according to Lawrence Rinder

T HE EXPERIENCE OF COLLECTING art and running the Lafayette gallery for thirteen years opened up a whole new world of pleasure and purpose for Barc and Sharon, in addition to putting them in the presence of working artists—both well established and those just starting out. Concurrently, they were getting increasingly involved with UC Berkeley and Girls Inc. from 1994 onward, tying together their love of art with Barc's long-term concerns about creating cultural and learning opportunities for under-resourced populations, with special focus on cognitive development in young children. *You teach a kid to paint or draw and that kid's mind opens up. You give them Shakespeare to perform and they do better in math, science, and English* (Barclay). In 1986, he accepted a position on the board of directors of the California College of the Arts (CCA), joining the UC Berkeley Art Museum board in 1988. These positions at two key East Bay arts institutions—along with his deep commitment to Girls Inc. and Sharon's to the California Shakespeare Theater (Cal Shakes)— were to become the principle (though not exclusive) focus of Barc and Sharon's considerable philanthropic energies during the rest of Barc's life.

California College of the Arts (CCA): Making the Familiar Beautiful

Barc's a true believer in art. He believes that it is transformative.
He believes art gives you something familiar made beautiful,
or something strange made comprehensible.

—Susan Avila, Sr. Vice President of Advancement, CCA—2000–present; see bio

EVEN BEFORE BARC AND Sharon set up the PSB Fund, and while the gallery was in its heyday, Barc was invited by Steven Oliver, then president of the board of trustees of CCA, to serve on the college's board. Connected to the nineteenth-century international Arts and Crafts movement, which focused on the role of artists and designers in "producing work that would address the social issues of the time and have a positive impact on the world,"[4] CCA had originally been called the California College of Arts and Crafts (CCAC), but changed its name more recently to CCA. The college had been founded in 1907 by Frederick Meyer, a German furniture maker involved in the Arts and Crafts movement, who moved to the Bay Area in 1902. His goal was "to provide an education for artists and designers that would integrate both theory and practice in the arts."[5] Being involved with an institution that explicitly aimed to integrate social purpose with aesthetic values was a perfect combination for Barc and Sharon. Citing one of the college's favorite mottos, "make art that matters," Susan Avila comments:

> *There are other wonderful art schools across the country, most geared toward artists who want to be alone in their studio to realize their personal vision, but the students who choose to come to CCA are the ones who really want to see their work in the context of the community. Barc particularly loved the programs where he actually got to interact with CCA students and elementary school kids in community-based collaborations.*

According to Sharon, *It was a fascinating time to be involved. I think it's a great organization. I feel very closely aligned with it.* She explains that when Barc was invited on to the board of trustees, CCA was *a small school trying to grow in interesting ways,* allowing him a hands-on role in making an impact on a still-fluid institution which had a much less formal hierarchy than UC Berkeley. Over the years, Barc and Sharon got to know each of the CCA's four presidents personally and felt intimately involved with the evolution of the college's changing mission and the development of specific community outreach programs. Said Susan Avila, *Every way you could possibly support a nonprofit, Barclay and Sharon have done it. They are our single most generous donors in the history of the college.*

For over twenty-five years, Barc and Sharon were involved with almost every new initiative from the Adopt-a-Book program, in which CCA tried to build its on-campus library through gifts by individual donors, to funding a substantial endowment for the Center of Art and Public Life, which has become the primary source of funding for CCA's community-based programs. This core institution within CCA has forged relationships with public schools and a range of community-based organizations in Oakland, San Francisco, Richmond, and a number of other municipalities in the greater Bay Area.

In addition to the Art in Public Life endowment, Barc and Sharon also made important capital gifts to the college, helping to construct a new library at CCA's San Francisco campus—which now bears Sharon's name—and the Simpson Glass Studio on the Oakland campus. But perhaps the sentimental favorite among their gifts has been the "Barclay Simpson Awards," a program they set up in 1986 to make direct donations each year to two to four MFA students, whose work is selected by a jury for exhibition and who receive $2,000–$5,000 directly from Barclay and Sharon to use however they see fit in launching their career. While the Simpson Fine Arts Gallery was still open, winners of the Barclay Simpson Awards would have their work exhibited and, if they were lucky, sold through the gallery. The annual openings for these exhibits were full of a very special kind of exuberance. Over the course of twenty-five years, Barc and Sharon made direct donations to seventy-four graduating students, providing a total of $116,000 to young artists just as they were starting out in life.

It is not just Barc and Sharon's generosity, but their motives for and methods of giving, that moves Avila for many of the same reasons cited by Cissie Swig:

> In my twenty-plus-year history as a fundraiser, I have worked with some very powerful, very wealthy philanthropists in the arts, including those associated with SF MOMA. Of the hundreds of donors with whom I've been professionally associated, Barclay and Sharon are my ideal of what a donor should be. They're the people I think of if I've had a particularly frustrating day, when I've dealt with a very difficult person, or somebody who's giving for all the wrong reasons, or someone who just doesn't understand the kind of constraints that a nonprofit organization works under. Barclay and Sharon are not like that at all; they respect what a nonprofit organization is trying to accomplish, but at the same time, they push that organization to do more and do better—but they do it as a partner. (Susan Avila)

She describes them as *unassuming,* even *humble,* taking *joy in giving and helping organizations, helping their community.* According to Avila their will to give has nothing to do with forging social connections—*Barclay and Sharon couldn't care less about that*—but they really want to make a difference for organizations that they believe can have an impact on things that matter to them. *They're just incredible human beings.*

Avila is particularly astute regarding Barclay's style of communication and his tactical understanding of timing and group dynamics: *He doesn't have to dominate a conversation or an issue. He's a fantastic listener. He's very respectful of everyone, but then when he says something, everybody else is quiet because you know it's going to be worth listening to. And, you know, he can express himself very passionately and persuasively in not too many words.* Echoed by Cissie Swig, Robert Birgeneau, Noel Nellis (member of the Berkeley Art Museum board from 1991–present; see bio), and Larry Rinder, comments such as these suggest that Barclay was consciously tactical regarding how to lead a group of people to consensus and positive action, skills he had honed as a businessman. In Avila's words, Barclay was a tremendous leader, not just in the generosity of his gifts, but in their *timing.* In this she saw him as *setting the bar high for all the other donors at CCA,* a comment that restates the degree to which he was both exemplary and strategic in his aim to attract other donors to causes he backed. As would be true with the major gifts he and Sharon made to UC Berkeley and Girls Inc., the method behind Barc's giving at CCA was always aimed at providing a core base of funding for a given project or program that would allow the college to raise additional money from foundations, corporations, and individuals.

Barc's skills as a philanthropist arose out of genuine passions and convictions that can't be modeled. Trying to put her finger on what made Barc so different as a CCA donor, Susan Avila points to his baseline belief in and *love for the intersection of education and the arts.* This in turn was deeply connected to his hope for social exchange and improvement, *bringing young people to an institution where they can realize their potential and train to go out and make the world a better place through art, architecture, and design.* In a cynical world, Barclay was an idealist, a man of pragmatic action, yet full of feeling. According to Susan Avila, for Barc art was miraculous:

Barclay talked about how art changed and enriched his life, how it helped him understand his individual humanity, but also our collective human- ity. He believed that art could show you something that, maybe, you al- ways knew was true, but it would show it to you in a new way or a way you never imagined, or you'd see something new beyond your imagining.

The Oakland Museum of California (OMCA): Art and Community

I called Barc to ask for a donation to our 2006 Capital Campaign, but before I could make my pitch, he told me that he and Sharon were going to donate $1 million. He took the initiative, didn't make me ask, and there were no strings attached. Later, at a celebration event for the campaign, he walked right up to one of our corporate donors, who had also made a gift of $1 million, introduced himself, and said straight out that, as a reflection of net worth, the gift made by the corporation was much too low. That was Barc. He gave several magnitudes more than I was going to ask for, and then called on another donor to consider a more generous gift.

—Lori Fogarty, executive director of OMCA, 2006 to present; see bio

BECAUSE OF ITS HIGH-QUALITY permanent collection combined with its emphasis on living artists, multimedia exhibitions, and its long tradition of reaching out to schools and the community at large, the Oakland Museum of California was a natural commitment for Barc and Sharon. Like CCA, it is an institution that consciously addresses the question of the role of arts in education, and of the intersections between individual and communal culture, a set of concerns that was part of the museum's founding mission and which were increasingly essential to Barclay's view of the "uses" of art. Undoubtedly, the public-private partnership aspect of OMCA's identity would also have appealed to Barclay, as a worthy example of the ways the two sectors can collaborate on ventures that create a range of value for a city and region. Although he never assumed any official leadership position at OMCA, he managed to lead in his own particular, exemplary way: supporting staff and exhorting other donors to step up.

For Lori Fogarty, it has been Barc and Sharon's approach to giving that distinguishes them. *I feel lucky to have known them. They become good friends of the people they support. They offer such a rich combination of attributes—it's their temperaments, their values, their not being complainers or negotiators, their positivity—it's their spirit.*

Lori speaks of her visits to the Lafayette gallery to meet with Barc over a lunch of burritos, or to the house in Orinda, or to events to which she was invited by Barc and Sharon, where she got to know their wide-ranging interests, from ceramics to the emergence of China as a determinative force in the world. *They are curious...always learning...always interested in you, where you were born, how you grew into the person you are.* Fogarty notes particularly how *the trappings of philanthropy*, the high society, name-recognition side of the business was of no interest to them. Rather than make the museum director *work for donations* as some donors do, they were supportive in more than simply financial ways, *asking good questions, pushing you to think deeper about an issue.*

In June 2011, OMCA was transitioning from being a department of the city of Oakland to becoming a quasi-independent nonprofit entity that still received some funds from the city. During that period, Lori explains how she drove out to see Barc at SST offices to discuss the museum's need to raise a higher proportion of annual funds to sustain the new nonprofit. She remembers that she was going to ask for $50,000, but that Barc again preempted the discussion, saying he had already decided on a contribution of $3 million to help get the new administrative structure of the museum launched. As was also true with his sizeable capital contributions to CCA, UC Berkeley, and Girls Inc., the extent of this contribution was strategically intended to create a base around which other financial gifts could cluster and breed. Maybe, Barc thought, the corporate sponsor he had challenged five years previously might find a way to amplify. *And, anyway, the Oakland Museum was a great investment* (Barclay).

Lori Fogarty explains that the $3 million pledge was fulfilled by November 2013, and that during the intervening time, Barc and Sharon also made modest annual gifts, along with gifts supporting gala fundraising events, including $25,000 in FY 2012 and $35,000 in FY 2014. In 2015 and 2016, following Barc's death in November 2014, Sharon made annual gifts targeted toward a couple of specific exhibitions. Then in 2017, during the current capital campaign for the museum, she pledged an additional $3 million, which she paid out within three years, while continuing to give sums ranging between $10,000 and $50,000 to annual fundraising efforts.

This substantial and consistent record of giving suggests that Sharon and Barc jointly regarded OMCA as an institution that fulfills the deepest of their philanthropic priorities.

In January 2020, at a directors' dinner in honor of major donors at the conclusion of the five-year capital campaign, Lori recounts how Sharon walked up to her, Barc no longer at her side, to say that the Simpson PSB Fund would be making yet another $3 million gift, matching the spirit that had animated Barc years before. She began the fulfillment of this new pledge in June 2020 with a down payment of $500,000. In Lori's words, *They have always been selfless donors, giving as much as they can. You never have to ask.*

California Shakespeare Theater (Cal Shakes): Sharon, Queen of the Revels

Barc and Sharon are not just philanthropists, they're working philanthropists.
They want to get the job done right.

—Jonathan Moscone

WHEN BARC AND SHARON decided to close down the gallery, one of the great beneficiaries was the struggling Cal Shakes theater of Orinda, to which Sharon devoted untold time and passion for over twenty-five years. Veterans of the East Bay may remember the early days of what was known in the seventies as the Berkeley Shakespeare Festival, where Othello, Lear, and Shylock cried to the gods for justice amid redwood trees before an audience ranged on a damp, pine-needle hillside in John Hinckley Park. This theater in the raw seemed both consistent with Berkeley's elemental sense of itself and with the idea that Shakespeare's greatness made him palpable in a multiplicity of settings and garbs. But, ultimately, Berkeley's Forest of Arden was a serious restriction on the theater's growth. Those interested in marrying Shakespeare to California's natural sublime went in search of money and location that could accommodate a larger purpose and an expanded audience.

In the late eighties, Barclay joined the theater's capital campaign to raise the money necessary to move and rebrand the enterprise. As Sharon was to do on behalf of countless other philanthropic campaigns in the coming thirty years, she assisted with fundraising galas and other theater-linked events at the Simpson home in Orinda. In 1991, with the help of a foundation grant of $500,000 from Sue and George Bruns—in memory of their son, Lieutenant

G. H. Bruns Jr.—the company built the new Bruns Amphitheater, facing the dramatic golden hills of Orinda, on land rented from East Bay Mud for one dollar a year. In this spectacular landscape, the East Bay could again listen to Elizabethan pentameter in *plein air*—where "surrounded by gorgeous eucalyptus groves, actors and audience share space under the sky for an experience like no other."[6]

The challenge of finding a compelling location for the refounded company having been met, George Bruns became president of the board, which was now faced with the daunting job of putting together a sound financial base on which to build a theater of artistic merit. As committed supporters, Barclay and Sharon soon pledged a substantial donation toward the operating budget of the theater to be paid out over a three-year period. In 1993, the board invited Barclay to join its ranks, an offer he declined because of other pressing board commitments at the UC Berkeley Museum, CCA, and Girls Inc., as well as continuing engagement with Simpson Manufacturing. As, in Sharon's words, *a kind of afterthought,* Board Member Michael Addison turned to her and said, *Well, how about you?* Somewhat taken aback by his offhand request, Sharon said she would think about it. She had wanted a break between the closing of the gallery in 1994 and taking on another major responsibility. Little did she know.

Eventually, in early 1994, she agreed to go on the Cal Shakes Board, but claims that she didn't say a word for the first six months. However, this changed suddenly when, listening to a report on the net earnings from that year's gala, the board learned that $9,000 had been paid to a party planner plus related expenses. By now a veteran of meals bought, cooked, and served out of her home kitchen with no help from caterers, Sharon suddenly entered the board conversation saying that she didn't think the struggling organization could afford to pay expensive event designers. The board member who had been responsible for the gala was furious and soon left the meeting. Upon her exit, George Bruns turned to Sharon, saying, *Honey* (still a permissible appellation in those years), *that was brilliant!* From that moment going forward, the foundling Cal Shakes was to be kept from a precipitous death by Sharon's increasingly essential and passionate ministrations.

In time, George Bruns was to ask Sharon to take over the presidency of the board, which she accepted with trepidation (and an under-the-gun review of Robert's Rules of Order)—but, luckily for Cal Shakes, also with fierce devotion, a natural gift for working with people, and unflagging will power. It was not a casual undertaking. For years, she worked forty- and fifty-hour weeks keeping the wobbly company from bankruptcy. Facing a range of difficult personnel issues that ranged from having to fire an alcoholic bookkeeper (after finding a bunch of unpaid bills stuffed into a desk drawer) to cleaning up behind a precious actor-turned-incompetent administrator, Sharon claims that those early years as president of the Cal Shakes Board were *one of the best experiences of my life,* providing her with an intensive education in business management as well as the therapeutic arts. Warm, generous, and supportive by nature, she had no experience, for instance, in firing people—but she did have Barclay as a counselor, who stiffened her spine, explaining that she had to do what was right for the organization without coddling the needs of people who were not doing their jobs. She rose to the challenge, *providing the glue* that kept the organization afloat until it could stabilize.

With the departure of one of the interim artistic directors of Cal Shakes, she took the initiative of organizing a thorough investigation aimed at identifying the key components needed to guarantee ongoing support from donors, foundations, and theater patrons. Sharon describes the message that emerged from these exhaustive meetings with important constituencies: *We were, then, regarded as a small, not very innovative summer theater, and we needed to up our game in order to stay in the game.* With this in mind, she established a search committee and hired a head-hunting firm to go in search of an exciting and savvy new artistic director to guide Cal Shakes into a more interesting and secure future. The name that popped out of this search was Jonathan Moscone, the then thirty-four-year-old son of slain mayor of San Francisco, George Moscone, killed in his office by a maniac colleague during tumultuous times in 1978.

At the time his name came up in Cal Shakes deliberations, Jonathan was working as the artistic director of an experimental theater in Dallas, Texas. Wanting to speak to him in person, the Search Committee ran into a dead-end when his agent insisted that all negotiations go through him. Frustrated but not deterred, Sharon flew to Dallas on her way to visit her son in Houston and lay in wait for Jonathan at the backstage door to his theater. They talked face-to-face and liked each other. Jonathan said he was very worried about returning to San Francisco where his family's history lay in wait. Sharon suggested that he would need to go home one day or other to confront the dragon, not to mention what it would mean to his mother.

Eventually, Jonathan came and met the Search Committee, interviewing for the job at an informal cocktail party at the Simpson house. Because he was so ambivalent about taking the job at Cal Shakes, Moscone remembers being totally honest in the interview. He told the Search Committee that as artistic director he would most likely throw out a lot of assumptions that protected Shakespeare from *really* being examined in our society in terms of relevance, entertainment, and accessibility. Moreover, he explained that if he were offered and accepted the job, he would take the programming beyond Shakespeare to showcase the work of other playwrights, including some moderns. And he would take a new look at Cal Shakes' arts education programming, which was skeletal and needed an overhaul. Commenting on his impressions of Barclay at that first meeting, Moscone says quite simply, *He thought I was authentic.* Then, as a follow-up, *Barclay has zero tolerance for inauthenticity. That's why politics don't interest him that much. He says most politicians whom he meets just don't follow through. To him, artists and teachers follow through.*

In the end, Jonathan did accept the Cal Shakes job, issuing in a ten-year period of transformation during which the company moved from small, community summer theater to being a regionally known and respected member of the Bay Area-wide performing arts world. Much of this major shift in fortune was directly linked to Moscone's artistic experimentations and broadening of the repertoire and theatrical talent base of the company. Additionally, he demonstrated skill as a fundraiser and provided the kind of visible leadership that attracted donors who had never before considered giving money to the Orinda-based company. Though being located in the East Bay as opposed to San Francisco was to be an ongoing issue for Cal Shakes, Moscone's vast San Francisco acquaintanceship and name recognition around the Bay Area helped the theater establish new sources of capital and operating money. These efforts were greatly assisted by Barclay and Sharon's ongoing donations of time, annual support, and foundational grants during the organization's capital campaigns. In 2007, the Simpsons made a capital contribution of $5 million to help build a new facility for the theater that bears Sharon's name. Around 2009, Sharon donated an additional $1 million to establish an endowment fund for the theater, named for Jonathan Moscone. As was true with many of the organizations they supported, Barc and Sharon's significant contributions drew in other donors who realized that Simpson support for an organization was a signpost of quality. This reciprocity was crucial both to Jonathan and to the overall evolution of the theater. *Through financial support, partnership, and leadership in promoting Cal Shakes, the Simpsons supported my most audacious concepts, not blindly, but with trust* (Jonathan Moscone). By then, supporting—in all senses of the word—the people they hired was a time-tested and successful practice that distinguished the Simpson name in philanthropy as well as business.

Chapter 26
University of California at Berkeley: Pole Star[7]

Barc and Sharon are a really extraordinary couple, both of them. They're humble and, at the same time, think very deeply about social issues and how they can contribute to them and to the betterment of the society around them.... I appreciated having someone like Barc as a partner in the number of things that we were doing because of his sophistication and his ability to make decisions quickly, and, of course, because of his high moral character.

—Robert Birgeneau

A S AN IMPECUNIOUS TEENAGER, Barc watched UC Berkeley football games from what was known as Tightwad Hill just above the stadium. In early January 2013, he received the Berkeley Medal[8] from the hands of then Chancellor Robert Birgeneau. In between those years, UC Berkeley was a pole star for Barclay, a kind of ongoing vital present rather than just a source of happy youthful memories. After leaving Berkeley to join the Naval Air Force during World War II, reenrolling after the war then dropping out again at the request of his father to *save the family business*, he finally received his Bachelor of Science degree in 1966 through night and continuing education classes at the university. But for Barc, graduation was genuinely more of a commencement than a moment of conclusion where UC Berkeley was concerned.

During his very long association with the university in a variety of capacities, Barclay was to interact closely with a number of UC Berkeley chancellors. Among these, Robert Birgeneau overlapped with Barclay during the Great Recession period that began in 2007—one of the most difficult times in Berkeley's history, particularly in regard to fundraising, racial diversity, and questions about the university's changing social mission. According to Birgeneau, it was a much more difficult period than even the Great Depression and its aftermath, for reasons that he connects with *the changing demographics of California, as well as the change in attitude of the California citizenry in regard to its willingness to support the public good.* Birgeneau's often-stated mission to promote "access and excellence" at the university came during an extended period of straitened financial circumstances at the state level, which, in turn, exacerbated the always heated battles over admissions, affirmative action, and the distribution of scarce resources available to a public institution.[9] Having allies within the private donor class was essential but not guaranteed. Birgeneau says he was very grateful to find committed confederates: *I met Barc and Sharon relatively early on during my service here. My wife and I were particularly impressed by their passion for Girls Inc. He pushed us strongly to be involved in it and for us to become donors. He was basically turning the organization around with his support. His passion is very deep and quite unrelenting.* It appears that Birgeneau felt Barclay's cudgel from the start.

Birgeaneau explains that he first met Barc when being introduced to university donors as the new chancellor. It was a pleasant encounter in the way of such events. But he could not anticipate the degree to which he and Barc would become partners in the promotion of a wide arc of university programs and capital investments over all of the years they were to collaborate. During that time, Birgeneau was to observe Barc regularly take over roles that he, as chancellor, or his vice-chancellor of University Development & Alumni Relations might have been expected to fulfill. He noted a special power in the way Barclay engaged people regarding the overall mission of the university, whether he was speaking about the art museum, Haas Business School, or university athletic facilities:

> *I was there when Barc got a number of awards such as being recognized by the Haas School....It was very hard for him to take credit for anything. Instead, he would talk about the importance of universities, of a public university like Berkeley, serving the entire population—the fact that it's our obligation, which I also feel deeply, to ensure that the playing field is level, and that everyone has an opportunity.*

Birgeneau states that it was never necessary for him to explicitly discuss shared values with Barclay. *I knew fair access was an aspect of Berkeley that mattered to him.* But it was also Barc's *relentless* methods that elicited Birgeneau's admiration and gratitude, including Barc's active solicitations to other private donors to step up and help the university meet its demanding range of commitments. He had *such credibility*, claims Birgeneau, because of his character and because of the sums he himself was willing to commit. Though the art museum was his deepest passion, Birgeneau explains that Barclay understood the full scope of interests that must be balanced in a public university.

The chancellor's early impressions of Barclay were to stand the test of time. Over a period of several years, the two were to collaborate closely on promoting and bringing to fruition a range of university projects. In addition to Barc's egalitarian values and holistic view of the university's mission, Birgeneau particularly appreciated the executive style that had made Barc so successful as an entrepreneur: *One of the things that differentiates successful people from others is their ability to make decisions quickly. If you can't decide quickly, then you're going to end up in a morass. I appreciated having someone like Barc as a partner in the number of things that we were doing because of his ability to make decisions quickly.* Barc's was an unusual "managerial style," according to Birgeneau, one that made partnering with him inspiring and efficient—which latter quality the chancellor knew was extremely hard to come by in the public arena: *Partly he persuades by example, partly he's quite directed and adamant. He knew how to focus discussions on the real challenges.* Adamancy and focus were traits Barc made famous at Simpson Manufacturing, and which he carried over seamlessly into his philanthropy. As many noticed, Barc could be tough—sometimes very tough—as when he fired a member of the Berkeley Art Museum Board whom he felt was falling short on her leadership obligations. The same had been true at SST when he thought someone wasn't performing up to standard. This toughness wasn't mean—but it was unsentimental.

While Barc's work at UC Berkeley was geographically local, its implications were broad in relation to his extensive role in helping to shape and adapt the mission of one of the greatest public universities in the US (and the world at large) during difficult economic and social times.

The UC Berkeley Haas School of Business (Haas)

It wasn't just the size of the gift. It was also the way he did it....
He's a consummate actor in the sense of action. But he's also super thoughtful,
and he questions the intellectual underpinnings of people's behavior
in a really fruitful way....The guy's got a core.

—Richard Lyons, dean, Haas School of Business, 2008–2018; see bio

THROUGHOUT THE LATE SIXTIES and seventies, as he was building Simpson Manufacturing into an ever-more profitable business, Barc took seminars for working business managers and executives at the UC Berkeley Haas School of Business. Starting in 1978, Barc served on Haas's board of directors, donating his time and $6.5 million in funds over a period of twenty-five years. These sums included an important donation of $1 million to the Young Entrepreneurs at Haas (YEAH) program,[10] in which low-income students are tutored by Haas MBAs on how to design and launch a viable business. Though, as Dean Lyons explains, Barc and Sharon didn't launch the program (now called BOOST), the focus of the initiative, which has been running for over twenty years, coincided strongly with their commitment to economically disadvantaged kids, particularly from the East Bay. Their sizable investment enabled the program to expand from the original target of a few East Bay high schools to include several middle schools as well. Lyons explains that Barc and Sharon's financial support of this program was essential to its precarious middle years in which it was either going to wither on the vine or flourish.

As an example of what may have gotten Barc and Sharon interested in YEAH, Lyons describes one of the program's memorable moments. It was a Saturday morning, Lyon's recounts, in one of the Haas classrooms, where Haas faculty and students and a venture capital panel comprised of industry people from the community joined with East Bay families to watch their seventeen- to eighteen-year-old kids make PowerPoint presentations, still a novelty at that time. *Some of the presentations by these kids would just knock your socks off...their MBA mentors beaming on the side lines...the families watching their daughters and sons presenting their proposals, a sight to behold.* Lyons remembers that one of the kids was talking about starting a T-shirt company:

The kid's name was Robert Reffkin and he was doing Rastafarian-style T-shirts, hats, products. It was very reggae oriented. This was in 1993, when I first heard his presentation. Then, later, when I was at Goldman Sachs from 2006 to 2008, I got an email from within the bank, and suddenly realized this kid had become a vice-president at the bank.

Stories like this fueled Barc and Sharon's involvement. Eventually the YEAH program was expanded into the middle schools, which pleased Barc, whose deeply held conviction that character and destiny were formed at a very early age made him push program directors in his target institutions to involve ever-younger children in order to shape hearts and minds at the source. Though the YEAH program didn't exactly serve Barc's very young target audience, it was nevertheless a classic example of the kind of outreach efforts to low-income kids that were to become a crucial focus of Barc and Sharon's giving from the late seventies onward.

Their ongoing relationship with Haas also provides an example of the other side of the Simpson donation strategy, that involving the making of significant capital gifts around which the given institution would be able to organize a comprehensive capital campaign for the expansion or restoration of core facilities. Dean Lyons remembers approaching Barc with the idea of thanking him for his many contributions, and to describe to him, as a member of the Haas Board of Directors, the school's plans to expand their physical complex. He and his colleagues found that Barc had done his homework:

We went to see him not expecting to give him a proposal—we wanted to thank him for everything he'd done for us and for the campus. In perfect Barclay fashion he says, "So why are you here?" He called the question. We showed him some pictures. He looked at them and said, "I'm in for five." Five million dollars. This is a huge gift for us. It wasn't like this was a whim; he'd more or less made his mind up, and he wanted to get to the conversation.

In Lyon's words, it *was a catalyzing gift,* like so many Barc and Sharon had made before and would make again.

According to Lyons, the school is trying to shape graduates who have what he calls *confidence without attitude,* a character combination that gets at what the dean thinks makes Barclay different:

With Barclay, the inner confidence is there, and it's unshakeable. But he never lords it over people. At Haas, we try to get at the three things he does so well: knowing, doing, and being. By the latter I mean self-awareness, about understanding who you are as a leader, what your values are. What are your nonnegotiables? What are your core values, and do you live in a way that's consistent with them? Is there an architecture among those core values? The knowing, doing, being triad is something that Barclay is so good at. You get a sense of his presence, the being part. There's a there there. You can't be around him and not get that feeling. The guy's got a core.

Perhaps, not strangely, this description recalls many of the things Barc's own children said about him as a father—about his presence, his consistency, his center. In 2005, Barclay was awarded the Haas School's "Business Leader of the Year" Award. The article memorializing[11] this event makes an absolute connection between the qualities of leadership that built Simpson Manufacturing and those which also gave a special shape to Simpson philanthropy. Article writer Marguerite Rigoglioso says:

Over the past half century, Simpson has built his company into an $800 million business, supported affirmative action in the workplace, and supported groups that work with disadvantaged youth. In recognition of his commitment to entrepreneurial success and his outstanding leadership in giving back to his community, the Haas School named Simpson the Business Leader of the Year for 2005.

The Berkeley Art Museum and Pacific Film Archive (BAMPFA): Passion, Tenacity, and Realignment

Barc believes that art provides a way for people to tap into their core humanity and to find points of commonality that cross over economic, racial, [and] cultural divides. I think he feels that art is an important catalyst for a kind of democratizing social engagement because it provides that common vocabulary where people can see their shared humanity.

—Lawrence Rinder

I don't know anybody as generous, thoughtful, and non-ego driven as Barclay Simpson....A lot of his capacity for leadership, a lot of his successes stem from the fact that anyone who associates with him becomes aware of these qualities of character.

—Noel Nellis

NINETEEN EIGHTY-EIGHT WAS A big year for Barc's career as a philanthropist. In the same year in which he and Sharon set up the PSB Fund, Barclay was invited to serve on the board of directors of what was then called the University of California Berkeley Art Museum. He was to serve in a leadership role with the museum until his death in 2014, first as a member of the board, then as president from 1996–2003, and finally as chairman, a position created especially for him. While on the board, Barc collaborated with such other impressive and unfaltering colleagues as Cissie Swig, the museum's first president of the board and longest continuously serving member, and Noel Nellis, originally recruited by Cissie Swig, two-time board president, passionate museum supporter, and active fundraiser.

The UC Berkeley Art Museum's roots go back to 1881, when Henry Douglas Bacon donated his library, several paintings, and half of the funds needed to construct what was known as the Bacon Art and Library Building, just the third structure built on the fledgling UC Berkeley campus. Among Bacon's most prized gifts to the new institution was Albert Bierstadt's painting *Yosemite Winter Scene* (1872). In 1931, the university converted an old brick power plant into a display space for its growing collection of prints and paintings. Designed in 1904 by architect John Galen Howard and known as the "Powerhouse Gallery," this was, according to Cissie Swig, a charming Art-Deco style building where she and a few others first convened as a board of directors for the museum during the sixties.

In 1970, the museum was moved from the old power plant into a dramatic, poured-concrete, modern structure on Bancroft Way along the southern edge of the UC Berkeley campus. The catalyzing force behind this new building, designed by San Francisco architect Mario Ciampi and associates Richard L. Jorasch and Ronald E. Wagner, was the 1963 donation by abstract expressionist artist and teacher Hans Hofmann of forty-seven of his paintings along with a $250,000 capital grant for construction of the new museum. In 1964, Peter Seltz, former curator at the Museum of Modern Art in New York City, was hired as director of the museum. Particular strengths of the UC Berkeley collection include Ming and Qing Dynasty Chinese painting, old master prints and drawings, and classic and contemporary art donated by a number of devoted patrons. This distinguished list includes Barclay and Sharon Simpson, who gifted sixty-one Whistler prints to the museum's permanent collection.

During the early years of Seltz's innovative and long tenure at the museum was the creation—in collaboration with Sheldon Renan, Albert Johnson, and Tom Luddy—of an internationally important film archive, under the museum's umbrella. What came to be known and revered as the Pacific Film Archive (PFA) was conceived along the lines of the Cinémathèque Française in Paris: "a place where cinema patrons, artists, students, and critics could watch the widest range of the world's films in the best technical and environmental conditions, that would also be a center for study, discussion, and exchange."[12] The integration of the film archive with the Berkeley Art Museum has been a crucial part of the institution's identity for nearly five decades, an essential resource for arts and film at the university, in the city of Berkeley, and throughout the San Francisco Bay Area at large. In 1996, the name of the museum was changed to the Berkeley Art Museum and Pacific Film Archive (BAMPFA).

In October of 1989, during Barc's first year as a member of the museum's board of directors, the Loma Prieta earthquake struck the Bay Area, bringing down a portion of the Bay Bridge and the Cypress Freeway segment that ran through West Oakland. At Simpson Manufacturing, this terrible event served as a major stimulus to the business, resulting in SST's active involvement with a number of Bay Area cities, including San Francisco, in consulting on the structural damage resulting from the earthquake and helping cities to develop more rigorous seismic regulations. The earthquake was also the impetus for the State of California to mandate systematic evaluation of the seismic reliability of its schools, colleges, universities, and other state-owned and operated facilities. At UC Berkeley, this brought about a comprehensive evaluation of the structural integrity of all campus buildings, known as SAFER (Seismic Action Plan for Facilities Enhancement and Renewal). In the summer of 1997, this evaluation resulted in the 1970 museum building being declared seismically unfit, scoring "very poor" on the safety rating—one of the worst buildings on campus.

Early estimates concluded that a thorough seismic retrofit of the existing building would cost in the neighborhood of $60–80 million dollars. Though striking in appearance, the 1970 museum building had a number of functional problems (beyond its seismic reliability) that led the UC Berkeley administration and museum board to consider alternative strategies, including tearing the building down and rebuilding it in a new form, or relocating to a university-owned site just west of the western entrance to the campus on Center Street near Oxford, at the location of the old UC Berkeley printing facility.

Birgeneau recounts a story regarding a meeting of the museum board on a Saturday morning in 2001, while staff and board were still seeking to define the alternatives and to start identifying their potential costs. During the course of that Saturday meeting, it became apparent that, in any form, the new or retrofitted museum wasn't going to move forward unless there was a foundational gift. *Barc stepped up and said he was going to give $25 million, which at the time was a significant portion of what we then thought would be the total cost—though, frankly I should have known better* (Robert Birgeneau). Noel Nellis, then president of the board, recalls the lead-up to Barclay's game-changing announcement: *Barc and I met that morning before the board meeting at the Café Roma at the corner of College and Ashby. I just plain came out and said that we needed a major gift to kick off the capital campaign and asked him if he could give $25 million. He said "no." Then, later, a half-hour into the meeting, he sent me a hand-scrawled note, "Okay, $25 M."* That was the beginning of what was to become a grueling fundraising campaign.

Partly to test the various alternatives being considered, and with Barc and Sharon's major commitment in their pocket, the museum leadership and staff decided in 2006 to hold an international design competition for the new building. This resulted in the selection of a Japanese architect named Toyo Ito for a concept that by everyone's account would have produced a truly spectacular and inventive building.[13] For a while, the aesthetic fever stimulated by this design kept at bay the daunting realization that opting for this level of beauty, estimated to cost $143 million in 2008 dollars, would require a capital campaign on a level not originally contemplated by the administration or the board. No one loved the design more than Barclay, who set out to fundraise it into being.

But Barclay wasn't the only enthusiast for the building. Another of the chief supporters for the concept was the then-director of the museum, who had staged and promoted the competition, and with whom Barclay had developed a close working relationship. Several of Barc's cotrustees were also enthusiastic. According to Birgeneau, *Barc worked passionately to try and raise the money for the Toyo Ito design.* However, these fundraising efforts ultimately ran into a major stumbling block: the problem of raising significant sums of private donor money for an art institution in the East Bay. Though, as Birgeneau explains, they were able to identify a number of people with the capacity to give at the same level as Barc and Sharon, most such people were not willing to make major gifts for an art institution outside of San Francisco, with its international art viewing public. *It was really hard slogging and actually the gap was just so large.* But Barc had taken his stand in the East Bay in general and on behalf of the University of California in particular. He didn't want to give up on the world-class design.

During the struggle to build on Barc's foundational gift, a potentially difficult problem arose that Birgeneau feared might cause conflict between himself and Barclay. At a certain moment, Birgeneau decided that although the existing director of the museum was an aesthetic "visionary," he did not have the skills required to raise the sums of money needed to get the project done. According to Noel Nellis, Barc had—uncharacteristically—been dragging his heels, "waffling" over whether to question the existing leadership. His excitement over the Ito design appears to have gotten commingled with his thinking about the director. The chancellor and Scott Biddy (UC Berkeley Vice Chancellor of University Relations, President of UC Berkeley Foundation, 2002–2017) were extremely anxious about Barc's potential reaction to Birgeneau's conviction that the museum director had to go. They decided they had to talk to Barc in person, outside of a board session, and ended up meeting him in a café in Lake Tahoe, where Barc was vacationing with his family.

> We were extremely nervous. But Barc's a very sophisticated man, and I think he'd been reading the tea leaves. We explained the logic of compelling a change in leadership to make this project happen. I remember him sitting there thinking. His first comment was, "We want to make sure that we're really fair to the previous director." Barc's such a fair man. But then, after a few moments he said, "Yes, I understand. We need to make a change." The knot in my stomach

disappeared. Having now made up his mind, Barc continued: "Let's just find a great new director, and we'll move forward with the project. You've got my 100 percent commitment. I'll do whatever I can to help with the transition."

Birgeneau saw in Barclay's capacity to hear the rationale behind a position quite different from his own the signs of effective executive leadership: *He processed the things that we had to say very quickly and assured us that his commitment was to the museum and to the university—not to any individual—which is the mark of a sophisticated manager.* For Barc, the most important thing was that there was now a road forward.

He continued to do everything possible to raise the money needed to bring the Ito design within reach. Birgeneau also thought the design marvelous, as did many others, and was deeply impressed by the intensity with which Barc pursued the goal. The chancellor describes how in all sorts of different public events, some not even related to museum business, Barc would *just get up and start talking about the art museum. If there were other donors present, he'd say, "You've got to step up. This is really important."* Here, again, the "cajoling" cudgel is visibly at work. But by 2009, as the Great Recession deepened, even Barclay realized it was time to modify the quest.

In that year, the board made the decision that they must put aside the Ito design and find a less expensive way to completion. Noel Nellis is philosophical about what he came to see as a necessary shift in direction: *Given the economic crash, it would have been wrong to have this magnificent, white, cloudlike building as a gateway to scruffy downtown Berkeley.* As the *LA Times* was to point out in its article written a month after the opening of the new building in January 2016,[14] instead of asking Ito to modify his design, the museum board hired the New York-based architectural firm of Diller Scofidio + Renfro (DS+R), who had been collaborators with the landscape architecture firm of James Corner Field Operations on the High Line project on the west side of New York City. Describing the building that emerged from the complex goals of the BAMPFA Board of Directors and financial constraints, the *Times* describes a poly-syllabic structure:

"The museum mixes Art Deco and contemporary architecture, combining a remade 1939 printing plant on the western edge of the UC Berkeley campus with a twisting new structure, clad in ribbons of stainless steel, that emerge from the sidewalk, slither over the existing building, and cantilever over the main entrance....Perhaps trickiest of all, given its history as a project born of post-2008 caution, it tries to make bedfellows of austerity and daring.... Cannily ambitious, the building is full of dramatic interior spaces and blasts of color. It gives the museum far more programmatic flexibility than it had before....It is clearly a boon for the city of Berkeley."[15]

By fall of 2008, the Ito design had been projected to cost $200 million, while a thorough seismic retrofit of the original Ciampi building was estimated to be in the range of $60–$80 million. In the end, the DS+R retrofit and new construction building came in at $112 million. To get to that number, Barc needed to bump up his original contribution of $25 million by nearly an additional $45 million. As Birgeneau remembers, *When we were getting close, but just needed one more push, Barc stepped up again.*

In reflecting on the massive joint effort that eventually brought the new museum into being, Noel Nellis concisely states that *without Barclay, there would be no newly expanded arts and film facility—period.* In honor of this bald truth, the university inscribed the entrance hall of the museum in bold, black letters against a white background: "Sharon and Barclay Simpson Galleries." To the public at large this is undoubtedly viewed as an acknowledgement that the Simpsons were lead donors in the project, which is certainly true in that they provided well over half of the total funds expended in its realization. But for Noel Nellis, there is a deeper truth regarding the effort that went into bringing the new museum project to fruition than the inscription can quite convey. This truth has to do with Barclay's personality—or, to be both more accurate and vaguer, his entirely unusual *way of being*:

> *Barc is a nonmaterial guy in his manner of dress, his car, his beliefs— he's such a "common man." I know a lot of wealthy people through my work as a lawyer, and as a board member of the San Francisco Museum of Modern Art and other charitable causes, but I've never known anyone like Barclay who cares so little about money, per se, who just cares so deeply about helping people out without taking credit.*

Nellis goes on to comment on how unusual it is to find a businessperson as successful as Barclay who does not complain about taxes, does not appear to believe in any political labels, who is not ideological except in his core belief that people of advantage have a bedrock responsibility to do everything possible to help the disadvantaged. *Barclay fits the great American myth of the self-made man, yet his success has led him to an overwhelming concern for the underprivileged. He leads by example, cajoling people into doing "what's right," to lift them up as they help others.* Nellis's description of Barclay as a certain kind of *common man,* entirely uninterested in the society beat, conjures a picture of a person both archaic and of the present—of presence, itself.

In magnitude, it is Barclay and Sharon's capital contributions to the museum project that are most visible; but Barc was also instrumental in helping alter the underlying mission of one of the key cultural institutions of a great public university. Situated at the exact transitional point where the university and the meleé of Berkeley's downtown are conjoined, the museum's new physical location makes manifest a set of commitments to intertwine the work of the "academy" with the needs of the community. For Barclay, this belief in an "open" university devoted to access as well as excellence, was at the heart of his and Sharon's UC Berkeley giving across decades and departments.

With the decision to move BAMPFA downtown, a whole new audience for its offerings was created. Instead of being isolated on the UC Berkeley campus, the museum and film archive now anchor the outer edge of the city of Berkeley's Arts District, are only three blocks from Berkeley High School, and are accessible to elementary school children and others from around the San Francisco Bay Area because of the building's proximity to BART. In the eyes of Larry Rinder, Director of BAMPFA, Barc's *most important legacy* was the broadening of the museum's mission to allow a focus on K-12 audiences.

This form of community outreach aligned with Barc's view that one of the most essential roles that art can play is as a catalyst for children's cognitive development. Indeed, the effect of art on the brains of very young children was a subject that had preoccupied Barc since the first days he became interested in psychology during the sixties. As he became increasingly involved in Girls Inc. during the nineties, his fascination with the arts' effect on cognition grew into conviction, a baseline belief that he communicated very directly to Rinder, and, undoubtedly, to others involved in carrying out BAMPFA's mission.

> *Barc felt that art is a very important catalyst for stimulating creative intelligence and cognitive capacity in young people (the younger the better), and that this is one the most important roles of art in society. He quotes studies that show that the cognitive capacities of very young*

children—kindergarten age or maybe even younger—are improved when they have an opportunity to interact with art and that such exposure can help them do better in math and science and just about everything. (Larry Rinder)

This conviction appears to have made a big impression on Rinder, who, while dean of CCA between 2004 and 2008, says he also read studies claiming that exposure to art can have a measurable effect on learning for young children through college-age students. Yet making these educational theories a central part of BAMPFA's mission was a shift Rinder attributes directly to Barclay's influence: *I believe that even if we hadn't moved downtown, even if we had stayed in the old location, we would have developed in this new direction because of Barc's conviction, which I've come to believe also. I wouldn't have necessarily gone down that path, though, if I hadn't been exposed to his passion for that point of view.*

In keeping with this belief that art should be central rather than peripheral to education, Rinder explains that the museum has run pilot programs with Barc's beloved Girls Inc., as well as with over six hundred second and third grade school children from the Berkeley and Oakland public school system doing participatory tours of museum exhibits combined with art-making workshops. Though originally the museum had no trained staff for conducting these programs, since opening the new facility they have hired a full-time staff person to support the museum's expanded mission *to lead the development and implementation of BAMPFA-linked programs for K-12 schools, families, and youth.*[16] This full-time staff person is supported on an ongoing basis out of the $2.5 million endowment established by Barclay and Sharon and earmarked for these purposes, while a part-time assistant for the museum outreach programs has been funded out of additional contributions by other donors. In both a financial and "exemplary" sense, this support model reflects Barc and Sharon's interest in using their money to expand and experiment while also providing a solid core around which other donors can cluster and contribute.

Like Cissie Swig, Robert Birgeneau, and Noel Nellis, Larry Rinder had a chance to observe Barclay up close during the long march to get the new museum built. This involved being exposed viscerally to the full impact of Barc's personality and principles. Rinder's comments are telling regarding the indivisible nature of Barc's beliefs and the particular management and leadership style that made them concrete: *Barc has given the institution a sense of social purpose, along with his passion, and his fundamental belief in the value of art and of museums in society. I think it's something that we all—the staff and the board—believe, but Barc was able to articulate it and bring it to the fore in a way that was very helpful and profound.…*Aware that Barc still had a leadership role at Simpson Manufacturing during most of the period from 2008 to 2014, and that he was concurrently serving on other boards and projects at the university and elsewhere throughout the difficult gestation of the new BAMPFA, Rinder marvels at Barc's capacity to focus and the essential "economy" of his participation, something for which Birgeneau was also acutely grateful.

> *When Barc is present, one does not get the feeling that he is diffused. He is very present. I think he is very efficient and economical with his time and his attention, so he does not like to attend meetings where he's not being useful. He doesn't waste time. He's very focused. He won't attend a meeting unless he knows that there's a specific reason why he personally should be there. I think he's able to serve on these multiple boards because he takes care not to waste his time.*

This capacity to be present also appeared to shape what Rinder felt to be a close relationship between himself and Barc:

> *He [was] a fantastic friend to the museum and very approachable and supportive of me personally as the director. I knew I could call him at any time for advice or support. As someone who reported to him in a way, I gained a direct sense of his leadership philosophy, which was based on the goal of finding people whom he believed in and then giving them all the support that he possibly could.*

Whether he knew it or not, Rinder here enunciates one of the core principles that Barc had pursued in building Simpson Manufacturing, a capacity to respect and support his employees and colleagues as a way of encouraging personal success as well as that of the company at large. This instinctive, yet intentional *giving of power to others* is a rare quality of the very best leaders. When combined with a certain kind of moral authority and charisma, this brand of leadership moves and compels rather than coerces. A keen observer, Rinder is eloquent on the subject of Barclay's special powers of delivery and persuasion:

> Barc has great timing. He doesn't talk a lot at board meetings, but there'll be moments when people are maybe feeling a little bit beaten down by the situation or the budgetary or political issues, and Barc will speak up and say something that is very powerful about the importance of art in society, and it will inspire people to keep going. I've seen him do that on several occasions, and when he talks, people listen. He's a powerful voice, particularly on the board. People have tremendous respect for him, and he has a way of leading, just in a very modest way.

Like a veteran actor—in both the theatrical meaning of the word and in the sense of one who takes action—Barc picked his moments, using moral force and silence in equal measure. He understood, as he always had, that the source of power springs from conviction, transparency, and tenacity. He didn't need to dominate, but he couldn't help but lead.

The Simpson Center for Student-Athlete High Performance[17] (The Simpson Center)

> I thought, "This is astounding." I had just heard him make that $25 million commitment to the art museum, and now he was making an additional, similar commitment to athletics. I thought to myself, this man really understands the breadth of activities at the university and why each one is important for a particular reason, making Berkeley the great place it is.
>
> —Robert Birgeneau

BARCLAY HAD BEEN WATCHING the Bears play football in or near the venerable California Memorial Stadium since Tightwad Hill days. He was an avid fan. Following the Loma Prieta earthquake, the stadium, like the museum, was identified as needing major structural, seismic retrofit. The master plan that emerged from this decision called for the upgrading of existing training facilities for athletes and expansion of office space for athletic staff members in addition to the necessary seismic shoring up of the old stadium. However, an early decision to preserve the original perimeter wall of Memorial Stadium made the related goal of improving student training and staff office facilities largely impossible. Identified early on, this key space limitation led planners to consider the addition of a new building on the western flank of the stadium, ultimately to be called the Simpson Center for Student-Athlete High Performance.

Going back to 1965, Barclay had been providing annual gifts and program support for UC Berkeley men's and women's sports programs, including endowment funds, totaling $1.4 million (1992–2002) to support tutoring and academic advising for student athletes. When the need to do a substantial seismic renovation of the stadium emerged as a university priority, Barc and Sharon made an additional pledge of $25 million (2004–2005) to assist with the retrofit. Ultimately, this funding helped make possible the construction of the expanded office space and state-of-the-art student athlete training and tutoring facility adjacent to the stadium.

Made around the same time that Barclay was making a series of significant grants to BAMPFA, the gift to UC Berkeley Athletics involved a reconsideration of Barc and Sharon's decision to focus the vast majority of their giving on the education of low-income children and on the arts, especially where these areas of focus could be brought together. Initially, it felt like a stretch to Barc to include a high-performance student athletic center in the mix of his and Sharon's philanthropic priorities.

According to Sandy Barbour, then-Director of Intercollegiate Athletics at the University (2004–2014; see bio), and Chancellor Robert Birgeneau, it took strong encouragement from Barc's oldest son, John, to make Barclay consider moving beyond his precisely defined philanthropic goals into the new territory presented by the university's desire to build a center for elite athletes. Barbour says that the first time she met Barc, he described an important conversation he had had with John, who was then provost at UC Santa Cruz, later to become president of the State University of New York at Buffalo: *Dad, you know, if you want Cal to be great, you need to support intercollegiate athletics because that can be a vehicle to promote its comprehensive excellence to the rest of the country and the world.* Barclay explained to Barbour that it was during this conversation that he came to fully realize the importance of strong athletic programs to the overall commitments of a public university and particularly for its fundraising capabilities.

Barclay was also swayed by the emphasis UC Berkeley puts on ensuring strong academic performance among its student athletes, providing them with major support systems aimed at guaranteeing that athletic achievement not eclipse a commitment to academics. Since the high-performance center would make recruiting the best of the best easier, it became increasingly clear to Barc how the athletic piece fit in with his deep interest in the myriad ways of bringing education to young people. *So, that really got Barc thinking about how supporting athletics could help the greater good of his beloved Cal. He came to understand that athletic contests—whether viewed by 65–75,000 people in the stands or countless other thousands viewing on TV—could offer a way to bring honor to Berkeley, to make a football game the stage for celebrating Berkeley's latest nobel laureate* (Sandy Barbour).

Having made up his mind, Barc went directly to Birgeneau to make his expanded, foundational gift of $25 million. For Birgeneau, this additional major pledge, coming on the heels of the millions already donated to the new museum, revealed something very important about Barc's capacity to understand the big picture and not just his own special passions.

As Barbour observed, the Simpson Center is a *huge building, but mostly hidden so that you don't feel its massiveness.* Designed by HNTB Architects and Studios Architecture, with the crucial structural engineering handled by Forell-Elsesser, the ingenious architectural strategy for the new facility made it a welcoming entrance to the retrofitted stadium rather than a clumsy impediment:

> *"The beauty of the design is that it maximizes views of the stadium and keeps that as the architectural focus....A key objective of the design was to better connect the whole stadium area with the campus and the city [and] to ensure the athletic center wouldn't obstruct views from the former to the latter."* (Berkelyside article author, Tracey Taylor, quoting Bob Milano, Assistant Athletic Director at UC Berkeley)[18]

Though the design was, indeed, sensitive to preserving the existing street scape, it nevertheless ran into a classic Berkeley-style protest action, which was stirred into being by the revelation that construction of the stadium and high-performance center were to result in the removal of over seventy-eight trees. Scheduled to break ground in 2007, the start of the project was held up until 2009 because of a twenty-one-month dispute with tree advocates, including a number of faithful protesters who logged hours, days, and months sitting in the doomed trees in defiance of chain saw and bulldozer alike. According to Tracey Taylor, "The trees in question were finally cut down in September 2008. The university has planted three new trees for every one it removed." Taylor goes on to explain that the roof of the new Simpson Center will consist of a "two-acre grand plaza, a spot she says formerly played host to a parking lot and a chain-link fence." Again, quoting Milano: "A number of trees have been planted into the 'ground' of the roof plaza, not an easy feat, and achieved thanks to ingenious engineering and the vision of landscape architect firm Olin Partnership. The plaza and open space give the project a human scale."[19] As a space for replacement trees within an open-air pavilion, the roof garden on top of the Simpson Center—known as the Lisa and Douglas Goldman Plaza—cleverly doubles as a ticketed area for the Memorial Stadium on game days, subtle proof that opportunity can lurk at the heart of controversy.

In fall 2011, nearly the entire Simpson family showed up for the dedication of the Simpson Center, which also attracted a wide range of Berkeley students, professors, administrators, and other university-linked celebrities eager to honor Barc and Sharon for their extraordinary generosity to the entire UC Berkeley community. Stating that the Simpson Center will have *a huge impact on this and future generations of UC Berkeley student athletes…leading to the promotion of the greatness of the entire university*, Sandy Barbour wryly remembers the way that Barc deflected such praise in his welcoming speech at the dedication event. Rather than bask in the glory of his and Sharon's donation, he shifted the focus to what he considered to be a real form of generosity: *the schoolteacher in Oakland who goes into their own pocket and buys pencils and erasers and paper and paint and supplies for their students, even when they can't afford to.*

Chapter 27
Girls Inc. of Alameda County, California
(Girls Inc.): Transformational Giving

Pat Loomes was such a pistol that I couldn't resist getting tangled up with her.

—Barclay

For Barc, it's always about the people, not just the project.

—Joseph Di Prisco

*I did tours of the San Leandro facility for Girls Inc. maybe once a year. Barc would
bring sometimes twenty-five or thirty girls...a lot from the Oakland area, many
were African American. Many had never seen someone like me in a position like
that. You could tell they were in awe of the facility and the scope of what we were
doing. It was like, "I see this Black man in charge of all of these people.
He's working for this company. Wow."*

—David MacDonald, SST

IN 1994, TWO "NEIGHBORS" in rough-hewn San Leandro met each other, formed an unlikely bond, and altered each other's lives—and the lives of many others in the process. The improbable match was between a successful businessman—who was in the same year to take the company he had built from scratch onto the New York Stock Exchange—and an Irish immigrant with a colorful past and present running a nonprofit storefront organization for low-income girls. Their mutual recognition across an apparently great divide was nearly instantaneous.

In 1977, Pat Loomes (First Executive Director of Girls Inc. of Alameda County; see bio) became director of a Girls Club based in San Leandro, California, that had come into being in 1958 with twenty girls, who met after school to learn the crucial skills of the day—sewing, cooking, and typing.

Girls clubs of this kind had emerged in New England in 1864 in the aftershock of the Civil War and during the upheavals brought on by the Industrial Revolution. In the 1990s all such US-based clubs changed their name to Girls Inc., which continues on to this day as a national organization with affiliate members across the country.

When Pat took over the San Leandro Girls Club, it was an organization with five staff members and a total annual budget of around $160,000. In the early nineties, what is now called Girls Inc. of Alameda County initiated a capital campaign to raise funds for the expansion of its existing facilities in a converted warehouse in San Leandro. A member of Pat's small staff who had been thumbing her way through the yellow pages suggested that they send their fundraising letter to Barclay Simpson, who had a factory in San Leandro and who might therefore demonstrate neighborliness through making a tax-deductible, financial contribution to a local nonprofit. *Who knows*, she said, *we might get lucky.* This suggestion came at a time when SST was entering its breakout transition into a global, powerhouse enterprise. Pat had never heard of Barclay Simpson but decided to follow her staff's advice and included him on the list they were compiling for the capital campaign. The letter she drafted explained to Barc and other potential donors the function of Girls Inc. along with the—at that time—rather arcane theory behind promoting the education of girls.

When Barc received Pat's fundraising letter, he'd never heard of Girls Inc. But something about the letter caught his attention. A few days after she had affixed the stamp to the solicitation, Pat got a personal phone call from Barclay: *I need to come see you people.*

Not very well-versed in the subtle arts of fundraising, Pat was taken aback, asking her development staff, *Now what do we do?* They envisioned a step-by-step process involving a slow introduction to show him what they were doing, then time to let the relationship develop, with the hope that he'd eventually want to donate. When Barclay showed up for their first meeting, they tried to follow this measured game plan by taking him on a tour of the organization's 13,500-square-foot threadbare warehouse while Pat spoke passionately about what they were attempting to accomplish. After about ten minutes, while she was still in the throes of explanation, Barc turned to her and said, *So, how much do you want?* Pat was stopped in her tracks. She didn't have a clue. Stumbling for an answer, she told the truth: *Well, you know, Mr. Simpson, we're just cultivating you right now.* He replied, *I know this fundraising business.* By this time, he was already a veteran of the CCA, the Haas Business School, and the UC Berkeley Museum boards. *How much do you want?* Flustered, Pat blurted, *$10,000 for our teenage program.* Barc responded, *Okay.* Pat thinks, *Oh, God, just like that.* Then he left. But he stayed in touch. According to Loomes:

> He obviously liked us, and to be honest, he liked me, and that always
> helps....It was some kind of chemistry. One of the things he liked about
> me was that I had a story. You know, I'm Irish, an immigrant, I'd been
> adopted, and I am a lesbian. He loved all of that. He loved difference.
> He loved the story, and he liked the work.

Apart from Pat's own story, Barc bought the narrative about why to invest in girls. In his words:

> It's because they mature more quickly than boys—brains and
> emotions—so you can make an imprint on them at an earlier age,
> because they are the ones who can make a conscious decision about
> when or if to have children and because the ones that do have children
> are the primary educators of the next generation.

It all made sense to Barc, the rationale as well as the chemistry with Pat Loomes. As it turned out, this concept and chemistry was destined to fuel major life changes for many low-income girls over the next decades.

Soon Barc began to fund Girls Inc. at a higher level, eventually getting to about $100,000 per year. Initially, he wasn't very interested in funding an expansion of the Girls Inc. facilities, though he had been brought in through a capital campaign solicitation. His interest, according to Pat, was in *direct service.* Among the programs that caught and held Barc's attention was the one called GIRLSmart (Science, Math, and Relevant Technology) for upper elementary school girls, which sought to combat the stereotype that girls were neither good at nor interested in science and math.

This emphasis on the traditionally "male" realms of study is in addition to the fundamental mentoring programs for middle through high school girls designed to increase the odds that they graduate from high school and go on to college. Besides the emphasis on doing well scholastically, the overall Girls Inc. program was focused on providing an emotionally safe and positive environment in which the girls bond with the adults mentoring them and with each other. In part because it was girls only, Girls Inc. is able to provide a place where it is possible to have open conversations about typical and not so typical coming of age issues—sex, peer pressure, drugs, and violence inside and outside of the home. The core goal of the program was centered on building self-confidence, transcending traditional gender stereotypes, and giving the girls a sense of how to take and exercise willpower in their own lives.

This broad, emotionally charged undertaking is expressed in the enduring motto and mantra of the organization: "Inspire girls to be strong, smart, and bold"[20]—*strong* through healthy living, *smart* through education, and *bold* through financial independence. The hope behind the motto is that in building these characteristics, girls will turn into women who can steer their own lives effectively, becoming agents of change, thus creating a ripple effect. The story of a fourteen-year-old girl who joined Girls Inc. in 1992 is one among many that puts a face to the motto.

Two years before Barc's fateful first meeting with Pat, Monica Manriquez had made a conscious decision to become a member of Girls Inc. She had known about the organization for years, but because her grades were excellent, she hadn't been one of the at-risk students recommended by teachers for their programs. Having always wanted to be part of the organization, she decided to join when she entered San Leandro High School, located directly across the street from the Girls Inc. warehouse.

> *I got involved because it gave me a platform to have some conversations I wasn't having anywhere else. I already had a lens for social justice and could see the unfair tracking that was taking place in school. I had witnessed a few instances of teachers not encouraging certain students to go on the path for higher education. I was one of two people of color out of a whole classroom of white and Asian AP students, so it was very blatant, very obvious. The expectation at Girls Inc. was that we were going to go to college and Girls Inc. offered a lot of opportunities and resources. I remember one of the group leaders had us meet other Latina professionals—a diverse group of women in careers I had never heard of.*

When it came time to apply to college, Monica's first choice was UC Berkeley, where she was accepted. She was elated but anxious: *I was debating* whether to even go or not. *I wasn't sure my family could afford it, plus it was such a huge step.* She confided this to her group leader at Girls Inc., who one day got permission to pull Monica out of class to make her a proposal. The group leader asked her if she was interested in a scholarship through Girls Inc. to be funded by a Mr. Simpson. This was in 1995:

> *I met Mr. Simpson in the spring during the application process. He told me to call him Barclay, but I told him I couldn't; I felt very disrespectful…. He took a risk in giving me the scholarship. I'm sure there were other candidates with higher GPAs. He sensed that I definitely needed the mentorship and the advice, and I always welcomed it. I had deep, deep respect for Mr. Simpson.*

When Barc suggested that she take an accounting course—not with the idea that she would become an accountant, but, as he told her, *it's part of becoming savvy about finances and will make you more independent,* she followed his advice. *With that venturing out, with that little push, I ended up taking economics as well and fell in love with it. The micro was fun, but the macro of what happens from our government all the way to our pockets was fascinating. It's the study of people.*

Also in 1995, Barc went to Pat Loomes and said he'd been doing a lot of reading on how learning takes place most effectively. In the course of this study, he had become convinced by the theory that if you can *get to children between zero and five,* you can make a huge difference in how they do in school, whether they go to college, and to how they perform in their work life. He had decided it was of critical importance to get young girls reading as soon as possible and asked what could be done at Girls Inc. to lower the age at which girls were recruited into the program. Pat told him most of their programs started at six, that they certainly could start programs at four and a half, maybe five years old—but that would be it.

By 1997, she had come up with a framework that came to be called GIRLStart—a literacy program aimed at girls from kindergarten to third grade, carried out after school every day. According to Pat, *We went in utterly naively,* basing the program on the premise that if you read to a child for twenty minutes every day, they would learn to read. *So, we thought we could do that. Anybody could do that.* They dove in, sending staff to a few schools in San Leandro before expanding into Oakland. In at least one of the pilot schools, the administration brought in someone to run a similar twenty-minute-a-day after-school reading program for young boys. But soon Pat came to realize that teaching reading, and *particularly teaching reading to low-income students and second language learners,* is *rocket science.* After the first year of the GIRLStart program, they realized they had to develop a much more intensive two-hour-a-day literacy program to replace the simpler concept of twenty minutes of reading after school. With the help of some outside consultants, they ended up writing their own curriculum.

Barc visited a few classrooms to see the program in action. According to Pat, he loved what he saw because the focus was on very young children—the population he was increasingly determined to reach. Believing that if you can't read and write, you're never going to succeed, he was now funding Girls Inc. at around $200,000 to $300,000 a year. Barc remembers with pleasure a prime example of the success of the GIRLStart program:

> *Among the first schools we took the program to was the Lockwood School in Oakland....When we put our program in after school, 4 percent of the kids read at grade level. We started the after-school program with thirty girls. Of course, we lost a bunch of them on the way, but we had fifteen who finished and got through to the second grade, still doing the program after school, and every single one read at or above grade level. Every one. If you can't read, you can't do anything. So, this is where we started.*

Meanwhile, Barc stayed very much in touch with Monica Manriquez throughout her years at Cal. She worked hard and often found the pressure enormous:

> *It was a very scary time for me. Cal is a huge institution and I think I had a fear of failing. Mr. Simpson often checked in to make sure I was okay. I think we had a personal connection. We met for either lunch or coffee every so often, sometimes at Café Strada, sometimes in Pleasanton. There were times I was tired and wanted to quit school, but I hung in there because of the support of Mr. Simpson and Girls Inc. Every time I met with him, he fed me positive energy and made me feel the sky's the limit; in fact, I flourished. I don't know if he saw something in me or if it was because he believed in me that I became what he saw.*

When Monica graduated from UC Berkeley, she was asked to join the board of directors of Girls Inc., her tenure lasting about four years until she had her first child. More recently she served a second term but had to resign again due to heavy demands at work, now raising two children and feeling unable to give the board her all. Following graduation from UC Berkeley, she had gotten a job in Silicon Valley where, during a number of years, she worked in a variety of high-powered, high-tech jobs in such roles as public auditor, securities and exchange advisor, and revenue analyst. The work was fast-paced and well-paid, but after five years she realized she was dissatisfied. She decided to leave the financial field and turn to education, which she felt had always been her calling. *It was my soul.*

Looking back, she wouldn't trade the circuitous route she took that ultimately returned her to her center. Studying economics gave her an intellectual base that applied to many aspects of her life as well as imbued her, she felt, with valuable leadership skills. She recognized that the decision to switch fields was radical, and she wanted Barc's blessing:

> *Not that I felt he wouldn't be understanding, but here was this great man and I didn't want to let him down. There was a lot of prestige working in finance in Silicon Valley. When I told him I wanted to go into education, he was the most supportive of anyone. Other people asked if I was serious and couldn't believe I was okay taking a major pay cut. He didn't question it. He told me, "There are kids out there who need what you have to give...." He also said, "You're still the best investment I ever made."*

With that emotional support, she was able to take the leap:

> *I've just taken off in education. I have a strong connection with my students and their parents. There's a deep reason I'm in education and a lot of it comes from the relationship I had with Mr. Simpson. What he gave me is what carried me through UC Berkeley and it's the same mindset I pass on to my students—find someone to believe in you.*

～

In 2003, Pat Loomes set out to develop a five-year strategic plan for Girls Inc. focused on how to grow individual programs as well as the institution at large, detailing the kind of money needed to implement the stated goals. By this point, there was a lot of interest in the GIRLStart program, including from funders who could see direct cause and effect at work in the program's very specific objective of having girls read at grade-level by the third grade. In figuring out how to grow and build on this program, Pat came up with a concept which she called a *continuum of service* in which Girls Inc. would begin working with girls on literacy in kindergarten and provide them with a variety of targeted programs all the way through to eighteen. From basic literacy, they would expand into math, science, and technology, inter-mingling intellectual, physical, and emotional skills training along the way. It was a vision of comprehensive learning, aimed at encouraging the girls to place their sights on higher education and to develop the emotional and intellectual base needed to make a leap from constricted opportunity to achievable possibility. Pat estimated that to realize these ambitions she needed to move from piecemeal funding to a new budgetary level of financing in the approximate range of an additional $10 million over five years. But to raise that kind of money, she knew she would have to institute reliable methods of program evaluation that would demonstrate concrete *returns on investment* to potential funders.

To get the ball rolling, the Girls Inc. development director at the time, Judy Glenn, suggested Pat start by asking Barclay to give $35,000 to conduct the evaluation. *Oh, dear...*Pat recounts, *Barc gives us all this money, and I'm going to nickel and dime him for $35,000....*She insisted that Judy go with her to make the plea. They bundled up the Five-Year Strategic Plan, with its colorful graphs, illustrations, and figures, and made their way out to Simpson Manufacturing's shiny new office complex in Pleasanton. With pencil poised, Barc was turning the report pages when Pat burst out, *So, if you could give us $35,000, that would be extremely helpful so we can do an evaluation.*

At that, he put his pencil down, looked Pat in the eye, and said, *I tell you what. I'll give you the $10 million.* Pat says she stared at him open-mouthed, paralyzed. A voice inside her head wanted to say, *But I was only asking for $35,000,* but there was another voice shouting over the first, *Don't say that!* Actually, she was incapable of saying anything. She turned and looked at Judy, who had tears rolling down her face but who managed to say, *Thank you, Barc; thank you so much.* Barc responded, *No, I need to thank you. This is the work I want done, you're doing it, and you're doing it very well. I'll give you up* *to $2 million a year for five years to carry out this expanded plan. If you don't spend it, then you don't get it.*

*But we did spend the $10 million....It was unbelievable to an organization like ours to have somebody make such a gift. It made a huge difference. But it also scared the hell out of me....*Pat realized she was suddenly in a whole new game, that she needed to figure out how to get the promised work done, which would involve growing the organization significantly. At that stage, Barc's contributions accounted for 60 percent of the Girls Inc. total budget; she understood that the stability and long-term sustainability of the organization depended on expanding its donor base. *Okay, we've got to work, she thought, and we did.*

Barc's next and continuing major contribution to Girls Inc. was *bringing his friends in*, helping Pat build a powerful advisory board to guide the organization and assist the staff with fundraising. He became an evangelist for Girls Inc., taking a small, hard-scrabble girls' club into the big time. As was true of Cal, he loved to talk about Girls Inc., bringing in people that the organization would never otherwise have had access to and getting them fired up about the work. According to Pat, *The buzz was tremendous. Barc put us on the map. We became his favorite charity—it really made all the difference.* At one point, the Girls Inc. Advisory Board numbered eighty. Although some eventually left because it just wasn't their cause, a solid core of forty stayed through many years. Among them and their contacts, there were a lot of sizable donors—nothing in the same league as Barc and Sharon, but people who gave $25,000, $40,000, $50,000 a year. In addition, Sharon and Barc opened their home in Orinda for regular Girls Inc. fundraising events. In 2010, the Clinton Global Initiative recognized Girls Inc. of Alameda County for its "Commitments to Empower Girls and Women."[21]

Throughout those years, Pat and Barc developed a close relationship. Pat describes how they would get together for lunch every few months at the cheap Mexican place across the street from Girls Inc. or at Barc's office in the Lafayette gallery.

What was wonderful about Barc, you could say anything to him. There was no sense of noblesse oblige or anything like that. It was like a partnership. He'd say to me, "You're doing the work and all I'm doing is writing the check. And my greatest joy right now is writing these checks," and it was, you could tell....He liked my strange story, that I was an immigrant, had had to be tough...and he had lots of interesting ones of his own, about business, about BART and politics, about the gallery they ran....He was just extraordinary and to be a businessman and to have that kind of heart and that kind of consciousness is rare.

It was a great partnership for both of them. In 2007, Pat retired form the organization after a full thirty years as its director—or at least she thought she was retiring. As part of her departing responsibilities, she helped with the recruitment and selection of another remarkable woman, named Linda Boessenecker (CEO of Girls Inc. of Alameda County, 2007–2016; see bio), who was to lead the organization for the following eight-plus years. In the course of giving Linda some background on the enterprise and its many personalities, Pat remembers joking with her as she described the special chemistry she and Barclay had always had: *Linda, it's going to be hard for you: married, white, native born—you'll have to think of something.*

But it turned out that Barclay wasn't ready to let Pat Loomes off the hook after a mere thirty years. In an attempt to help Linda find her footing in the first few weeks on the job, Pat accompanied her on a few of Linda's early meetings with Barclay. During one of these, Barc turned to Pat and said, *Okay, now that you're retired, how would you like to take the GIRLStart program across the country?* Surprised, Pat nevertheless started immediately to imagine taking their creation on the road: *In some ways, I'm an entrepreneur and as nutty as he is.* She looked up at him and said, *Oh, okay. I'll do that,* although neither of them had a clue how to pull this off. Barc's daughter, Jeannie Simpson, joined the effort, making the case to Barc that maybe they should focus the new initiative on boys and girls, not simply girls. But Barc was, by now, adamant about the pro-girl rationale: *I get more bang for my buck with girls.* In spite of Jeannie's arguments, he wouldn't budge. Five years later, Pat and Jeannie had set up girls' after-school literacy programs in a number of locations across the country, including in New Hampshire; Jacksonville, Florida; Omaha, Nebraska; Brooklyn; New York City; San Rafael, and San Francisco, California.

When Pat Loomes retired from Girls Inc. in 2007 and passed the directorship to Linda Boessenecker, the organization had grown from five to eighty staff members, with an annual operating budget that had increased from $160,000 to $5.4 million. With the rundown building in San Leandro bursting at the seams and an ever-increasing demand for programs for more and more girls, Girls Inc. launched a capital campaign to fund new facilities. In late May of 2011, Barc and Sharon made a $2 million contribution that helped kick off a fundraising effort that ultimately resulted in attracting $11.4 million in donations for establishing a new home for the program. In July 2012, Girls Inc. purchased the old East Bay Water Company's 1919 building in the heart of Oakland's distinctive, early twentieth-century historic district.[22] Beyond committing to the restoration and repurposing of an architecturally noteworthy building, Girls Inc. was also now able to build an important presence in the heart of the East Bay, steps away from mass transit and a network of public schools and multiracial, low-income communities. Anne Phillips, Principal of Anne Phillips Architecture, was hired to draw up the plans with ongoing input from the girls then enrolled in Girls Inc. programs to ensure that form and function would be mutually reinforcing. Renovations on the building began in July of 2012.

The final design of the expanded facility was, according to Linda Boessenecker, a direct reflection of the important needs brought to the fore by the girls. Chief among these was their desire for a space large enough for them to involve their families in Girls Inc. activities:

> One of the ideas behind the design of the new building was to have a large area where families could come together....Our girls have said part of the importance of having their parents involved with us is if you're a first-generation young woman and your parents are new here, trying to explain to them why you should be taking the PSAT and getting ready for college is difficult without some help.

The girls also asked for a teaching kitchen where they could learn to cook. So, we also incorporated that into the final design, because health and nutrition are huge issues for families and young women (Linda Boessenecker). Other important features are a library, gym with state-of-the-art exercise machines and free weights, yoga center, and an internet café. These top-of-the-line facilities are a concrete representation of Girls Inc.'s concern with physical and mental health and their interdependence. The age-old principle of "a healthy mind in a healthy body" is a crucial element in this approach, designed to get at the subtle interactions between the somatic and the psychological. As part of its emphasis on physical practice, Girls Inc. designs field trips that offer the girls experiences—such as sailing, surfing, and camping—that provide a set of mental, emotional, and physical challenges that they may never have imagined meeting in their own lives.

On October 12, 2013, in the new building's soaring double-story lobby and internal courtyard, people from all over the Bay Area gathered to celebrate the grand opening of the Simpson Center for Girls. The beautiful, old, tiered ceiling had been revealed from under a drop ceiling, and other architectural details were preserved to honor the past while new design elements and spaces give the restored building a modern feel, emphasizing immediacy and the future.

The first floor has two classrooms, the "Girls' Space"—a large, sunny, comfortable room with round tables, couches, and large windows onto the street—and the "Learning Center"—a smaller room with modular rectangular tables. In addition, there is a courtyard where girls gather upon coming into the center as they check in at the front desk. The second floor includes an atrium overlooking the first-floor courtyard. It houses the staff kitchen, the mailroom, and the boardroom, which transforms into two classrooms, and an open desk space.

Through its architecture, the building itself provides tangible evidence of the girls' importance, collectively and individually—a concrete message that there's a larger, outside world accessible to them, and that they are free to dream their own dreams into being.

⌒

REFLECTING ON BARC'S SEMINAL contributions to the creation of Girls Inc. in its current, much-expanded form, Linda Boessenecker emphasizes the extraordinary importance of his early and continuing conviction that literacy must be at the heart of the organization's mission—and that getting girls involved early is the key to achieving success. The dark corollary to this was his belief that illiteracy often engenders a vicious cycle of poverty. *Barc really, truly saw the impact of literacy on the future of girls. He understood that there's a huge link between being able to read at grade-level in the third grade and future success in school* (Linda Boessenecker). Like Barc, Linda believes that the inverse is also true, that *girls who have low literacy rates engage in more risky behavior. It really comes down to self-confidence and self-esteem.*

Barc also bought into the argument that by touching a girl's life, Girls Inc. could touch her community, making larger changes possible, including those involving the next generation. According to Boessenecker, there is a lot of current research—especially involving underdeveloped countries—that to change a culture, it is essential to educate girls. Suggesting that the US also has lots of under-resourced communities, Linda says it is time for the country at large to learn from this research. *Women are the early educators*, says Linda, recounting a telling comment from one of the Girls Inc. young women: *Girls Inc. not only helped me succeed in my own dreams, but now I know what could be different for my three-year-old son, what I can dream for him.*

Like Pat Loomes, Linda describes Barclay as having been an extraordinarily important advocate for Girls Inc. who—in addition to making substantial annual contributions—also continued to promote its programs to the important donor class to which he and Sharon had access. As had been true in his relationships with Pat and staff in other institutions he backed, Linda found him to be a ready and key source of counsel in difficult times. When the Great Recession hit, she remembers seeking him out repeatedly for advice and moral support, his shrewd business sense and ability to take the long view providing a rare kind of solace. *We were getting ready to go into this capital campaign. What did he think? Did he think I should go forward? He's a good advisor because he's accessible, clear, and understands business.* Linda's description of this full-service support model recalls Jonathan Moscone's comments about his own experiences with Barc and Sharon's special kind of philanthropy when he was artistic director of Cal Shakes: *When you have been branded as an organization that matters to the Simpsons, that means a lot, and they put their money where their mouth is. But they don't do that and say, "Now, you're on your own." They introduce you to people. They stand by you. They provide counsel. They care.*

～

THERE'S NO QUESTION THAT Girls Inc. and its executive leaders were striking exemplars of the Simpson brand. This was to prove true once again with the hiring in February of 2016 of the organization's third CEO, who—though she never met Barclay—is an extraordinary embodiment of his deepest beliefs in the power of education and personal will to help build a fairer world.

Born and raised in Oakland, Julayne Virgil (see bio) was the third generation of her family to live in the city. During the Great Migration,[23] her grandparents had moved from Louisiana when her mother was eighteen months old, establishing a new base for the family half a continent away from their southern home. Virgil grew up a few miles from the Girls Inc. warehouse in San Leandro, though the organization was never to figure in her own early development.

Not having had the opportunity herself to attend a four-year college, Julayne's mother nevertheless wished a larger world for her daughters. With this supporting vision, Virgil won a scholarship to University High School, one of San Francisco's most prestigious private academies, and was later admitted to the University of Pennsylvania, graduating cum laude with a bachelor's degree. Throughout this successful trajectory, Julayne remembers that she was, nevertheless, acutely aware of the gross *disparities in educational equity* suffered by many of her peers. Recounting how, together, she and her mother had to learn the arcane process of selecting and applying to college, Virgil emphasizes the multiple hurdles faced by children applying to college as the first member of their family to do so. There's a whole structure of expectation as well as information that is the birthright of some students, while others must cobble together the strange complex of emotional and practical decisions required with no precedents to guide them.

Following the signposts provided by her elite education, Julayne says that she quite naturally entered the private sector upon graduation, moving to New York City with all the attendant promise of prestige and high income. But, in the aftermath of 9/11, she switched her professional aspirations to the public sector, where she worked for several years until, in fall of 2005, Virgil enrolled in the Sol Price School of Public Policy at the University of Southern California, graduating with a master's degree in public administration. Her graduate school application essay focused on her desire to run a youth development organization in her hometown.

Following graduate school, Julayne was hired as the founding managing director of the Chicago office of a national nonprofit organization called Education Pioneers. After a few years in Chicago, Virgil took on a national rather than regional role within the organization, allowing her to move back to Oakland. One day, walking down Sixteenth Street near Broadway, Julayne happened to spy a newly renovated building named the Simpson Center for Girls. The encounter was unlikely at best—maybe, she muses, *uncanny or fated*.

She wanted to get involved immediately, but the timing wasn't right given her other professional obligations; however, a few years later, in 2015, when Girls Inc. advertised for a new CEO to replace Linda Boessenecker, who was retiring, Julayne felt she was fulfilling an important part of her *destiny*. Interviewed by fifteen board members, including Sharon Simpson, Virgil was hired as CEO of the now venerable organization, which celebrated its sixtieth year of operation in 2018.

From the start, Julayne viewed her mission as maintaining the spirit and programming that had put Girls Inc. on the map while at the same time building new business and technical *infrastructure* that would make it possible for the organization to meet new challenges and changing or evolving target populations. In honor of its sixtieth anniversary, Julayne launched an ambitious, three-year strategic plan (2018–2021) christened "Thriving Girls, Sustainable Futures." The key objectives of the plan included greater infusion of mental health services into programs; strengthening the focus on community leadership, college prep, and career planning; and shoring up the organization's core procedures in order to ensure ongoing operational strength.

In fiscal year 2020–21, Julayne Virgil reports that Girls Inc. now has a budget of $7.025 million, with a staff of approximately ninety. By 2020 (pre-COVID), Girls Inc. had outreach programs in over twenty schools and satellite centers throughout Alameda County, annually serving more than a thousand girls with hundreds of hours of programming for each girl. Unusual for its focus and its wide reach, Girls Inc. remains the only agency in the Bay Area offering such extensive programs aimed at the specific needs of girls. This is a far cry from the important but significantly more limited reach of the small educational program run by Pat Loomes when she first wrote a fundraising letter that landed on Barclay Simpson's desk in 1994. It is a testament to Barc and Pat's deep commitment and that of Linda Boessenecker and Julayne Virgil and all the fellow travelers incited by this remarkable gang of four that so much could have been accomplished in the intervening twenty-six years.

Currently, the population served by Girls Inc. includes an overwhelming majority of girls who identify as people of color, with approximately 39 percent identifying as Latina and roughly 30 percent as African American.

As of FY 2019–20, 44 percent of the girls served by their programs speak a language other than English at home and 90 percent are eligible for free and reduced-price lunches under federal and state programs.

Under Virgil's leadership, the "continuum of service" programming model first developed by Pat Loomes, with Barclay's support, and carried forward by Linda Boessenecker, is still at the heart of Girls Inc.'s daily practice. The organization's signature literacy program, GIRLStart, which focuses on *"essential reading, writing, speaking, and listening skills,"* currently serves approximately four hundred girls a year in K-3 grades in after-school programs administered at nine local area schools. Each year the students are tested by an outside evaluator using the standard *Dynamic Indicators of Basic Early Literacy Skills (DIBELS)* assessment tools, an evaluation process that has been crucial to Girls Inc.'s methods since the time of Pat Loomes. Recent results show GIRLStart particpants continuing to perform above grade level in relation to their peers in the Oakland Unified School District (OUSD). In addition to maintaining their after-school literacy programs, Girls Inc. has recently expanded its outreach by agreeing to house EMERGE, the Alameda County Office of Education's program for girls for whom the traditional school experience is not working. This new group of students attend school at Girls Inc. during the day and get PE credits for using the gym and yoga studio, and health credits for using the kitchen.

To Girls Inc.'s basic "continuum of service" model—with its focus on the interconnections between physical, psychological, and cognitive development—Virgil has recently added a new element called *trauma-informed programming*. This component is based on the premise that under-resourced communities often see severe forms of dislocation and distress among their members, stemming from such factors as inadequate housing, high unemployment among older family members, and violence inside and outside of the home. To respond to this and to deal more effectively with the daily disturbances many of their girls' experience, Girls Inc. has set up referral structures through which their girls—and their families—will have ready access to needed mental health support.

In addition to literacy and expanded mental health services, Julayne's strategic plan continues to place emphasis on STEM education, exposing students to a range of nontraditional careers for women, and on Girls Inc.'s fundamental goal of helping their girls to cross the big divide into higher education. Crucial to all of these are mentorship opportunities with women (and men), community and business leaders who may be able to open the girls' eyes to opportunities in the big world outside their neighborhoods. Drawing on the network of resources available through the current members of their advisory council, Girls Inc. attempts to identify special aspirations among the girls and to match them with professionals who can offer concrete assistance at critical moments, and/or provide organized mentoring or targeted internships. Such exposure offers the girls role models who have a range of struggles, tragedies, cautionary tales, and triumphs to share regarding careers and spheres of interest the girls may not have even known existed. Inspiration—which was always central to Barclay's form of philanthropy— remains a kinetic element in Girls Inc.'s daily practice.

Among Girls Inc.'s most important long-term commitments is the program that appears in Julayne's strategic plan as "College Access Now" (CAN). At present, approximately forty-five to sixty girls split between the eleventh and twelfth grades participate in these college preparation efforts. The process begins with thirty eleventh graders being selected by staff to undergo "an intensive school year and summer college readiness program that will provide college-bound girls and their families with vital information and resources to pursue their college dreams." Specifically, this involves furnishing them with SAT/ACT test skills training, information on a wide array of schools and financing options, trips to colleges, discussion of possible majors, and detailed assistance in meeting application requirements, including the shaping of entrance essays and the preparation of financial aid applications (FAFSA) in three languages.

Additionally, the program includes careful education of the girls' families as to why their child might aspire to continue their academic training. In the case of most of the girls in the CAN program, they will be the first in their families to pursue or achieve the goal of going on to college. This involves a cultural shift as well as a simple outlining of the actual steps required to leap across this major experience gap. As of spring 2020, 100 percent of the CAN program seniors won entrance to a post-secondary institution, while a majority of these are the first in their families to do so. The CAN results have held steady for the past five years.

As part of the 2018–2021 strategic plan, and in keeping with Barclay's emphasis on regular evaluation of outcomes, Julayne Virgil introduced an entirely new initiative focused on building an alumnae network aimed at capturing information on the long-term impacts on girls who have participated in Girls Inc. programs through the years including, particularly, the CAN graduates. The first of these alumnae surveys was conducted anonymously online from April to May 2018, using Qualtrics Survey Software, and was open to anyone who had participated in any Girls Inc. programs. The survey resulted in 111 total responses. In the section devoted to attendance at an institution of higher education or certificate program: "Ninety-two percent of all respondents either completed a post-secondary degree or certificate program (33 percent) or were currently enrolled in an educational institution (59 percent). Nine alumnae had completed a master's degree or MS in the areas of applied behavior analysis, writing, public policy, education, business administration, environmental science, geology, and educational leadership. Three respondents had obtained doctorates in clinical psychology, medicine, and pharmacology." Of those who had completed a post-secondary degree, 77 percent were working either full- or part-time. The college attendance and employment results of the survey are ones that Barc would have particularly loved.

A flesh and blood example of what these statistics mean in the life of a particular girl is captured in the story of Tayo Ogunmayin,[24] a Girls Inc. alumna who is now in her senior year at UC Davis, majoring in civil engineering. Tayo recounts that she entered Girls Inc. on the threshold of puberty, suffering from low self-esteem and with no confidence in her own will or capabilities. While in middle school, she attended a Girls Inc. presentation by a group of engineers, focused on how bridges are built. Until that moment, she says, she had never given any consideration to the web of bridges surrounding her home on the edge of San Francisco Bay. Although she knew she had always loved math and science as a kid, she had no clue how to build on that interest, nor did she have the confidence to try. In this regard, she speaks of how Girls Inc. afforded her a *safe* community in which she could experiment both emotionally and intellectually with a pile of jumbled feelings and thoughts. She speaks of being permitted to experience personal vulnerability without its attendant fears. Strikingly, she talks of learning the skills of *empathy and active listening* that made her able to express her own opinions and think those opinions were of value, while also listening to the opinions of others.

It was through a Girls Inc. summer internship that she came to realize that she had a *passion for engineering* and began to understand the skills required by different possible career paths. By the end of this experience, she knew she wanted to become a civil engineer. In pursuit of that goal, she speaks of being provided with the technical skills required in writing a résumé, practicing how to interview, learning how to seek a career that would best match her interests with her training. Perhaps most importantly, she was introduced to and worked with professional women pursuing careers similar to the one she was starting to be able to visualize for herself. These role models were crucial bulwarks against self-doubt when people would point out to her that she didn't resemble most of the people who went into civil engineering—by which they meant that there were few or no African Americans, or women, or both, in engineering positions. But she came armed; Girls Inc. had provided her with the vision and concrete tools to combat the obstacles to her believing in the possibility of her own success—including those coming from within her own family. Now, she says, no one could be prouder than her father in her achievements as she approaches the threshold of graduation from an elite university with a highly specialized degree.

Like that of Monica Manriquez, Tayo Ogunmayin's story demonstrates a level of commitment and tenacity that would reassure Barclay that Girls Inc. remains one of the very best of his investments.

Notes for Part VI

1 Arts Access School Time Program, DRAA. Through this program, DRAA provides free tickets and transportation throughout the year to more than 4,000 K-12 Contra Costa County students who live in underserved neighborhoods and whose schools are in districts that have coped with tough budget choices by reducing or entirely eliminating classroom arts programs. https://www.draa.org.

2 Artistic Engagement at Cal Shakes grew out of explorations of how theater, artists, and community members could be equal partners in discovering and sharing the profound stories of our times. https://www.calshakes.org.

3 https://www.simpsonpsbfund.org.

4 https://www.cca.edu.

5 Ibid.

6 https://www.calshakes.org.

7 As per the UC Berkeley Development office, a break-out of the Simpson's giving to CAL through 2016 includes the following highlights::

—Berkeley Art Museum and Pacific Film Archive—$77.3 M+ (1989–2016)

—BAMPFA—Center Street—$70M (2000–2014) (opened in 2016)

—Endowment for school and family outreach programs—$2.5M (April 2014)

—Regular gifts supporting annual, curatorial, and acquisition programs (beginning in 1989)

—Intercollegiate Athletics—$28.75M (1965–2014)

—Simpson Center for Student-Athlete High Performance—$25M (2004–2005) (opened in 2012)

—Endowment and program support for Student Athletic Study Center—$1.4M (1992–2002)

—Annual gifts and program support for men's and women's sports teams (beginning in 1965)

—Haas School of Business—$6.5M (1978–2013)

—Chou Hall (Haas School North Building Project)—$5M (2012)

—Simpson Manufacturing Youth Leadership Academy and Community Programs Funds—$1M (1999–2003)

—General support (beginning in 1978)

—Library—$1.25 M (1983–2006)

—Gifts include support for the University Library, Bancroft Library, and Oral History Center (beginning in 1983)

—Student Affairs, Cal Performances, and Division of Equity & Inclusion—$900K (1982–2015)

—The Simpsons' support in these and other areas includes a focus on outreach and educational opportunity for youth in the community through programs such as Young Entrepreneurs at Haas, Ailey Camp, and the Young Musicians Program, as well as an anonymous investment in the Cal Forensics Debate program.

8 See chapter 36 regarding Barclay's receipt of the Berkeley Medal.

9 *At Berkeley, we have the same number of Pell Grant recipients in our undergraduate body as the eight Ivy League universities put together* (Chancellor Birgeneau).

10 Former YEAH program is now called Boost. For a full description of the program, see https://www.haas.berkeley.edu/boost.

11 *Putting Something Back: Business Leader of the Year Barclay Simpson Brings a Humanitarian Touch to Work and Giving* by Marguerite Rigoglioso, "CalBusiness," winter 2006 cover story.

12 https://www.bampfa.org.

13 "[Ito's] proposal for a three-story box of gallery space and screening rooms inside a thin container of curving, white-painted steel would have ranked among the most ambitious cultural buildings in California in a generation. It was abandoned as too costly by the museum in 2009, in the wake of the global financial crisis." *LA Times Architecture Review,* Feb 12, 2016, "The New Berkeley Art Museum is a Study in Extremes," by Christopher Hawthorne, Los Angeles Times Architecture Critic.

14 Ibid.

15 Ibid.

16 The position is called the Sharon and Barclay Simpson Associate Curator for Education, School and Family Programs, BAMPFA.

17 "The 142,000 square-foot center is designed to be an all-encompassing facility for Cal student-athletes. In addition to a weight training complex and locker rooms, the facility houses a sports medicine department—including four pools for aquatic therapy, sports physiology, and biomechanics laboratories. There are also separate team meeting rooms. The center features academic service rooms, nutrition and food services, and a full-blown medical clinic with X-ray and ultrasound imaging equipment." https://www.berkeley.edu/map?simpson.

18 From "Berkeleyside," Berkeley, CA's independent news site, by Tracey Taylor, Aug. 8, 2011.

19 Ibid.

20 The local website is https://www.girlsinc-alameda.org. This motto is also used by the national organization https://www.girlsinc.org.

21 https://www.clintonfoundation.org/clinton-global-initiative/commitments/girls-inc-eureka-stem-career-development-girls.

22 "Built at the turn of the century as headquarters for the East Bay Water Co., the early version of today's East Bay Municipal Utility District, the Gothic Revival edifice has a terra cotta façade, replete with cornice moldings, strong vertical lines, and multiple panes of windows." Jessie Schiewe, March 12, 2012 from https://www.oaklandnorth.net.

23 The Great Migration, sometimes known as the Great Northward Migration or the Black Migration, was the movement of six million African Americans out of the rural Southern United States to the urban Northeast, Midwest, and West that occurred between 1916 and 1970. https://www.wikipedia.org.

24 2020 Girls Inc. Gala Webinar [https://www.girlsinc-alameda.org].

PART VII

Success and Succession: New Cooks in the Sauce

It was thrilling to be up on the balcony overlooking throngs of traders and assistants of all kinds at this most important stock exchange in the world. Everyone down there was waiting for me to get the trading day started....It was exciting to be standing there with a big sign above us saying Simpson Manufacturing Company, Inc. and then to strike the opening gong.

—Barclay

Chapter 28
Tone at the Top

What public auditors look for in publicly held companies is what is called "tone at the top." We do well with that, and it is Barclay that has really set that tone. The dominant characteristic of his leadership is his very strong sense of propriety... and that sense of propriety is also egalitarian.

—Earl (Budd) Cheit

A CCORDING TO BARCLAY AND others at the company, the decision to take Simpson Manufacturing public was not to raise money to cover debt or for expansion purposes, but to allow long-term employees who held Simpson private stock to monetize their holdings: *The business didn't need the money. We did it so the employees would feel even more that it was their company* (Barclay). Barry Williams confirms Barc's version of the story:

> *I wasn't a part of the decision to go public, but my understanding is that Barclay wanted to provide a way for people like Tom, who had all their holdings invested in a private company, to have some liquidity. It wasn't because Barc or the company needed the money.*

In Barc's mind, providing liquidity to his employees was the most concrete way to acknowledge their contributions in building the company, to help ensure that they would stay, and to remain competitive in attracting and retaining new talent in the future: *We are a successful company, and attracting and keeping the best people has made it all possible. Great people. That's the whole secret* (Barclay).

On May 26, 1994, one day after Barclay's seventy-third birthday and thirty-eight years after the company had been established, Simpson Manufacturing Co., Inc. sold stock equaling approximately 20 percent ownership of the company through an initial public offering (IPO) on the NASDAQ exchange.

This first offering of stock was fully sold. Soon after, the company was also admitted to the *New York Stock Exchange* under the NYSE abbreviation, SSD. According to tradition, the CEO of the company, who in 1994 was Tom Fitzmyers, was invited to ring the bell that opens the exchange on the first day of the company's admission into this august financial club. Graciously, Tom deferred to Barclay, who remembered the experience with gusto:

> *Sharon and I went to New York, checked into a hotel on Fifty-Sixth Street, and the next morning started to walk down to the NYSE. This was one time when my aversion to taxis was not too smart. It got to be about ten minutes from the opening, and there still was a mile to go. We grabbed a cab and got there just in time.*

Standing on that dias, chiming that very particular bell, Barc must have dwelt, for at least a nanosecond, on what a long way he had traveled from the moment in 1956 when Warner Odenthal rang his back doorbell, holding in his hand a metal joist hanger.

Chapter 29
The Simpson Manufacturing Company, Inc. Board of Directors[1]

I like companies with strong positions that want to work on strategy, and, most important, also have the resources to implement a strategy. Frankly, I was fascinated by the company. Many things were very different.

—Barry Williams

APPOINTING SIMPSON MANUFACTURING'S FIRST board of directors must have been a dramatic moment for both Barc and Tom as they ceded ultimate authority to a group of people whose first responsibility was to shareholders rather than to the company's founders and employees. Though this was a significant adjustment leading away from Barc and Tom's freewheeling command, their somewhat eccentric, charismatic leadership remained a constant in the daily life of the company and its board for the eighteen to twenty years they continued at the helm. Yet, naturally, there was some tinkering with the sauce.

At the time the company went public in 1994, the Simpson Manufacturing Board of Directors was made up of five independent directors with Tom Fitzmyers and Barclay as the two inside directors. Like the employee base of SST, the company's board of directors has a very high retention rate with a majority of directors having served for over ten years, and twenty years in the case of founding directors Budd Cheit and Barry Williams.

Representing a wide arc of interdisciplinary talent, the board comprised an educator (Budd Cheit) and a politician (Sunne McPeak) in addition to top-level business owners and CEOs from local and international companies: the range of entrepreneurial, academic, and political expertise assembled for the Simpson Manufacturing Board guaranteed that employee, community, and public policy concerns would be commingled with the analysis of shareholder financial interests. Indeed, the first group (as well as its impressive successors) functioned as a kind of philosophical as well as practical think tank for Barclay and Tom. As had been true in their recruitment of staff, they had wished to build a board that could introduce complex visions for the Simpson Company's future, not just provide the public enterprise with a stamp of Good Housekeeping. Leaders recognizing, attracting, and retaining other leaders was, as always, a critical ingredient in the Simpson "secret sauce."

Going public is a major transitional moment for any company, in which the intimate personality of an enterprise is exposed to outside scrutiny and an essentially impersonal set of exigencies. What is intriguing is the extent to which the very particular Simpson culture was transmitted and diffused among the company's elite group of directors, and how this figured in their attempts to guide the company into new waters. The navigational trick here was to transform Simpson into a truly modern global company without destroying the fine mixture of ingredients that had brought the company this far.

This challenge was particularly apparent as the Simpson board attempted to introduce certain institutional processes and forms of standardization that had always made Barclay impatient. Among these was a human resources department within the company, the lack of which was a serious anomaly in relation to most American businesses of Simpson's stature. Given Barc's distrust of lawyers, Simpson Manufacturing had also never had an office of internal counsel, the majority of Simpson's legal work having been conducted by the firm of Shartsis Friese LLP of San Francisco. Alluding to these looming gaps, Jennifer Chatman, wittily summarizes the challenges that the Simpson directors were up against in their efforts to make sure that the company's very strengths not become stumbling blocks:

> God forbid that we [the board] wreck the "secret sauce." I certainly hope that we never do that. But at the same time, the company is getting big, it's growing, it's international, it's exposed to all kinds of possible legal challenges, as every company is. The board is challenged to do this as elegantly and productively as possible without killing the goose that laid the golden egg.

Among the first group of independent directors, Barry Williams, entrepreneur, and Budd Cheit, dean and professor, loom large as key advisers to Barc and Tom in the transition of Simpson Manufacturing from a private company to an international, publicly owned enterprise with manufacturing and distribution facilities throughout North America, Europe, Asia, Australia, South America, and the Middle East. Side by side with other distinguished board colleagues, Williams and Cheit each helped in major ways to write the story of the modern company and are among its most insightful interpreters. First as pioneers and then as veterans, they served on the Simpson Manufacturing board for twenty years, the maximum term of service allowable under the board's governance regulations, originally drafted by Budd Cheit. In anticipating their departure from the board in 2014, Jennifer Chatman commented on the tremendous gap they would leave behind: *How to replace Budd and Barry? We are not exactly sure how we are going to survive without them even for ten minutes.*

Chapter 30
Salesman in Chief Again

*Barc hates to waste a nickel of shareholder money....He was the only person
I knew who took the bus in from JFK to downtown rather than a cab. And that
applies to all aspects of his leadership style.*

*Barc has no BS in him, his investor relations were open. Because of his large share
of the ownership of the company, he could get away with some things that other
people couldn't, but he was just remarkable, always stressing the long term and
never speculating about how we're going to do next quarter.*

—Earl (Budd) Cheit

THE IMMEDIATE CONSEQUENCE OF the SSD IPO was that Barclay was back
in the saddle as salesman in chief of the Simpson Company. John Herrera
comments that during the years between Barc's hiring of Tom Fitzmyers in
1978 and 1994, Barclay had withdrawn a bit from the down and dirty of the
daily business, surrendering his role as chief salesman, the occupation that
had always been at the heart of the company's identity. But once the decision
was made to undertake the initial stock offering, Herrera said that the old fire
returned and Barc was on a charge as he took over the selling of the company
with the same intensity that he had once had for selling SST products.

Initially, Barc went on the road along with Tom Fitzmyers and Steve
Lamson, Simpson's chief financial officer (CFO). They were accompanied on
the first trip to visit mutual fund managers and analysts in the US and the
UK by two people from JPMorgan Chase and one from Robertson-Stephens,
who had assisted in the first stock offering. Barc remembered these latter
professionals *shuddering* at the SSD team's desire *to tell it like it was*, to discuss
with fund managers potential losses as well as gains. Blunt truth-telling had
always been the earmark of Barclay's sales style and continued to be the key

to his considerable success selling Simpson Manufacturing to investors over the next eighteen years.

Following that initial trip, Barclay single-handedly took over the role of head of investor relations, freeing Tom Fitzmyers and Steve Lamson to continue running the company without having to worry about this whole new element of the business. As Barc says, the investors were *totally stuck with me.* The decision was that in this new realm, there would be only one mouthpiece for the company, and it was Barclay's contact details alone that appeared on all the investment and presentation materials. He seems to have felt entirely comfortable in the new role, already armed with the experience of having made all of the investment decisions for the company's pension plan for close to four decades. *I knew pretty much what questions the analysts might ask and could prepare for them—I'd been there.* What this experience as pension plan manager had taught him was that *it is earnings, not investor relations departments, which drive the long-range price of a stock.* Characteristically, he decided on a one-man-band presentation format rather than building a bloated fiefdom to aggrandize his new role. *Most presenters had a team of people backing them up at the podium. I was alone. I saw the job as relatively simple.*

Commenting on this stripped-down approach, Barry Williams echoes Budd Cheit in describing the ways that Barc shaped his message and managed his audience's expectations:

> *Barc never would make a prediction. No guidance on stock price, no predictions. What you saw was that these shareholders had a tremendous respect for Barclay because he was very consistent in what he said. He didn't candy it up. He said the good with the bad. He was very measured. And what else was fun was that Barc got away with a lot. He just wouldn't answer certain questions that were too specific or too closely tied to aspects of our "secret sauce." The analysts are always trying to get more information. Barc would just say, "I'm not going to answer that," and he got away with it because they had tremendous respect for him. They trusted him. Another CEO would have had difficulty.*

Another shrewd observer of Barc's tactics with investors was Jennifer Price, who had in 1991 answered a newspaper ad for a technical writer at

Simpson Strong-Tie—*thinking it was a neck-tie company*. Since then, she has served in a variety of marketing jobs at the company. Shortly after Simpson Manufacturing had gone public, Barclay came into Jennifer's office, asking that she help him do a PowerPoint presentation for investors. She had no idea he even knew who she was, and she remembers, *It was like God walking in*. This was the beginning of a long and close collaboration between Barc and Jennifer as they began designing Barc's road show for stock analysts.

Witnessing Barc's tactics from the front lines, she wittily describes a rare combination of likability, reliability, and toughness: *Barc came across as very casual, delightful, a charming fellow…but, in fact, he was extremely calculated in the amount of information he would share….*Though the analysts would try to pry predictions from him, he refused to embellish or forecast the economy or markets. Rather than oversell Simpson Manufacturing, he knew that the more you gave the analysts, the more you might end up disappointing expectations, which in turn might drive the stock price down. According to Jennifer Price, Barc always walked into the presentations or phone calls, knowing exactly where he was going to draw the line, no matter how hard he was pushed. *He was very direct with them. There are many things about Barclay that one could admire, but, most of all, he had an honesty and an integrity that the analysts learned they could absolutely trust. If he told them something, that was the fact of it.*

Jennifer also appears to have gotten a big kick out of Barclay's wackier side, which may account for the length of their collaboration and their mutual appreciation of each other. *Barc had such a wicked sense of humor. Some of the things he'd want to put into the presentation, we'd think, Oh, Lordy, I don't know what these people are going to think.* One time, she remembers, he wanted to emphasize the flexibility and adaptability of Simpson Manufacturing. She found a picture of a lady in her nineties doing the splits with her leg up on a bus stop pole. As a joke, she said, *How about this?* To her amazement, Barc was thrilled and had her put it into the PowerPoint. *I thought to myself, I can't imagine these analysts when he shows this up on the screen. They'll look at this and think, "What the…"—but they'd just crack up.* She recognized Barc as a particularly *savvy* performer, simultaneously corny and concise, ever the brilliant salesman: *He was an older man standing up in front of all of these young suits, very well-off guys who were whiplash sharp. The minute he stood up he just had them eating out of the palm of his hand.* Among the tricks of Barc's trade was the half-satirical attempt to educate the Wall Street guys by flashing pictures of Renaissance paintings on the screen between financial charts. *Our presentations were artistic and fun,* says Price. In these descriptions, Barc's exuberance and intensity appear to have been as much on display in these later years as they ever were.

Also on show were his attention to detail and his refusal to gild the truth. Price, who wrote the scripts for the presentations, remembers, *Barc would rewrite and rewrite, going back and forth, until I would want to throttle him.* Once when they were choreographing a presentation, she remembers that he told her she would never make a good salesman. *He was very, very honest—brutally honest.* But Jennifer seems to have weathered both his editorial nitpicking and his rough candor. Indeed, he remains for her a model of certain quite miraculous and intimate virtues: *Barc honestly cares about people. He'll come in and ask about my kids, and I'll want to tell him about their successes. There are not too many other people that I care to do that with, but I so want him to be proud of them…*

When she was working in the position of CFO for the company, Karen Colonias accompanied Barc on several investor calls, recalling the challenge of selling investors on a fundamental, unglamorous product in the era of Apple and other emerging tech giants, who can offer high drama through the regular introduction of innovative devices as well as the sheer exhilaration of gambling for great riches. *Okay, we make this metal angle. How are we going to convince people how important this is? No short-term gratification. But if you look at how our financials are doing and what our return is from building materials of US manufacture, we're a pretty good-looking company to invest in.* In an era of blockbuster tech businesses and a hypersell mentality, Barc's style was to stick with the unadorned facts, managing expectations through understatement rather than blowing a big horn. As Colonias put it, he wooed potential investors using *an inch-by-inch rather than rosy picture approach,* preferring to surprise with results rather than mislead with puffed-up predictions.

As usual, Barc appears to have thoroughly enjoyed designing and playing the role of renegade, once again an *outlier* in his new career as head of investor relations. Fun as it may have been for him, it was also a demanding occupation according to Williams, who comments on its attendant rigors: *So, if anybody ever wondered what Barc was doing in his sort of semi-retirement, investors require a lot of time.* In Barc's mind, the most difficult part of the job came with the realization that a very significant segment of investors is entranced with short- rather than long-term bets. It was a challenge, swimming upstream against a countervailing interest in quick gain.

Chapter 31
End of an Era, Beginning of an Era

One test is worth a thousand opinions.

—Karen Colonias

I N A CAREER THAT spanned thirty-eight years, SST's Designer-in-Chief Tye Gilb developed thousands of new connectors, many of which were patented. He was well into his eighties when he retired in 1998. Five years before that, around 1993, the growth of Simpson Manufacturing occasioned a change in the daily life of the company that was both logistically and symbolically important. The old San Leandro facility on Doolittle Drive needed new warehouse and office space, as well as a training facility, necessitating the transfer of the now-global "home office" functions of the business to a new location, first to a shiny suburban office park in Pleasanton, then to Dublin, then back to a new one in Pleasanton, where it has remained since 1995.

Though the company still resists the use of titles, this was the first time that senior management was physically separated from the rumble and tumble of production. This transition of the business—from its crowded place of origin to new dispersed quarters that separated operations from management—found Tye himself refusing to budge from the old plant in San Leandro, long after the majority of the company's white-collar staff had embraced the comforts of modern office space.

By 1998, the reorganization of functions in San Leandro and Pleasanton had already proven inadequate to the expanding requirements of the company. The new plan was to leave the head office in Pleasanton, but to move forward with an ambitious plan to build a mega-complex in Stockton to entirely replace the old San Leandro plant, warehousing, shipping, training, and administrative offices of the original Northern California branch of the company. In addition to these core functions, the new complex would also include Simpson Shear-Wall manufacturing operations that had formerly been located in Visalia and Manteca, California, and a truly innovative, state-of-the-art product testing facility. Massive in size, this new multipurpose twenty-first century complex—which opened in July 2003—sprawls across eleven acres of industrial park, comprising 600,000 square feet of building space—a far cry from the humble San Leandro flagship enterprise.

Housed in its own separate building within the complex, the 25,000-square-foot Stockton test facility is the crown jewel among the many Simpson test labs now sprinkled throughout the company's plant facilities around the globe and may be the most sophisticated testing facility of its kind in private hands. Christened the Tyrell H. Gilb Laboratory, this major component of SST's modern physical plant pays dramatic tribute to the company's founding technical genius and to the spirit of experimentation that animated his hand-fabricated and tested creations over years of a long and fertile career.

If Tom's Amada was an early sign of Simpson Manufacturing's accelerating shift toward sophistication and engineering excellence, the construction of this extraordinary laboratory is the most dramatic expression of the company's commitment to investing major resources in R&D. Built at a cost of $12 million, the lab was designed specifically for the testing of construction-linked products under simulated conditions that replicate the gigantic force fields created by wind and earthquake. The metrics for these simulations are drawn from a range of natural disasters from around the world, from Loma Prieta, to New Orleans, to Kobe, Japan—traumatic events and locations to which SST has been called to study and assist in damage assessment, innovative product design, retrofit, and international-level testing.

Director of the Tye Gilb Lab since its inception, Steve Pryor (Advanced Research Manager; see bio) is the company's current lead testing and design specialist, known worldwide as an expert in the construction of earthquake-proof structures. He and other Simpson engineers, such as Randy Shackleford (Manager of Codes and Compliance; see bio), one of whose specialties is design and testing of products for buildings in hurricane zones, are worthy acolytes of the Gilb method of integrating constant testing into the process of product design.

Among the most important of the Tye Gilb Lab's testing mechanisms is the shake table, largely designed by Pryor with help from other technicians responsible for the table's sophisticated hydraulic and control systems. Though not as large as the shake table used in the 2009 NEESWood Capstone tests near Kobe, Japan,[2] where Pryor was among the lead technical minds at work on these simulations, the Tye Gilb table is nevertheless impressive in its own right, able to sustain the weight and dimensions of a three-story wood-frame building and test its structural integrity under violent and varying conditions. At the press of a button, Steve Pryor can dial in a Loma Prieta or Northridge-scale earthquake. Though this level of sophistication is a far cry from the original handheld test presses used by Tye in the sixties, the emphasis on innovation and experimentation is consistent with Tom and Barc's joint vision that the ongoing success of the business was directly linked to creating products capable of preventing man-made structures from collapsing.

One wonders what Barc must have thought, walking the floors of the gleaming Stockton facility and Tye Gilb Lab, remembering the old plant in San Leandro with all its battle scars and "familial" memories, recognizing many members of that family still now working in the mega-plant under scientifically adjusted lighting and acoustical conditions, seeing the ways in which his passions and principles had played themselves out in whirring machinery, lives lived, and lives saved.

During the early years of the new millennium, as the Stockton megaplex was under construction, there was a three- to four-year-long phasing out of the old facility on Doolittle Drive in San Leandro as various functions gradually moved eastward to Stockton. This physical transition—during which many long-term Simpson employees had to decide either to retire or move—signals the end of an era. While some long-term employees like David MacDonald picked up stakes and moved to Stockton, in his case to take on the management of the Stockton manufacturing plant, other old-timers waited until the last possible moment to make the change to the shiny and the novel, lagging behind until the old San Leandro buildings were finally fully vacated in 2007. To the extent that this delaying behavior was linked to a reluctance to let the old world go, Barc himself may have had at least one toe in the laggers' camp. John Herrera recalls that Barclay—always, ostensibly, a pioneer eager for change—also seems to have hesitated on the brink, though whether for nostalgic reasons (which sentiments he wouldn't have approved), it is impossible to say:

During the 2002 through 2007 period, when Barclay was showing possible investors around the SST plant facilities—instead of taking

*them to this beautiful, brand-new facility up in Stockton—he'd bring
them to San Leandro. In Stockton, the floors were clean, the ceilings
were thirty-five feet high, the lights were state of the art, there was
scientifically modulated sound.* (John Herrera)

Even as the old plant was emptying out—a kind of skeleton in the
making—he'd bring them to Doolittle Drive:

*The San Leandro plant was clean for San Leandro and for a forty-year-
old building, and it was properly taken care of, but it wasn't a showcase.
Yet, Barc never blinked an eye about taking potential investors there,
never explained—just showed them around. If you were trying to woo
an investor, you've got this beautiful factory in Stockton, and he takes
them to San Leandro....That was his home.* (John Herrera)

Undoubtedly for Barc, the heroic days of the original company still had
a hold on him. It is also equally likely that he was in some way testing his
potential backers to see whether they were "worthy" of investing in Simpson
Manufacturing, or he was managing expectations in the manner he was
famous for with asset managers and stock analysts. Perhaps, he wanted to
find out whether they could glean quality without the charm of fabulous
surroundings, whether, in Herrera's words, they just wanted to be courted
versus knowing what really happened.

Maybe Barclay wanted to impress upon these would-be investors that a
major part of the story of the company was not in its new spit-polish finishes,
but in its historic frugality—its essentialist nature. Around about the same
time, Herrera recalls pulling up beside Barclay as he arrived in the San
Leandro parking lot in his famous, dusty, black Ford Taurus:

*Barc's side-view mirror was hanging. He gets out and says, "I guess
I got a little too close to the guard station. Do you think some of that
glue that we bought, you know, from that epoxy company we just
purchased, do you think that might work here?" A couple of days later,
I see he's got duct tape wrapped all around the mirror.*

And he got investors anyway.

During this same period, another important symbolic alteration took
place that signaled changing times. To acknowledge the broadening of

their product line, the old SST logo (Simpson Strong-Tie Connectors) was shortened to Simpson Strong-Tie. Thus was the central *strong-tie* metaphor retained, but without limiting the scope of the metaphor to "connectors," a word that had always been used within the company lexicon to denote a metal part. To accommodate the company's expansion into epoxies and other non-metal parts, the logo needed to be altered to reflect the new, expanded variety of products. However, the removal of the old wording from company stationery, promotional materials, and packaging elicited an immediate and impassioned reaction on the part of many of SST's long-term employees.

According to Kristy Lincoln, *You would have thought that a sacrilege had been committed.* Tom and Barc received countless protest phone calls, one guy from the San Leandro plant pleading with Barc, *What's going on, man? I've been running this press for thirty years, and you can't just change my logo on me* (Kristin Lincoln). But the times they were a-changing—except that the guy in the plant still didn't hesitate to make a direct call to Barc, knowing the chairman would pick up the phone himself without any screening interference from a secretary. Some things remained sacred at the company.

Chapter 32
Tweaking the Sauce and the Big Hand-Off

The downside of being a strong culture organization...is that it's hard to bring in new people at higher levels...there are always trade-offs....In order to be totally inebriated by the "secret sauce," do you have to come through the ranks of the organization, or can we spot people from the outside who would be amenable to it and could fast-track...? If you don't have all the expertise you need inside your existing operation—and we don't—these are serious issues for growing companies.

—Jennifer Chatman

BARCLAY'S NINE PRINCIPLES HAD for nearly four decades guided the business's growth before the decision to take the company public in 1994. But like most inspired commandments and constitutions, the Nine Principles represent a set of precepts, more ethical than pragmatic, whose enduring strength depends on interpretation and, even, amendment. While the board was largely convinced of the power of Barc's core principles, they were also aware that their fiduciary responsibilities as independent directors required them to evaluate possible changes made necessary by new and fluid exigencies.

Barc's final chapter as spiritual leader of the company encompassed the eighteen years from 1994–2012, a period during which the philosophy and practice of the business he had built from scratch both changed out of necessity and redoubled in intensity. It was, for instance, an article of faith with Barclay that the business was not for sale, a statement that Budd Cheit remembered Barclay repeating to securities analysts and potential investors as well as to his employees. Yet, since the board of a publicly owned company owes its primary allegiance to shareholders, it is required by law to consider serious purchase offers. In steering the company forward, the board had, for instance, to seriously consider how to balance this legal obligation with the company's long-held precept that employees could reasonably expect to make a career at the business. For Barclay it was essential that SST employees need not fear losing their job through a merger or acquisition initiated from the outside, or from one of Barclay's seven children being moved peremptorily into an executive role that they might not have been skilled to undertake. To avoid any whiff of nepotism, Barclay made clear from the beginning that Simpson was not a "*family*" business in the blood sense of the term.

This idea that employees could build a career at the company, in turn, affected the way Barc first constructed Simpson's rather unusual compensation system, as well as shaped his commitment to hiring and promoting from within the company wherever possible. In both instances, his methods were aimed at giving his employees a tangible stake in the business and in rewarding loyalty in direct and transparent ways. One could also argue that the exercise of these principles created a kind of closed, circular, and possibly ingrown system that could cut Simpson off from fresh blood available outside the company. There are obvious dangers inherent in a system in which the rules are written to support an existing vision.

Analyzing the sources of Barc's beliefs, Budd Cheit observed, *Barc feels that we've built a very special kind of organization, that there are a lot of mutual commitments to people who have cast their lot with you, and you don't want to treat that relationship as being subject to the whims of a financial transaction....* The idea that mutual commitments involving employees might impede certain financial transactions is well outside of mainstream business practices. Barry Williams, a veteran of countless company boards, parses one of the dilemmas presented by Simpson's creed, acknowledging the extent to which he accepted Barclay's underlying premise:

> *We continue to get offers to buy the company. You know, as a director of a company, you should never say you'd never sell the company because your primary focus is on shareholders. There may be a price out there where it is in the best interest of shareholders to sell. That would be very difficult at Simpson because if we sold, I don't think anybody could honor our particular "secret sauce." It just wouldn't work. It wouldn't be good for our people. So I, too, believe we should never sell because it would be harmful to our people, and I think it would be harmful to our customers. We could make a lot more money and drop a lot more*

to the bottom line if we cut back on quarterly distributions. We could make a lot more if we cut back on R&D, if we cut back on servicing. But these things are what we are about.

The contradictions and trade-offs alluded to here are of the utmost significance to any for-profit business. By 1994 and beyond, it was the board's job to navigate the company's passage between the crashing rocks of competing demands.

Among the most challenging of these double-edged demands was the issue of how the company was to move beyond the era of charismatic leadership that had shaped its purposes and practices from its inception. Barc himself identified one of the moments when this issue emerged in dramatic fashion. During the 2007 "crash," for the first time since Simpson had gone public in 1994, SSD's sales and earnings did not exceed those of the prior year. His phone was ringing off the hook with agitated securities analysts. Their probing questions included one that would concern the company and its board of directors for years to come: *With an eighty-six-year-old chairman, who is also the largest stockholder in the company, and an over sixty-five-year-old CEO, does company management have a viable succession plan in place?*

Though Barc had implemented his first-generation succession plan single-handedly through the selection of Tom Fitzmyers, it was now clear to everybody at Simpson that Barc's 1978 selection process was not replicable for the modern company in the post-millennial business climate. It was time to put in place a succession plan that would reassure investors and guarantee effective next-generation management of the company in an increasingly competitive industry. Such a plan would involve both exploiting and adjusting the distinctive culture of the company established by its founders. In Barry Williams's words:

So, we knew the two people who developed, spread, and lived the culture were going—inevitably—to step back. It was not only that we were getting bigger, but it was also the question of how to ensure that the good parts of the culture would survive, and to consider how some parts of the culture might evolve, because maybe we didn't want all of the old culture. We wanted most of it because it served damn well, but we didn't want to be confined by a culture that was set for a prior time.

As Williams and others on the board realized, establishing a sound succession plan would, in turn, compel them to reevaluate the company's unusual compensation formulas as well as to confront a range of other core precepts at the heart of the business's particular, not to say peculiar, identity. The very strength of the company culture—from which the enterprise continued to derive its vitality—was also the source of certain knotty contradictions that the board had to overcome in steering Simpson Manufacturing toward modernity.

In 2007, the board started to deal head-on with the succession issue by focusing on the recruitment of a CEO who would be able to replace Tom Fitzmyers when the time came. According to Williams, from the beginning of these discussions, Barclay was firm in his belief that it would be a sign of failure if they were to go outside the company in search of candidates for the top leadership position, a conviction consistent with his commitment to promoting from within the company whenever possible. He argued that there was a pool of talented mid-level management people, many of whom had already been with the company for two decades or more.

Though the board agreed to search diligently for prospects within the company, they were unambiguous about their intention also to look outside Simpson if they believed the internal talent base did not offer the range of leadership capacities they were seeking. *We made that clear to Barc. We agreed to disagree. If you've met Barclay, you know what I mean.* [Laughs.] *He wasn't buying it, but yes, we made it clear. He wasn't buying it…we're messing with his baby* (Barry Williams). In Jennifer Chatman's words, *I have never seen a senior leader cling to the philosophy of promoting from within more than Barc.* She goes on to observe: *There's huge continuity in the Simpson senior team. The downside of that is that it's really hard to bring in anyone at a senior level.*

What is particularly interesting here is that Barclay's resistance to going outside for candidates was not linked to any desire to guard the interests of a relation or hand-picked successor, as is often true in family-owned and operated businesses. His concern was to maintain the strong ties that underpinned the structure he and Tom had built over decades. *Why mess*, he wondered, *with a winning formula and a beautiful design?*

In keeping with their commitment to Barclay to thoroughly develop and evaluate internal candidates in their search for a new CEO, the board proposed trying various Simpson employees in a range of different jobs within the company to give them experience beyond their existing specialties. According to Williams, this was a decision potentially fraught with risk and resistance: *When you have good people performing well in a critical position, there's reluctance to move them around. This again is part of the mastery of Barclay. This is something the board came up with and discussed with Barc. He agreed. He allowed this to happen because he so much wanted an internal candidate.*

Among the pool of potential Simpson contenders for the top job was Karen Colonias, by then head of the engineering department. As early as 2004, the board and management of SST placed her in the position of branch manager at the Stockton plant in order to broaden her knowledge and experience within the company. Then, in 2009, Barry suggested she move again, this time into the role of chief financial officer to round her out, a change that in turn triggered a series of other reassignments of upper-level personnel. *She didn't know anything about finance, but she's a damn smart person, and she learned it, and she did a good job, and it made her a better candidate.* And so it went over a period of several years. *We also did that for other internal people who were contenders. Karen was a strong candidate, yet she wasn't the only one initially; but over time, she was clearly the one* (Barry Williams).

In 2012, several batons were passed simultaneously. Barclay retired as chairman and head of investor relations, though he remained on the board through 2013. Tom took over Barc's role with investors. And, exactly twenty-eight years after being hired into the nascent engineering department at SST, Karen Colonias became the company's third CEO, moving into mythically large shoes. But by now, she also had her own fabled history at the company.

Notes for Part VII

1 **Original board members:**

Officers:

Barclay Simpson, Founder, President, and Chairman of Simpson Manufacturing

Tom Fitzmyers, CEO of Simpson Manufacturing

Steve Lamson, Vice President and CFO of Simpson Manufacturing

Independent directors:

Earl (Budd) Cheit, Professor and Dean of the UC Haas School of Business

Alan R. McKay, founder of A. R. McKay & Associates and principal in geotechnical engineering firm, Hallenbeck-McKay & Associates.

Sunne McPeak, Member of the Contra Costa County, CA, Board of Supervisors, President and CEO of the Bay Area Council, and Secretary of the California Business, Transportation, and Housing Agency

Barry Lawson Williams, Entrepreneur and director for multiple private and public corporate boards

Current board members:

Officers

Karen Colonias, President and CEO of Simpson Manufacturing Company, Inc.

Independent directors:

James S. Andrasick, Chairman and CEO, Matson Navigation (retired)

Michael A. Bless, CEO, Century Aluminum Company

Jennifer A. Chatman, Paul J. Cortese Professor of Management, Haas School of Business, UC Berkeley

Gary M. Cusumano, Chairman, The Newhall Land and Farming Company (retired)

Philip E. Donaldson, Executive Vice-President and CFO, Andersen Corporation

Celeste Volz Ford, Founder and CEO, Stellar Solutions

Robin Greenway Macgillivray, Senior Vice President, One AT&T Integration, AT&T (retired)

2. In 2009, just outside Kobe, Japan, a seven-story wood-frame tower (40 x 60 perimeter) was constructed atop one of the world's largest shake tables. Led by Colorado State University with Simpson Strong-Tie as its technical collaborator with Steve Pryor at the helm, the NEESWood Capstone Project pursued ambitious testing—under major seismic activ-

ity—of new design methods for building wood-frame, multi-story structures. Simpson Special Moment Frames constructed of steel secured the first floor, and Anchor Tiedown Systems and numerous structural connectors provided the hardware to fasten the remaining six wood-frame stories together. The tower was submitted to a series of earthquakes, culminating in a brutal forty second, 7.5 magnitude simulation, 180 percent the size of the Northridge quake. Stunningly, the structure survived with only minor drywall damage, proving that if such a structure is built using Colorado State's design philosophy of going above the code minimum, along with using Simpson connectors, it and its inhabitants would survive. https://www.strongtie.com.

Part VIII

Retirement

Hello Board members:

There is a crazy idea going around that I might be having some sort of physical problem & here to drop off of the Board!

Actually, its true & while I'll miss the association with all of you interesting & productive people, I really have no choice but to resign.

Three couple of requests which I hope are OK:

1. Continue to have Samantha send me the info on Board meetings

2. If financially reasonable, raise the dividends.

3. Do not agree to sell the company no matter what the price.

We are able to attract & keep the best people because they come here for a career, not just a bus stop.

Thank you all for the great job that you have done, & Budd & Barry are going to be hard to replace.

Barc

Handwritten note from Barc to the Simpson Manufacturing Board of Directors, announcing his retirement, 2013.

Chapter 33
The Wager

Health is not a condition of matter, but of mind.

—Mary Baker Eddy

IN 2009, BARCLAY WAS diagnosed with cancer that had metastasized into his spine. Used to being in vigorous good health and having a firm belief in the power of attitude in conquering afflictions of all kinds, he had long been resistant to having physical checkups, believing the less time spent with doctors, the less chance of being ambushed by illness. By the time he was diagnosed, it was too late for surgery. The doctor explained that there was a drug protocol that might slow down the progress of the disease. But Barc was a guy who didn't take aspirin, let alone a cocktail of drugs. He asked how much time he had if he didn't do anything. Five months or so was the answer. Those odds were longer (that is, the time was shorter) than even he, an expert poker player, thought worth the gamble. Well, he guessed, he might take the pills—since he still had a lot to do. So, he started the medicinal regime. But many of the pills went astray, falling out of his pockets and rolling under tables, chairs, beds, across parking lots. When he did take them, his face and feet got puffy. When next he saw the doctor, he announced, *I am not going to die a fat man.* Instead, he had decided to take the long odds, betting on his innate physical strength and prodigious will to buy him time without benefit of pills and chemical therapy. Looking the consequences square in the eye, he raised the bet. He lived for five years following the original five-month diagnosis. There was serious encroaching pain near the end, yet the five years were full, the mind definitely tricking the matter into line until it couldn't anymore. But, by then, Barc had won the wager.

Chapter 34
Letters to and from a "Servant Leader"

Hello, Barc, You have made such a difference in my life and the life of my family. Simpson Strong-Tie has been a blessing to work at. Simpson paid for my education in computers and project management and also has provided a good living wage and health care for my family (I have a little boy now). On top of that, it's such a respectful and fun place to work and I think you had a lot to do with all those things. You've been an inspiration as a servant leader.

—Tim Koss, Project Manager, IT, Pleasanton, California

Dear Barc, What happened to those twenty years we worked together on the board? They slipped by, but in the process created a bond of respect, admiration, and affection that is not subject to procedures like retirement.

—Earl (Budd) Cheit

WHEN BARC ANNOUNCED IN 2012 that he would be stepping down as chairman of Simpson Manufacturing, his business family responded with an outpouring of letters. They came from board members; engineers; packers; shippers; new employees and those who had been with SST over decades; old friends in the company as well as those who may have only glimpsed Barclay from afar as he led the New Employee Orientation Sessions; and from those in North America and those based well beyond her shores:

Hello, I'm a relatively new employee with Simpson. I absolutely love my job and this company. I recently attended orientation and didn't get the opportunity to tell you in person what a wonderful company you have built. Every day is a pleasure to come to work. It is the hardest job I've ever had in terms of training (so many products to learn), but I love a good challenge. I am happy to work for a company that has such integrity, and pride in its products. (Deb Fontaine, Customer Service Representative, SST, Stockton Branch, California)

Hi, Barclay, This is Ricardo Arevalo, VP of Engineering. I wanted to thank you for creating a company and culture that has changed the lives of so many people in a positive way....Over time, I really began to understand what you infused as a culture by your example, your mentors, your generosity. (Richard Arevalo, VP of Engineering)

Barclay, I have been with Simpson almost ten years now and the only regret I have is not finding this wonderful company twenty years ago when I was working at another company that didn't have the Secret Sauce...I just wanted to personally thank you for making Simpson a great place to work, and for making quality products here in AMERICA, as well as taking care of your employees like they are your own family and I guess we really are. (Kevin Posey, Inside Sales, McKinney, Texas)

Dear Mr. Simpson, My name is Omar Aranda, General Manager for Simpson Branch 95, our warehouse in Santiago, Chile, South America.... We are a small warehouse, 8,600 Sq/Ft, a team of five employees, and lots of dreams....For me [it] was a real pleasure to have met you in person and had the honor to talk to [you] in my orientation week class, a master class in our secret sauce and values. In that conversation, you told me that you would love to hear from us in ten years and have the Santiago Warehouse be a winner. We are working hard to make that promise a reality, we will never forget your wise words and the values that make our company a not equal company. (Omar Aranda, Gerente General I, Simpson Strong-Tie, Santiago, Chile)

Hi, Barclay, ...It means the world to me to work for a company that had such humble beginnings. (Rachel Holland, PE, Simpson Strong-Tie, Branch Engineer)

Mr. Barclay Simpson, Thank you for providing me the opportunity to work here, for a company built on integrity and doing things right. I find comfort and faith in knowing these values are not only competitive, but thrive in a marketplace riddled with short-cutting and bottom-line interests. (Dustin Muhn, R&D Engineer, SST)

Hello, Barclay,…I met my wife at the Brea office in 2000. We have now been married for over eleven years and have two children. It is always wonderful to mention to somebody that I work for Simpson and see them light up. (Joe Polder, Brea Branch of SST, California)

Thank you for a company that is a good corporate neighbor and not a poster child for greed. Thank you very much. (Kenneth F. Diggins)

Dear Barclay, Several years ago I attended an orientation training in California. You spoke at one of the sessions and I have never forgotten one of the things you said…that it is the company's job to take care of employees, and the employees' job to take care of the customer…and the sales will come. That was so impressive to me as most companies are all about the sales and the bottom-line. (Kathy Stevens, Collections Manager, SST)

You have led this company through a great journey, which your legacy will survive forever. (Kevin Logsdon)

Barc,…Very few people really ever get the chance to make a career out of doing what they love. You have provided that opportunity for me with Simpson and have taken care of me and my family. (Roger J. Dankel, Branch Sales Manager, SST)

You are living proof that if you want it, you will make it happen. (Ann Horne, Branch 53, Ontario, Canada)

Barclay, From the team in Australia, New Zealand, and South Africa….We have only been part of the business for a short ten years; however, in that time you have been an inspiration with your passion and commitment to the people in the business as well as the leadership you have shown. (Herb Kuhn, Managing Director, SST-Australia)

Dear Barc, It's hard to believe that in just two weeks I will have been with Simpson for twenty-nine years. I can remember my interview with Dick Perkins. I was only eighteen years old and scared to death. I also remember the first time you called our office in Texas...and when I realized it was you on the other line, I was really nervous. Once I met you, those nerves just went away by how kind you are....Hugs, Cyndi (Cyndi Chandler, International Accounts Manager, SST, McKinney Texas)

Hello, Barc, I am less than a couple of weeks from my retirement and I wanted one last opportunity to thank you for giving me a chance to participate in this incredible phenomenon called Strong-Tie for over forty-three years. Thank you...for asking me to be your warehouse manager at the ripe old age of twenty-two. Not many companies took those types of risks with their employees in those days....With companies being bought, sold, or just failing, Simpson Strong-Tie has always been there for me. (John Herrera)

Dear Barc, I can't tell you how much I've learned about running an organization from you—from your successful operations, to the incredible culture, and secret sauce you and Tom nurtured all those years. It has been my deep honor to serve on the Simpson board, and even more so to have a chance to understand, up close, how you have thought about and developed the company. You are an inspiration to me, and you have inspired so many others!! (Jennifer Chatman)

Barc, You will always be the company. What a wonderful run. What a legacy. What a friendship. (Barry Williams)

And dozens more...

In December 2013, one year after retiring from the chairmanship of Simpson Manufacturing and four years after the bleak medical diagnosis, Barc retired also from the board of directors of the company, leaving behind this handwritten note:

Hello, board members:

There is a crazy idea going around that I might be having some sort of physical problem and have to drop off the board.

Actually, it's true, and while I'll miss the association with all of you interesting and productive people, I really have no choice but to resign.

Three requests which I hope are OK:

1. *Continue to have Samantha send me the info on board meetings.*
2. *If financially reasonable, raise the dividends.*
3. *Do not agree to sell the company no matter what the price. We are able to attract and keep the best people because they come here for a career, not just a bus stop.*

Thank you all for the great job that you have done, and Budd and Barry are going to be hard to replace.

Barc

As a valedictory note, this was pure Barc:

No handwringing over illness.

No officialese in the moment of leaving a central passionate commitment of his life, after fifty-seven years of command.

No imposing memorandum from the top; a personal letter, written by hand.

A repeated commitment to both his shareholders and employees; a reminder of the central tenet of the Nine Principles.

Nearly twenty years after taking Simpson Manufacturing public, Barc was still unchastened by the impersonal realities governing publicly held companies. For him, the key to success remained what it had always been: taking care of his employees and running his very particular kind of "family" business even from within the jaws of the global marketplace.

Chapter 35
Sightings: Brilliant Plumage

*He's such a wonderful man. He was in the building yesterday
just for a few hours, but I love it when he comes here.*

—August 2012, Receptionist at front desk of SST Head Office,
Pleasanton, California

O N A SUMMER MORNING, Barclay was spotted walking around the floors
of the SST headquarters carrying a handwritten note with discussion
points he wanted to communicate to new employees. Sharon was gone for
a few days and he had reverted to his sartorial norm, selecting a striking
version of his famous, preferred plaid-themed multi-wear. *So, he comes to
work with tennis shoes and knee-high socks, plaid shorts, and a plaid shirt, all
different colors. But you know what…the thing that was always so great is that
he was there. It didn't matter what he was wearing* (Terry Kingsfather).

From the time he officially retired from his role at the company as head of
investor relations until he finally withdrew from the board in December 2013,
Barclay continued to do New Employee "Master Classes" at SST's orientation
sessions. Inevitably, he spoke of the company's core values, imprinting the
Simpson creed on new generations of workers. Other SST luminaries hated
to follow Barc at these events:

*He made an impression on everybody. At the end of these training
sessions, there is a critique written by every single person. There
could be as many as forty people in the class, and the class is just an
orientation class to get new employees up to speed with Simpson and
what's going on. So, I always read the reviews….Hardly anybody doesn't
mention Barc and I almost get jealous….They always say how great it
was to have Barc get up and tell them that this company is not for sale.
We're a long-term company. We're a people company, and we're here*

to stay. Almost all of them talk about Barc. They don't say much about what I said, which is the day-to-day operations and how we're going to get to where we're going. That's why nobody likes to follow Barc in a presentation. (Terry Kingsfather)

Chapter 36

Acknowledgments from the Community: The Berkeley Medal

The Berkeley Medal was established in 1981 as UC Berkeley's top honor. On very rare and special occasions, it is bestowed on individuals whose exceptionally distinguished contributions to society advance the university's ideals and goals and whose careers have benefited the public beyond the demands of tradition, rank, or direct service to Berkeley. The chancellor works closely with an advisory committee to confidentially select each recipient. The medal is given at a public function on campus, and recipients must be present to accept it. [1]

IN THE YEARS BETWEEN his retirement from Simpson Manufacturing in 2012 and his death in November of 2014, Barclay's achievements in business and community philanthropy were celebrated in commemorations organized by Simpson Manufacturing as well as by many of the grateful nonprofit institutions that had benefited from his leadership and his and Sharon's ongoing financial support. Among these—in May 2012—was a staged retrospective show by the California College of the Arts, "Celebrating 25 Years of the Barclay Simpson Award."[2] This show gathered together exceptional work by many of the students enrolled in the Graduate Program in Fine Arts at CCA who had been recipients of the award in the year of their graduation from the college. A quote from one of these students captures some of the whacky flair that Sharon and Barc loved and supported through their long tenure at CCA:

> *I was really honored to receive the Simpson Award. The Simpsons were incredibly gracious. I had in mind an installation that suggested that they had secretly begun drilling for oil inside their gallery. It wasn't earth-shattering, but it was certainly disruptive and not at all*

commercially viable! I don't know if Barclay and Sharon cared for it, but they were supportive and cheerful and cared deeply about the lives of students. (Kurt Kiefer, one of four CCA student winners of the Barclay Simpson Award in 1992)

The jewel in the crown of these celebrations occurred in early January 2013, when UC Berkeley's Chancellor Robert Birgeneau awarded Barclay the Berkeley Medal, the university's highest form of acknowledgment for extraordinary *service to society*. The celebration took place on a cold Berkeley day on the construction site of the future Berkeley Art Museum and Pacific Film Archive (BAMPFA) building. Barc's partner in nearly a decade's worth of struggles and campaigns to bolster core university institutions and programs, Birgeneau spoke feelingly and simply as he placed the medal with its golden sash around Barc's neck: *In everything he does, Barc has a positive effect on the lives around him.* Highlighting Barc's crucial role in the BAMPFA building campaign, Birgeneau also went on to mention his important contributions to Cal Athletics, the Haas Business School, scholarship programs for Cal students, and a number of other key programs aimed at expanding access for low-income students to the educational and cultural resources of the university. He ended by reciting Simpson Manufacturing's motto: *We learn. We grow. We put something back.*

Following Birgeneau, Lawrence Rinder, Director of BAMPFA, handed Barclay a brick dug up during excavation of the site of the future museum, upon which he had inscribed a message celebrating Barc's leadership in bringing the project to fruition. This tribute by Rinder followed on a previous appreciation ceremony honoring Barc and Sharon at the museum in May of 2012.

Stepping up to the lectern in a midnight-blue suit, highlighted by the golden sash of the medal and a burst of colored balloons behind him, Barc said he didn't really think he deserved the medal, especially once he learned the names of his distinguished medal recipient predecessors. Among many other eminences, these included Herman Wouk (1984), Mary Robinson (1991), Earl Cheit (1991), Walter Haas (1991), Peter Haas (1996) Karl Pister (1996), Kofi Annan (1998), Bill Clinton (2002), Jimmy Carter (2007), Walter Hewlett (2008), Ernesto Zedillo (2004), and Li Ka-shing (2011). It is doubtful that Barclay could have imagined that he would be keeping such rarified company when he was carousing in the Sigma Nu fraternity in 1939, soon to be a fighter pilot over the Pacific.

At the conclusion of the ceremony, Sharon recounts that she was busily clearing the back seat of their car—still covered with pine needles from Christmas decorations—in order to provide room for the chancellor's wife, who was to accompany them to the chancellor's house, where a select group of twelve had assembled at the mansion to further honor Barc at dinner. Lacking a dustpan and brush, Sharon surreptitiously asked Jeannie, resplendent in a new red winter coat, to slide across the back seat as a human duster to prepare the way for the chancellor's wife. As she was explaining that she would have the beautiful coat dry-cleaned the next day, Sharon heard a strange bumping as the trunk opened. When she was able to go to the back of the car to see what was going on, she found Barc hurling the prized Berkeley Medal into the morass of household things littering the compartment. Gulping, Sharon pleaded with Barc to replace the medal around his neck. *I don't wear necklaces* was the response. It was with great difficulty that Sharon was able to persuade him that he needed to wear this one—without the chancellor's wife being any the wiser.

Chapter 37

2014: Passages

I see here a small piece of the magnitude he has given.

—Monica Manriquez, Girls Inc.

IN 2014, THE COMPANY underwent another set of historic passages: Budd Cheit's death on August 2; Barclay's death on November 8; and Barry Williams's departure from the board, in keeping with the body's twenty-year statute of limitations. Almost all at once, Simpson Manufacturing's extraordinary conclave of "Big Bs" left the field forever. The earth shook, the wind roared, but the structure held. Tom and many other long-standing employees and members of the board of directors stayed in their essential positions—a skilled and passionate praetorian guard, which was itself twenty, thirty, and more years in the making. Having planned their own eventual withdrawal for years, the B's didn't leave a void, but rather riches, behind. Barclay, Budd, Barry, and Tom were transmitters as well as leaders—maybe two ways of saying the same thing.

Following Barclay's death, Girls Inc. held a "life celebration" event, honoring their most passionate supporter. Among the many speakers was Monica Manriquez, who spoke about Barc in a manner that he would have approved for its simplicity and transparency. Looking out over the large group of people who had assembled in his name, Monica summed up what Mr. Simpson had meant in her life:

> *I see here a small piece of the magnitude he has given, the massive impact. It has brought my thinking about him to an even greater level, which is amazing because I didn't believe I could think more highly of a person. He was a man who was gracious in blessing people with his energy. I'll miss him, but in honoring him it gives me courage to do*

*more things. Mr. Simpson and Girls Inc. instilled in me the feeling that
I belong wherever I feel I want to be.*

No achievement would have ever meant more to him. Monica sums up both
the goal and the genius at the center of Barc's being.

Chapter 38
Legacy: Measuring Value

The great use of life is to spend it for something that will outlast it.

—William James

The Economics of the Secret Sauce

We have one of the best balance sheets in the world, and Barc and I have always been really proud of that. Maybe he's been less proud of it than me, because he's always been the one saying, "Take a big risk! Do something! Buy something! What are you going to do?" But I'm a banker. More cautious. So, we have no debt and a big cash position. That helped us get through the downturns.

—Tom Fitzmyers

AT THE END OF December 2013, anticipating his own impending retirement six months later, Terry Kingsfather wrote a celebratory email to Sharon to give to Barclay. As well as honoring Barc's long tenure, this communication gave a thumbnail sketch of the arc of Simpson Manufacturing's growth during the over thirty-four years that Terry would have worked for the company:

> *Hard to believe July 1 I will be leaving this wonderful company. As a matter of fact, I was thanking Tom the other day for hiring me back on December 9, 1979, and was hoping to catch Barc to tell him the same….Candy [Terry's wife] and I always reflect on the wonderful opportunities I was given when coming to work for Simpson Strong-Tie. Finishing my career as president of Simpson was more than I could ever imagine.*

Recently I have been giving presentations to the branches on the directions of the company going forward.....Please tell Barc I am using bullet point number three when talking about the company and the opportunities for all Simpson employees.....I dug up some numbers to point out the growth of our company during that time. When I started in 1979, annual sales of the company were about $17 million.....My territory in Oregon was only $500,000. We had two US manufacturing branches [San Leandro and Brea] supporting our sales. We will finish 2013 with sales of $706 million, with fifty-five Simpson locations throughout the world and the company has made it through five recessions.....That same territory in Oregon is now selling $16 million a year of Simpson products, almost as much as the whole company when I started in 1979. I have been pointing out these facts to let everyone know how far we have come, but the fact is we are just getting started. Barc's right, this company is not a "bus stop" and he should be so very proud of what he has done for so many people.

Kingsfather's optimistic predictions reflect a four-year period of recovery following the "Great Recession" that began in 2007, hitting construction-related businesses with a multi-year ferocity not seen since the advent of the company. In 2009, Simpson Manufacturing showed net sales of approximately $526.5 million and a roster of 1,789 employees—significantly down from the 2006 prerecession sales of $863 million and a worldwide employment of 2,711. Yet because of the company's strong balance sheet, the business was able to weather the ruinous downturn in the worldwide construction industry, again showing year-over-year increases in net sales and employment by 2010, with totals that finally surpassed those of 2006. From that point onward, Simpson Manufacturing was to continue to show resiliency and the same capacity for consistent annual growth that had marked its prerecession records.

By 2020, eight years into Karen Colonias's stewardship of the company as its president and CEO, the Annual Financial Report for Simpson Manufacturing documents results that more than bear out Kingsfather's predictions, and that would have delighted its founder. Net sales reached $1.27 billion, the highest in the company's history and an 11.6 percent improvement over 2019. As a result, Simpson Manufacturing generated record earnings of $4.27 per diluted share, up 43.3 percent over 2019.[3] Sixty-three years after its incorporation and modest beginnings with a handful of employees working in constricted circumstances in East Oakland and San Leandro, Simpson Manufacturing now employs 3,337 people working in multiple locations across the globe through its operating segments in North America, Europe, and Asia/Pacific.[4]

These numbers suggest that the company's founding vision is still producing prodigious results, even after Barc and Tom's withdrawal from the scene. Much of this ongoing success has to do with how they passed on a coherent set of beliefs to the next generation of company leaders.

Another Form of Accounting

FOLLOWING SIMPSON MANUFACTURING'S LISTING on the New York Stock Exchange, corporate counsel advised that having the chairman of a publicly traded company manage the company's pension funds created an unacceptable level of liability. Their strong recommendation was that the company outsource the management of the funds to an established Wall Street firm. Having successfully navigated the markets for thirty years on behalf of his employees—investing his own money in the same portfolio of funds he developed for them—Barclay was deeply concerned about handing this responsibility off to an impersonal entity.

Nevertheless, against inclination and instinct, in this rare instance, he bowed to legal opinion and set out to find a Wall Street firm to manage the company pension funds. His selection process took the form of a trial run in which three different reputable firms were asked to compete for the business by investing Barc's own money over a period of twelve months and then comparing returns. Ultimately, a young man named Simon Baker from Credit Suisse was awarded the management of Simpson Manufacturing's $100 million pension fund (Simon Baker, CEO and Founder of Baker Ave. Asset Management; see bio).

Baker, a British expatriate who came to the US on a soccer scholarship to Hartwick College in upstate New York, was a rising star at Credit Suisse. With his clever wit and straightforward approach to asset management, he immediately established a rapport with Barclay. However, as the bank's proposed menu of investment options for employees began to develop, Barclay grew ever more concerned that the approach being designed would leave Simpson employees without enough informed guidance. He was worried that, left entirely to their own devices, many of the Simpson workers were not financially literate enough to make the kind of sound investment decisions required if they were to protect their long-term financial security. For years he had argued with his union employees about the wisdom of taking the long view rather than pressing exclusively for short-term, up-front wage increases that would be taxed. He knew firsthand the difficulty of selling patience over risky short-term gains.

The preparation period for rolling out the bank's proposed program culminated in Barclay and Simon making a five-day tour around the country to meet with employees at the various Simpson locations to explain the shift in procedures and to answer questions. During this time together, Simon came to understand just how deeply concerned Barclay was about employees being suddenly expected to make unguided investment decisions that could harm their security in retirement.

On the final night of the employee listening tour, troubled that Barclay was fundamentally uncomfortable with the investment choices being offered, and equally aware of the unwillingness of Credit Suisse to adjust its model, Simon approached Barc with a radical proposal, succinct even by Barclay's standards: *My recommendation is that you fire me and Credit Suissse tonight. I would only ask that I have an opportunity to continue to work with you and Sharon on a personal level.* Barc accepted the proposal, hiring Baker on the spot as his ongoing personal financial confidante and advisor. After all, it was Simon who had won the business for Credit Suisse by investing Barc's personal money during the trial period. Moreover, Barc's swift instincts about people had always been at the heart of his decision making.

After taking Baker's advice and firing Credit Suisse, Barclay continued to manage Simpson Manufacturing's pension funds for another year or so until he found another Wall Street firm that would allow both self-directed and fixed-asset allocation investment plans for his employees. In the end, this double-faceted solution satisfied the corporate lawyers buzzing louder now that the company was a publicly traded entity; more importantly, it reassured the company's founder that the long-term interests of Simpson employees would be protected even though Barc was no longer able to manage the pension funds he had strived so hard to build for them. On a more personal level, one of the happy outcomes of the solution concocted that night over dinner and drinks was that Simon was to name his firstborn son Barclay—

paying the profoundest kind of tribute to a friend and mentor while hoping also to confer upon his son some of the deep powers of his namesake.

In his long-term tutelage of his employees' pension benefits, Barclay established a special and enduring legacy for the business he had created, driving home one of his central principles: that taking care of employees is central to the mandate of any business and the key to its enduring success. Indeed, this principle and its long-term effects appear to be borne out by Simpson Manufacturing's continuing growth, even in the wake of Barclay's death in November 2014.

Yet the business is only part of Barc's legacy. The other institution he created that continues to carry forth the core principles that guided his life is the Put Something Back (PSB) Fund. As Simon Baker and others suggest, the PSB Fund may be as important an achievement as Simpson Manufacturing itself. Reductively speaking, the business made the fund possible, yet if you scratch the surface, it is hard not to see these two very different entities—one for the generation of concrete profits, one for the promotion of other kinds of value—as aspects of the same whole. Certainly, the principles of leadership that guided the profit and the giving are inextricably intertwined.

Following Barc's death, Sharon has carried forward the simplicity of purpose and essential spirit of the fund in a way Barclay would approve, and she has made decisions that will ensure that it continues to channel support to the community in perpetuity. The original emphasis on education and the arts for children and their families remains integral. While the beneficiaries of the fund may expand over time, it is likely that they will continue to include a group of nonprofit organizations and programs with which Sharon and Barc have been working for decades. As one example, in 2018, Sharon made an additional gift to BAMPFA of $11 million to support ongoing operations and innovative program development. Five million dollars of this donation was in the form of a Challenge Gift (already met), aimed at inspiring expansion of museum membership and stronger giving from other donors, always a key element of Barc and Sharon's philanthropy.

As in the past, the newest version of the PSB Fund website simply, explicitly reaffirms the founders' "passionate" commitment to "education for young children"—and particularly those from low-income backgrounds. In this core statement resides Barclay's deepest belief that children's brains and characters are constructed at very young ages and that literacy and access to the arts are essential to opening up the possibilities for a productive life. The corollary of this belief is that all of society has a responsibility to guarantee this flourishing, and not only for its luckiest members. Similar to the pledge Barc made to his employees, this baseline commitment is the essential prerequisite and binding codicil of the Simpson creed.

For the foreseeable future, the PSB Fund will continue to disburse between $5 and $6 million a year. Still operating without a paid staff, Sharon echoes Barc's words to Pat Loomes regarding their gifts to Girls Inc: *It is one of my most satisfying jobs. How many people have the pleasure of giving away money and helping to make a difference in someone's life or the life of an institution?* Given this consistency of belief, the PSB Fund stands a strong chance of becoming a major beacon for education and the arts in the San Francisco Bay Area and beyond, long after its founders have ceded the field.

Skeptical by trade and experience regarding the evolution of publicly traded companies, Simon speculates that there is the possibility that Barclay's Nine Principles and the memory of his compelling presence may not always be able to shape the fortunes of Simpson Manufacturing from beyond the grave. For instance, it is impossible to guarantee that the publicly traded company will never be sold, as Barclay insisted. Yet Baker believes that, come what may, the PSB Fund *can guarantee the Simpson legacy*, as a literal embodiment of Barclay and Sharon's doctrine of gratefulness and giving back.

More of a romantic than Simon, Barclay probably would have a hard time accepting the idea that *his baby*, as Barry Williams called the company, might with the winds of fortune move away from some elements of the SST core belief system. But then, giving rein to his pragmatic side, Barc would probably quickly shrug off these disappointments, believing, along with his beloved Epic tus, that *there is only one way to happiness and that is to deny all worry about things that are beyond the power of our will.* Perhaps armed in this knowledge and with his usual exuberance, Barc would not look backward, but would celebrate the fact that the Simpson creed will live on at UCB, BAMPFA, CCA, OMCA, DRAA, and Girls Inc., and among the many other people and institutions the PSB Fund has in the past, and may in the future, choose to sustain.

Of course, there is also a good chance that the Simpson Strong-Tie brand—with its sixty-plus-year history, its consistency of belief, and its unusual people—may continue to prevail according to the company's uncommon lights for a long while yet; certainly, memory of what the creed meant will continue to reign among the Simpson employees who have lived it on a daily basis—will remain ingrained in those who knew Barc personally as their "servant leader."

Notes for Part VIII

1 https://www.awards.berkeley.edu/berkeley-medal.

2 https://www.issuu.com/californiacollegeofthearts/docs/barclay25_catalog_lowres/13.

3 See 2020 Annual Report. https://www.simpsonmfg.com.

4 2019 Annual Report. The company is organized into three operating segments consisting of North America, Europe, and Asia/Pacific. The North America segment includes operations primarily in the United States and Canada. The Europe segment includes operations primarily in France, the United Kingdom, Germany, Denmark, Switzerland, Portugal, Poland, the Netherlands, Belgium, Spain, Sweden, and Norway. The Asia/Pacific segment includes operations primarily in Australia, New Zealand, China, Taiwan, and Vietnam. These segments are similar in several ways, including similarities in the products manufactured and distributed, the types of materials used, the production processes, the distribution channels, and the product applications.

Epilogue
Back in the Gallery

IN JANUARY OF 2014, ten months before Barc's death in November, I returned to the gallery. This time Sharon answered the door, alone. Instead of walls covered with prints and paintings and a warm light shining from Barc's library/office, the dull whiteness of the block-like front room of the gallery seemed forbidding in its emptiness—its vertical spaces sightless, opaque, and refusing to give up memories of the color, conviviality, creativity, and personality that had clustered in this space, overflowing its boundaries. At the end of the room, the beautiful, built-in maple drawers designed to hold rare prints were tugged open, laying out their once carefully tissued and concealed wares to nothing but the cold morning air, Sharon, and me. I felt as if I had stumbled into the scene of a robbery, except that it was a theft of time.

Sharon was whirring between boxes and open cupboards, pulling out and laying bare intriguing tools of the art trade, old notebooks, rare correspondence—her sheer physical activity and focused intentness the only remaining embodiment of the vital energies she and Barc had poured into this enterprise and coaxed from its many converts and fellow travelers when the gallery was in its heyday. I was amazed by the palpable life of objects—brought up short time and again by Barclay's precise and pleasing handwriting on the flyleaves of books, the backs of prints, inventories, and ledgers—including the carefully ruled sheets on which he kept track of naval air sorties during World War II and industrial production numbers from the fifties. The alluring, recondite artifacts ambushed me, along with his so-familiar script.

Now and then, Sharon would stop and join me to look at drawings, attributions, and inventories—the rare jewels spilling forth from the strong box that had been the gallery. But she was on a mission, organizing gifts of prints and books for universities, auction houses, family, and friends. I could see her face open and close as she brought objects in and out of focus, relying on competent action to short-circuit the sting of memory and the knowledge of loss looming.

Moving through feeling to dispassionate efficiency and back again, she cannibalized boxes, storage racks, and desk drawers, took swing after swing at the job that needed doing—Barclay sitting on her shoulder. I could picture him watching her, proud as always of her beauty, her dancer's precision, her capacity for action—the refusal of useless brooding or sentimentality.

Interviewees

Bios

The Family

Barclay Simpson "Barc" (1921–2014) was the founder of Simpson Manufacturing Company, Inc. and its primary subsidiary, Simpson Strong-Tie, which he led from 1956 to his retirement from the company in 2012 and from the board of directors in 2013. From 1976 to 1988, he served three terms as the elected representative from Contra Costa County on the BART board of directors. Along with his second wife, Sharon, he ran the Barclay Simpson Fine Arts Gallery in Lafayette, California, from 1981–1994, and was a member of the board of directors of the California College of Arts (CCA) and the Berkeley Art Museum and Pacific Film Archive (BAMPFA) from the mid-eighties onward. From the early nineties until the end of his life, he was a primary supporter of Girls Inc. as well as of a long list of other nonprofit arts and education institutions.

Sharon Hanley Simpson, born in 1938, married Barc in 1974. She was a cofounder of the gallery and one of its principal salespeople. Side by side with Barc, and following his death, she has been an active participant and financial supporter of all of their primary nonprofit organizations. She was on the board of directors of the California Shakespeare Theater (Cal Shakes), based in Orinda, California, from 1994–2020, and served as president of the board from 1995–2000.

John Barclay Simpson is the oldest child of Barc and his first wife, Joan Devine Simpson. A neuroendocrinologist, he is a former president of the State University of New York at Buffalo and professor emeritus of physiology and biophysics (2004–2011). He was the executive vice chancellor of UC Santa Cruz (1983–2003). Before this, he served for twenty-three years on the psychology faculty of the University of Washington, ending there as dean of the College of Arts and Sciences (1994–98). He is an alumnus of the University of California, Santa Barbara.

Anne Katheryn Simpson Gattis is the second of Barc and Joan's three children. She attended UC Berkeley and married Bob Gattis, who also graduated from Berkeley. She has been a contributor to Girls Inc. She lives in Orinda and is the mother of Sean Barclay Gattis.

Jean Devine Simpson is the youngest of Barc and Joan's children. She was a teacher in the Oakland public school system; was a salesperson for the gallery, specializing in corporate sales; and later worked with Pat Loomes to replicate some of Girls Inc.'s early education reading programs in educational institutions throughout the United States. She has served on the board of directors of Cal Shakes, where she was president of the board from 2012–2019.

Jeff Gainsborough is the oldest of Sharon's children from her first marriage. He started in the mortgage lending business in 1992, and in 1997 founded Foremost Mortgage Company. In 2008, he founded Gainsborough Holdings, LLC and moved into the mobile housing market, founding Mobile Housing of Texas (now AmeriCasa Dream Homes), which has grown into one of the top independent dealerships in Texas. In 2014, he founded MHOT Financial and MHOT Insurance Agency, and in 2016 became the cofounder and president of AmeriCasa Solutions and AmeriCasa Communities.

Julie Simpson is Sharon's second child from her first marriage. She was a design fellow in Nagoya, Japan, and worked at Sotheby's in New York. Working with some of Barc and Sharon's premiere nonprofits, she has served on the board of directors of Girls Inc. and is a Lifetime Trustee of BAMPFA as well as an Honorary Trustee of Alice Waters' The Edible Schoolyard Project.

Amy Simpson and her twin, Elizabeth Simpson Murray, are the youngest of Sharon's children from her first marriage. Amy is a chef and lives in Lake Tahoe.

Elizabeth Simpson Murray (Lizzie), along with Amy, is Sharon's youngest child from her first marriage. After graduating from Northwestern University, Lizzie moved to Los Angeles, where she had a career as an actress and a voiceover artist. After the birth of her second child, she became a full-time mother and an active volunteer.

Simpson Manufacturing Company, Inc./Simpson Strong Tie (SST)

Jennifer Chatman joined the Simpson Manufacturing board of directors in 2004. She is the Paul J. Cortese Distinguished Professor of Management at the Haas Business School, having joined the faculty in 1993. In addition to her research and teaching at UC Berkeley, she consults with a wide range of organizations and is the faculty director of the University's Executive Leader Program. She is a Trustee of Prospect Sierra School.

Earl F. Cheit (known as "Budd") was one of the original and longest-standing members of the board of directors of Simpson Manufacturing, drafting its first set of bylaws and serving on the board for twenty years, from 1994 to 2014. For nearly three and a half decades, from 1957 until his retirement in 1991, he was a professor at Haas, serving as its dean twice (1976–82 and 1990–91) and presiding over the school's growth and modernization. Other key positions he held at UC Berkeley included roles as executive vice-chancellor (1965–69), athletic director (1993–94,) and trustee of the University of California, Berkeley Foundation. He also served as vice president of financial and business management for the University of California system from 1981–82. Other professional activities included service as a trustee of Mills College, board member of the University of California Press, board chairman of Shaklee Corporation, board director of CFC Transportation, associate director of the Carnegie Council of Higher Education, and a senior advisor on Asia-Pacific relations for the Asia Foundation.

Karen Colonias was hired as SST's second licensed engineer, serving in the company's R&D Department from 1984 to 1998. She rose through the ranks of SST, becoming the president/CEO of Simpson Manufacturing in January of 2012 and a member of the board of directors in 2013. In arriving at this pinnacle, she served from 1998 to 2004 as VP of engineering, responsible for the design and testing of new products and code development; from 2004 to 2009 as VP and branch manager of the company's mega manufacturing, distribution, and testing facility in Stockton, California; and from 2009–2012 as CFO/Treasurer/Secretary of Simpson Manufacturing.

Thomas Fitzmyers was vice-chairman/investor relations of Simpson Manufacturing from 2014 to 2017 and served as a member of the company's board of directors from 1994 to 2017. From 2011 to 2014 he served as chairman of Simpson Manufacturing. Hired in 1978 as the head of acquisitions for SST, in 1983 he assumed the position of CEO of SST, serving in that position until 1994, when he became president/CEO of Simpson Manufacturing, until he took over the role of chairman in 2011.

John Herrera was hired at SST in 1970 to work in the shipping department. Over his forty-four years at the company, he held many increasingly responsible positions, working his way up to VP of operations services, retiring from that role in 2014.

Terry Kingsfather started as a salesman for SST in Portland, Oregon, in 1979. From that date onward, he served in various capacities at the company, joining the management team in charge of Anchor Systems in 1998, from which he was promoted to VP of Anchor Systems in 2003, a position he held until August of 2006. From then until February of 2009, he served first as president and COO, moving into the position of president and CEO from 2009 until his retirement in July of 2014 after thirty-five years of service at SST.

Kristin Lincoln was hired at SST in 1995 and worked her way up to senior vice president of Global Marketing of Simpson Manufacturing, retiring in 2016 after twenty-one years at the company. She currently owns a leadership and organizational development consulting firm, LiveWire Consulting, based in Walnut Creek, California.

David MacDonald was plant manager at SST from 2004–2014, having been hired in 1984 as a packer in the automatic department. He is a graduate of Chabot College.

Jacinta Pister has been senior vice president of Global Manufacturing at Simpson Manufacturing from 2005 to the present. Previously, she held a variety of positions within the company including VP of manufacturing (1998–2005); manager of manufacturing engineering and tooling (1993–1997); manager of manufacturing engineering (1989–1993); and business analyst (1986–1989). She holds degrees in engineering and business administration.

Mike Plunk was hired at SST in 1972 as a part-time packer. He was soon moved into a full-time position and was tasked with setting up the warehouse at the San Leandro Plant when the back building was acquired. He became the supervisor of warehousing until his retirement in 2013 after forty-one years with the company.

Jennifer Price has been an employee of SST for thirty years, joining the company in 1991. Hired as a technical writer, she managed the marketing services team while working with Barc on analyst communications. She also worked as Simpson's sustainability analyst and currently manages the company-wide SAP implementation Training Program.

Steve Pryor, PE, SE, has held several important positions at SST including advanced research manager (2019–present); director of innovation (2016–2019); and international director of building systems (2009–2015).

Randy Shackelford has been with SST for twenty-seven years, having joined the company in 1994. Currently he holds the position of manager of codes and compliance and is located at the SST Branch in McKinney, Texas.

Lauren Versluysen, based in France, was vice president for European Operations from 1994–2018.

Barry Lawson Williams served on the board of directors of Simpson Manufacturing from 1995–2015, one of the company's first and longest-standing members, along with Budd Cheit. He is a retired entrepreneur and director for fourteen corporate boards. Since 2012, he has focused on promoting diversity on corporate boards and on mentoring Black professionals. He has developed and taught a Black entrepreneurship course at Haas School of Business at UC Berkeley.

Bay Area Rapid Transit District (BART)

Michael Healy is the retired director of media and public affairs for BART. Known as Mr. BART, he served as BART's chief spokesman for thirty-two years. A recognized expert on the San Francisco Bay Area's premier mode of public transportation, he published the definitive history of the system in his book *BART: The Dramatic History of the Bay Area Rapid Transit System,* which was published in 2016.

Arthur Shartsis was elected as a director of the BART board for three terms starting in 1976, serving as president of the board in 1984. He cofounded the San Francisco law firm of Shartsis Friese LLP in 1975 and is currently the senior manager of the firm. For many years Shartsis Friese LLP served as outside counsel for SST.

Joan Van Horn was legislative analyst at BART from 1973 to 2004. She attended UC Berkeley, then worked on the Hill in DC prior to working at BART.

The Barclay Simpson Fine Arts Gallery, Lafayette, California

Lynda Dann joined the gallery in 1984, working there until 1993 in administration and sales, and her paintings were exhibited at the gallery. Prior to her work at the gallery, she attended the Academy of Art College, San Francisco, California from 1980 to 1983. Her studio is in Oakland, California.

Joseph Way is an artist whose work was represented by the gallery from 1986 to 1993. From 1993 to the present, he has worked at SST, first as an assistant to Tye Gilb and then in the marketing department as an artist, prototype fabricator, and in-house photographer for trade shows and other marketing activities.

The University of California, Berkeley, including the Haas School of Business (Haas); the Berkeley Art Museum and Pacific Film Archive (BAMPFA); and the Simpson Center for Student-Athlete High Performance (Simpson Center)

Anne Saunders "Sandy" Barbour was the athletic director of UC Berkeley from 2004 to 2014. Subsequently, she went on to be VP for intercollegiate athletics at the Pennsylvania State University.

Robert Birgeneau is a Canadian American physicist and university administrator. He was the ninth chancellor of UC Berkeley from 2004 to 2013, and the fourteenth president of the University of Toronto from 2000 to 2004. He is particularly known for his efforts to recruit a racially and economically diverse student body and to promote the idea that both "access and excellence" should be the guiding principles of a public institution of higher education. During the 2011–2012 academic year, Birgeneau unveiled the Berkeley Middle-Class Access Plan, a new financial aid model that caps the total annual cost of an eligible student's education at fifteen percent of the family's total income.

Jennifer Cutting has served as executive director, philanthropy and principal gifts in the University Relations Department at UC Berkeley from 1997 to the present. Previously, she was in Alumnae Relations at Westridge School from 1993 to 1997.

Neil Henry is an American journalist and professor, who is a former dean of the UC Berkeley Graduate School of Journalism. Between 2012 until his retirement from the faculty in 2016, Henry served as director of the Oral History Center of UC Berkeley's Bancroft Library. During this period, he undertook an oral history of Barclay Simpson, which is available from the center. Before becoming a professor at UC Berkeley in 1992, Henry was a staff writer for *Newsweek* and then worked for thirteen years for *The Washington Post*. He is the author of *Pearl's Secret*, an autobiographical family history that explores issues of mixed African-American and White-American heritage. He is also the author of 2007's *American Carnival: Journalism Under Siege in an Age of New Media.*

Richard Lyons is a professor of Economics and Finance at Haas, where he served as dean from 2008 to 2018 and acting dean from 2004 to 2005. In January 2020, he became the first chief innovation and entrepreneurship officer for UC Berkeley. His research and teaching are mostly in international finance, though his more recent work explores how business leadership drives innovation and the importance of culture in shaping organizations. From 2006 to 2008, he took a leave from Berkeley to serve as Goldman Sachs' chief learning officer, focusing on leadership development for managing directors.

Noel Nellis has been a member of the BAMPFA board of directors from 1991 to the present, serving as its president from 1991 to 1997. Currently, he is also serving on the board of trustees of the University of California, Berkeley

Foundation; the board of trustees of the San Francisco Museum of Modern Art; and the policy advisory board of the Fisher Center for Real Estate and Urban Economics. He is an adjunct professor at Haas. Formerly he was a partner at Orrick, Herrington & Sutcliffe.

Lawrence R. Rinder is the director emeritus of BAMPFA, where he served as director and chief curator from 2008 to 2020, having previously served as a curator as well as assistant director for audience and programs from 1988 to 1998. During his tenure as director, Rinder oversaw a period of exceptional growth and transformation for BAMPFA, beginning with the transition from its former home on Bancroft Way to a new building in downtown Berkeley. Previously, he was the dean of the college at CCA. Rinder also served as the Anne and Joel Ehrenkranz curator of contemporary art at the Whitney Museum of American Art in New York City and was founding director of the CCA Wattis Institute for Contemporary Arts in San Francisco. In 2005, he was appointed to the San Francisco Arts Commission by Mayor Gavin Newsom.

Roselyne "Cissie" Swig has served on the board of directors of BAMPFA from the sixties to the present, acting as its president in the early years. Other major arts and education organizations that she has supported as trustee and donor include the San Francisco Art Institute; San Francisco Museum of Modern Art; the Contemporary Jewish Museum; and the National Gallery of Art, where she served as cochair of the Collector's Committee. In 1994, she was appointed director of the US Department of State Art in Embassies Program by President William J. Clinton, serving in this position until 1997. She is founder and president of ComCon International and Artsource and has devoted decades to philanthropic and community service efforts at the local, national, and global levels, with focus on women's empowerment, social welfare, fine art, political advocacy, and education.

Girls Inc. of Alameda County (Girls Inc.)

Linda Boessenecker served as CEO of Girls Inc. from 2007 to 2016. During her tenure, the organization was moved out of its old quarters in San Leandro to a newly restored building in the heart of Oakland, which was the product of a major, successful capital campaign. Previously she was COO for the Girl

Scouts of the Bay Area from 2003 to 2007, and executive director of the Girl Scouts of Napa and Solano Counties from 1995 to 2003.

Pat Loomes was the executive director of Girls Inc. in San Leandro from 1977 to 2007. During her thirty years as head of the organization, she took it from a glorified girls club with a handful of participants to a major East Bay regional nonprofit with an enrollment of more than seven thousand girls. Originally from Ireland, Loomes came to the United States at age twenty-three, eventually receiving a master's degree in sociology from San Francisco State University, where she later became a lecturer.

Monica Manriquez joined Girls Inc. in San Leandro at the age of fourteen. With scholarship help from Barclay, she attended UC Berkeley, graduating with a degree in economics. Following graduation, she served for a time on the board of directors of Girls Inc. After five years working in private sector firms, she decided to switch to a career in education. She served as the English learner coordinator for the Hayward Unified School District and is currently the principal of Palma Ceia Elementary School in Hayward, California.

Julayne Virgil has served as the CEO of Girls Inc. since 2016, charged with taking the organization to the next level through the expansion of programming, as well as the optimization of infrastructure and administrative practices. The success of those initiatives enabled Girls Inc. to successfully pivot during the pandemic to deliver programming remotely while continuing to be a critical resource to girls and families. Previously, Julayne was a VP at Education Pioneers from 2011 to 2016 after launching the Chicago office as the founding managing director in 2008. Prior to receiving her master's degree in public administration from the University of Southern California, Julayne managed digital social service campaigns for The Advertising Council while facilitating a girls' leadership program in Brooklyn.

Arts Organizations: California College of Art (CCA); the Oakland Museum of California (OMCA); California Shakespeare Theater (Cal Shakes); and Diablo Regional Arts Association (DRAA)

Susan Avila is a career nonprofit leadership professional with over twenty-five years of experience in the San Francisco Bay Area. She joined CCA as

324 ~ Katharine Ogden Michaels

VP for advancement in 2000, helped lead the school as interim copresident during 2007, and was promoted to senior VP in 2008; she continues to serve in this position at the present. Previously, she served as director of development at the San Francisco Museum of Modern Art from 1998 to 2000. She has served on numerous accreditation committees for the Western Association of Schools and Colleges and has received the Smithsonian Institution Award for Museum Leadership as well as the Girls Inc. "Woman of Distinction" award.

Joseph Di Prisco is the founding chair of the Simpson Family Literary Project, which is named in honor of Barclay and Sharon Simpson, a collaborative effort of the UC Berkeley English Department and the Lafayette Library and Learning Center. On an annual basis, the project awards a cash prize to a mid-career fiction writer. Additionally, it promotes literacy and literature, focusing on underserved young people in the Bay Area of California. Previously, he served on the board of directors of Cal Shakes (2001–2014) and was the board chair of Redwood Day School in Oakland for seven years. Additionally, he has been involved in numerous nonprofits, including the Ann Martin Center, Playworks, and Girls Inc. He has published fourteen books of fiction, memoir, nonfiction, and prize-winning books of poetry.

Lori Fogarty has been CEO of OMCA from 2006 to the present. In this capacity, she has overseen museum program and administrative operations. In 2011 she helped transition OMCA from its status as a department of the City of Oakland to becoming a private nonprofit entity that still receives some support from the City of Oakland. Currently she serves on the board of the Association of Art Museum Directors. Her previous roles include executive director of the Bay Area Discovery Museum (2001–2006) and senior deputy director of the San Francisco Museum of Modern Art (1999–2001).

Jonathan Moscone was the artistic director of Cal Shakes for sixteen years from 2000 to 2016. In 2009 he received the inaugural Zelda Fichandler Award given by the Stage Directors and Choreographers Foundation for his transformative work in theater. Currently, he serves as the chief producer for the Yerba Buena Center for the Arts in San Francisco.

Peggy White has, since 1994, been the executive director of Diablo Regional Arts Association (DRAA), the nonprofit partner of the Lesher Center for the Arts. With a lead gift from Barclay Simpson in 2006, she launched the Arts Access School Time Program, which has made it possible for over fifty thousand East Bay students from underserved schools to experience the joy of the arts.

Put Something Back (PSB) Fund

Simon Baker is the founder and CEO of BakerAvenue Wealth Management, headquartered in San Francisco with offices in NYC and Dallas. Chairman of the executive committee and a member of the investment committee, he also has responsibility for the firm's family office clients. Before launching BakerAvenue in 2004, Simon was a managing director at Bank of America Securities; Donaldson, Lufkin and Jenrette (DLJ); and Credit Suisse First Boston (CSFB).